D0771838

Apple Pro Training Series
Motion 5

Mark Spencer

Apple
Certified

Apple Pro Training Series: Motion 5
Mark Spencer
Copyright © 2012 by Peachpit Press

Published by Peachpit Press. For information on Peachpit Press books, contact:
Peachpit Press
1249 Eighth Street
Berkeley, CA 94710
(510) 524-2178
www.peachpit.com
To report errors, please send a note to errata@peachpit.com. Peachpit Press is a division of Pearson Education.

Apple Series Editor: Lisa McClain
Project Editor: Nancy Peterson
Development Editor: Bob Lindstrom
Production Coordinator: Kim Elmore, Happenstance Type-O-Rama
Contributing Writer: Dion Scoppettuolo
Apple Reviewer: Anne Renehan
Technical Editors: Brendan Boykin, Jem Schofield
Copyeditor: Darren Meiss
Compositor: Chris Gillespie, Happenstance Type-O-Rama
Indexer: Jack Lewis
Cover Illustration: Kent Oberheu
Cover Production: Chris Gillespie, Happenstance Type-O-Rama
Media Producer: Eric Geoffroy

ISBN 13: 978-0-321-77468-2
ISBN 10: 0-321-77468-X
9 8 7 6 5 4 3 2 1 Printed and bound in the United States of America

Acknowledgments I'd like to thank Dion Scoppettuolo, without whom this book wouldn't be in your hands; Kent Oberheu, another trailblazer; the Santa Monica brain trust; Sharon Franklin, who introduced me to Peachpit; and Marjorie Baer, who started it all.

Contents at a Glance

Table of Contents

Animation

Motion Graphics Design

Visual Effects Design

An Introduction to 3D

Getting Started

Welcome to the official Apple Pro Training course for Motion 5, a behavior-driven motion graphics application that allows you to create stunning visual effects for a wide variety of projects.

This book is a comprehensive guide to designing with Motion. It covers the use of behaviors, keyframes, particle dynamics, text, audio, keying, painting, tracking, creating effects for Final Cut Pro X, and working in 3D.

Whether you've been creating motion graphics for years or are encountering these techniques for the first time, Motion's design approach is different from anything you've used before. The real-time design engine and behavior system are easy to learn, yet they open the door to expansive creativity.

The Methodology

This book takes a hands-on approach to learning the software. It's divided into projects that methodically introduce the interface elements and ways of working with them, building progressively until you can comfortably grasp the entire application and its standard workflows.

Each lesson in this book is self-contained, so you can jump to any lesson at any time. However, lessons are designed to support the concepts learned in the preceding lesson, and newcomers to motion graphics should go through the book from start to finish. In particular, the first three sections—Fundamentals, Animation, and Motion Graphics Design—comprise eight chapters, teach basic concepts, and are best completed in order.

Course Structure

The lessons are project based and designed to teach you real-world techniques for completing the types of motion graphics projects most commonly encountered in a professional setting. As you progress through the book, you will learn Motion's features and capabilities while you build several animated title sequences; create visual effects including retiming, keying and tracking shots; and construct Smart Motion Templates for use in Final Cut Pro X as a title, a transition, and an effect.

The lessons are organized into the following sections:

▶   Lessons 1–2: Motion Fundamentals

In Lesson 1, you build a project while becoming familiar with Motion's user interface. You learn how to import video files, transform them, and add filters, behaviors, and masks; apply blend modes; and create and animate text. Lesson 2 explores compositing in depth, including working with layers and groups, blend modes and filters, and masks and clones; as well as editing in the Timeline.

▶   Lessons 3–4: Animation

After mastering the basics, you are now ready to try animation. Lesson 3 focuses on using behaviors, and Lesson 4 is devoted to keyframing.

▶   Lessons 5–8: Motion Graphics Design

Having acquired basic skills in compositing and animation, you turn your attention to designing motion graphics using Motion's tool set. In Lesson 5, generators, shapes, and paint strokes are used to create animated content. Lesson 6 covers text styling and anima-tion. Lesson 7 examines particle emitters and replicators, and Lesson 8 covers multiple ways to work with audio.

▶   Lessons 9–10: Visual Effects Design

This section explores visual effects design. In Lesson 9, you create speed changes; in Lesson 10, you explore stabilizing, tracking, and keying while creating a visual effects shot.

Lessons 11-12: An Introduction to Publishing and Rigging

This section introduces you to creating motion graphics for use in Final Cut Pro X. In Lesson 11, you learn how to publish Smart Motion Templates to Final Cut Pro, and how to publish specific parameters of those templates. In Lesson 12, you build and publish parameter rigs that allow an editor using Final Cut Pro to change the look of an effect with a single control.

▶   Lessons 13–14: An Introduction to 3D

The final section provides an overview of Motion's 3D capabilities. In Lesson 13, you build a 3D scene; and in Lesson 14, you animate a camera through the scene, adding lights, reflections, depth of field, and shadows.

Because this book is project based, earlier lessons sometimes call on you to use features and techniques that aren't explained in detail until later lessons. When this occurs, you'll see a note indicating that the technique is covered in more detail in a later lesson.

Some Terminology

Here are two key terms used throughout the book:

▶   Composite—Most often this refers to your final work: the image you see on the screen. You could also think of this as a *composition*. The term is occasionally used as a verb: You *composite* several objects together to create the final product.

▶   Objects—This is the word used by Motion to describe the individual elements of a composite. *Objects* can include QuickTime movies, image sequences, still images, and text. The objects are layered together to create the composite.

For a full list of motion graphics–related terms, a glossary is included at the end of the book.

System Requirements

All systems are not created equal, and the more power you have in your hardware, the more you can do in real time (that is, without rendering) in Motion.

Here's a brief explanation of how Motion leverages your hardware. If you're thinking of upgrading your system to run Motion, it might help you to decide what configuration will give you the best results.

The following sections are a little technical, so if you start to lose track, don't panic. Just remember: Faster equals better, more RAM equals better, and a more powerful graphics card equals better.

System Memory

Motion uses system RAM to cache all the objects that make up your composite throughout your preview range (see the Glossary if these terms are new to you).

Here's an example. Let's say you are combining three QuickTime movies in Motion to create a final, single image: your composite. Imagine that you have a moving fractal background clip (Element 1), a rotating web (Element 2), and some random boxes (Element 3).

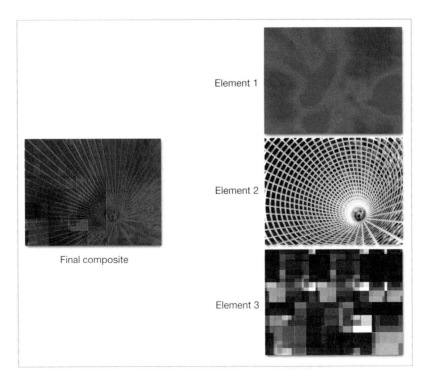

Element 1

Element 2

Element 3

Final composite

Each frame of 8-bit NTSC video contains 720 pixels horizontally and 486 pixels vertically (480 for DV). When you add the memory required to store every one of those pixels in the computer's memory, it works out to about 1.3 MB (including an alpha channel). A full raster 8-bit 1920 x 1080 HD video requires about 8.3 MB for each frame.

So if you want Motion to generate a real-time preview of your three-layer composite that lasts for 120 frames (about four seconds), you need to multiply the memory requirement for a single frame by the number of objects onscreen at the same time, and then multiply that by the number of frames you want to play in real time: 1.3 x 3 x 120 = 468 MB. For HD video, the memory requirement would be about 3 GB.

To adjust the three clips in your hypothetical composite in real time, you need at least 468 MB of free RAM, or 3 GB for HD. And that's beyond the RAM used by the operating system, Motion, and other background applications. So for this scenario to work well, you need at least 1 GB of system RAM for NTSC, or 4 GB for HD. (PAL-format video requires essentially the same amount of RAM as NTSC video: Although the images are 720 x 576, there are only 25 frames each second.)

But all you really need to know is that if you have more system RAM, you can play more objects in real time and watch a longer preview of your composite than you can with minimal RAM. However, this is only part of the story.

Video Card Mcmory (VRAM)

In addition to your system RAM, your Macintosh also has memory on the graphics card, known as *VRAM* (*video RAM*). It's used by the graphics card while performing calculations to draw an image to your computer monitor. Your graphics card also has its own processor, called a *GPU* (*graphics processing unit*), that calculates how images should be drawn.

Every time Motion draws a frame of your composite on the monitor, it sends one frame of each object in your composite to the VRAM of the graphics card, along with a set of instructions telling the processor on the graphics card what it's supposed to do with each image. The processor might be told to scale down one image, blur another, or color-correct still another before combining them into a single image. This is where the real-time aspect of Motion takes control.

Because the graphics card's processor can render only what's put into its VRAM, the number of layers that can be processed in real time is limited by how much VRAM the card has.

In the NTSC example, each of the three layers of video takes up 1.3 MB of memory per frame. In theory, you need only 3.9 MB of VRAM to draw a frame; but in reality, overhead is created by other processes, and certain filters and effects will use VRAM over and above that used for the video layers.

After a single frame is drawn, the VRAM is free to load the objects for the next frame. So the amount of VRAM affects how many layers and effects can be combined at *one frame* of the sequence, not the whole sequence. In other words, the number of frames being previewed is not affected by how much VRAM you have. The VRAM amount affects only the number of objects that can be composited in a single frame.

Finally, even when you reach your VRAM limits, Motion has a clever RAM-caching feature that allows you to render a real-time preview and still manipulate individual objects in real time using a soloing feature.

CPU Speed

You've always been told that a faster CPU is better. That's also true for Motion, but not in the way you might think. Because the processor in your graphics card is doing all the heavy lifting, the CPU doesn't have much to do with the actual construction of the composite.

The main system CPU comes into play when Motion uses it to calculate behaviors, particle trajectories, motion paths, and curves before sending them to the graphics card. So if you use a lot of complex behaviors in your projects, you'll definitely benefit from a faster processor.

Summarizing Hardware Requirements

The good news to be gleaned from the preceding technobabble is that if your system meets the minimum system requirements, improving Motion's performance doesn't necessarily mean buying a faster computer. You may only need to upgrade your graphics card.

Here's the story in a nutshell:

▶   System RAM determines how many frames of animation you can preview in real time; and to some degree, how many objects in a composite you can view in real time before you have to perform a RAM Preview render.

▶   VRAM (video RAM on the graphics card) determines how many objects in a composite can be rendered in real time before a RAM Preview render is required. If you want to place more objects on the screen with more filters and effects, you'll need more VRAM.

▶ CPU speed determines how many complex behaviors and simulations can be applied to composite objects in real time. Processor speed has less impact on the number of layers that can be drawn to screen. The amount of available VRAM is more important for layers.

Visit www.apple.com/finalcutpro/motion/specs/ for a current list of system requirements and supported hardware. In addition, be sure to install any Apple updates to the Motion 5 software.

Using Motion on a Laptop

Some of the keystrokes identified in this book work differently if you use a MacBook Pro. Specifically, you need to hold down the Function key (Fn) at the bottom left of the keyboard when pressing any of the F keys (F1 through F8) along the top of the keyboard. To avoid this, open the Keyboard section of System Preferences (the Keyboard & Mouse section in Mac OS X prior to Lion), and in the Keyboard pane, select the "Use all F1, F2, etc. keys as standard function keys" checkbox. In addition, when you are using Mac OS X Lion, click the Keyboard Shortcuts button in Keyboard Preferences to disable all the Mission Control shortcuts.

Even with this checkbox selected, however, you will still need to press the Fn key when using the Home and End keys, located at the lower right of the keyboard (marked with left and right arrows).

Gestures

Motion supports two types of gestures: gestures that you perform on the Multi-Touch trackpad of a MacBook Pro; and the native gestures language in Motion, which is a set of patterns that you draw using a Wacom Intuos tablet and pen. (Motion gestures are available exclusively for tablets in the Wacom Intuos family.)

Multi-Touch Gesture Support

You can use two-finger scrolls, three-finger swipes, pinches, and rotation movements on the Multi-Touch trackpad of a MacBook Pro to perform actions such as scrolling through a list of files, resizing icons, opening the Project or Timing pane, and moving the playhead.

Motion Gestures

Unlike gestures performed on a Multi-Touch trackpad, Motion gestures are movements that you make using a pen and graphics tablet to address a larger variety of tasks, such as playback control, Timeline navigation, editing, and general command execution.

To use gestures, you need a Wacom Intuos tablet connected to your computer, and you need to enable Handwriting Recognition in Mac OS X Ink preferences, which can be accessed through the Motion Gestures preferences pane.

For information on how to enable and use gestures, and view a table of all available gestures, see Appendix D in the Motion 5 User Manual, which you can open by choosing Help > Motion Help.

Copying the Motion Lesson Files

Apple Pro Training Series: Motion 5 comes with a DVD containing all the files you need to complete each lesson. The project and media files are contained within the Motion5_Book_Files folder.

Installing the Lesson Files

1   Insert the *Apple Pro Training Series: Motion 5* DVD into your computer's DVD drive.

2   For best results, drag the entire Motion5_Book_Files folder from the DVD to your Desktop or to an attached media drive.

    The disc contains approximately 3 GB of data.

Reconnecting Broken Media Links

For any number of reasons, you may need to separate the lesson files from the media files. For instance, you may choose to keep the project files in a user home directory and the media files on a dedicated media drive. In this case, when you open a project file, a window will appear asking you to reconnect the project files to their source media files.

Reconnecting files is a simple process. Just follow these steps:

1   When you open a lesson's project file, a dialog may appear listing one or more files as missing. Click the Reconnect button.

2   In the window that appears, navigate to Motion5_Book_Files > Media, and open the appropriate project folder.

3   Select the highlighted file and click Open.

4   Continue to connect files as necessary until the window closes.

5   Be sure to save the newly reconnected project file, or you will have to perform the reconnect operation the next time you open the project.

About the Apple Pro Training Series

Apple Pro Training Series: Motion 5 is both a self-paced learning tool and the official curriculum of the Apple Pro Training and Certification Program.

Developed by experts in the field and certified by Apple, the series is used by Apple Authorized Training Centers worldwide and offers complete training in all Apple Pro products. The lessons are designed to let you learn at your own pace. Each lesson concludes with review questions and answers summarizing what you learned, which can be used to help you prepare for the Apple Pro Certification Exam. For a complete list of Apple Pro Training Series books, see the page at the back of this book or visit www.peachpit.com/appleprotraining,

Apple Pro Certification Program

The Apple Pro Training and Certification Programs are designed to keep you at the forefront of Apple's digital media technology while giving you a competitive edge in today's ever-changing job market. Whether you're an editor, graphic designer, sound designer, special effects artist, student or teacher, these training tools are meant to help you expand your skills.

Upon completing the course material in this book, you can earn Apple certification. Certification is offered in all Pro applications, including Aperture, Final Cut Pro, Motion, and Logic Pro. Certification gives you official recognition of your knowledge of the Apple professional applications while allowing you to market yourself to employers and clients as a skilled user of Apple products.

Apple offers three levels of certification: **Apple Certified Associate**, **Apple Certified Pro - Level One**, and **Apple Certified Pro - Level Two**. Please note that not all applications include three levels of certification; Motion currently only includes Level One certification. Certification exams do not require class attendance. Students who prefer to learn on their own or who already have the necessary skill set in the chosen application, may take an exam for a fee.

Apple Certified Associate status validates entry-level skills in a specific application. Unlike an Apple Certified Pro exam, you can take Associate exams online from the comfort of your own home or office. Apple Certified Associate status is appropriate for students, for someone who is preparing for a first job out of school or a college-level program, or for anyone interested in validating entry-level credentials.

An **Apple Certified Pro** is a user who has reached the highest skill level in the use and operation of Apple Pro Applications as attested to by Apple. Students earn certification by passing the online certification exam administered only at Apple Authorized Training Centers (AATCs). Apple Certified Pro status is appropriate for industry professionals.

For those who prefer to learn in an instructor-led setting, training courses are taught by Apple Certified Trainers at AATCs worldwide. The courses use the Apple Pro Training Series books as their curriculum and balance concepts and lectures with hands-on labs and exercises. AATCs are carefully selected to meet Apple's highest standards in all areas, including facilities, instructors, course delivery, and infrastructure. The goal of the program is to offer Apple customers, from beginners to the most seasoned professionals, the highest-quality training experience.

For more information, please see the page at the back of this book, or to find an Authorized Training Center near you, visit training.apple.com.

Resources

Apple Pro Training Series: Motion5 is not intended as a comprehensive reference manual, nor does it replace the documentation that comes with the application. For more information about Motion, refer to these sources:

▶   User Manual. Accessed through the Motion Help menu, the User Manual contains a complete description of all features. You can also access the help at help.apple.com/helplibrary/.

▶   For a list of other resources, please visit www.apple.com/finalcutpro/motion/resources/.

▶ For details on the Apple Training and Certification programs, please visit training.apple.com.

▶ Peachpit's website—As Motion 5 is updated, Peachpit may choose to update lessons or post additional exercises as necessary on this book's companion webpage. Please visit www.peachpit.com to register this book. To do this, click the Account Sign In link at the top of the page and follow the instructions to register the book. Enter the 10-digit or 13-digit ISBN that appears on the back cover of the book. Registering ensures that you receive access to download files, updates and any errata.

Motion Fundamentals

1

Lesson Files	Motion5_Book_Files > Lessons > Lesson_01
Media	Motion5_Book_Files > Media > Skier
Time	This lesson takes approximately 60 minutes to complete.
Goals	Navigate the Motion interface
	Add video to a project
	Make transformations
	Add and modify effects
	Apply blend modes
	Create and animate text
	Use Library content
	Output your project

Getting Around in Motion

With its intuitive interface, Motion lets you immediately combine video and graphics, animate text, or create dazzling particle effects. But don't confuse efficient design with simplicity. Motion is a deep application that can help realize your creative vision, no matter how intricate or complex.

In this first lesson, we won't focus on what things are or why they work. You'll learn more details in the lessons that follow. In this lesson, you'll jump right in and start building a new project to quickly get a feel for what's unique about Motion and why it's so much fun.

Following a New Paradigm

With Motion, you can do things on a desktop or portable computer that were unthinkable only a few years ago: create compelling, professional-looking motion graphics and visual effects in a real-time design environment.

Whether you answer to a producer, agency, corporate client, or to your own creative muse, you can design motion graphics in a way that is natural and addictive.

Motion makes it easy to perform the primary motion graphics tasks: *compositing* and *animating*. Compositing involves layering together disparate elements to create a single complete image. Animating involves changing properties of those elements over time so that they fly, drift, grow, fade, spin, or wriggle. The interactive, real-time design engine and unique *behaviors* of Motion allow you to design and animate elements as your project plays.

With its intuitive 3D design tools, you can spread out your elements in 3D space; add lights, reflections, and shadows; and fly virtual cameras around a 3D world.

Finally, you can use all of these features in Smart Templates that can be published to and modified in Final Cut Pro X.

Whether you're designing an opening title sequence, producing a series of lower thirds, or doing green screen work, Motion makes motion graphics and visual effects more accessible, more interactive, and more enjoyable.

Opening Motion

Before you get started, install the Motion application, if necessary, and copy the lessons and media from the book's DVD to your hard disk. Instructions for doing this are in the Getting Started section of this book. After those two tasks are complete, let's start by opening Motion and creating a new project.

1   From the Dock, click the Motion icon to open the application.

The first window that opens is the Project Browser, where you can create a new project, open a recent project, or choose a template. In this exercise, you'll create a new project. The sidebar to the left of the Project Browser lists project categories and themes. The center project stack displays thumbnail previews of projects based on the sidebar selection. An information column to the right includes project settings options.

2   Verify that the Blank category is selected in the sidebar, that Motion Project is selected in the project stack and that the Broadcast HD 720 Preset is selected in the information column.

> **TIP** To see the projects you've recently worked on, from the sidebar list, select Recent.

In this lesson, you'll work with a video clip recorded in 1280 x 720 HD resolution at 59.94 frames per second (fps). Because these are the default project settings, you needn't change the Broadcast HD 720 Preset in the information column.

> **TIP** You usually choose a project Preset setting based on the format of your video material and the target output specifications. For example, you might choose one preset to create a spot for standard-definition television and a different preset for HDTV content. If you consistently create projects using the same preset, you can choose to bypass the Project Browser by changing an option in the Project pane of the Motion Preferences.

3   Click Open.

A new, empty Motion project opens.

Importing a Video Clip

The Motion interface, called the workspace, consists of a single window with components you can show or hide. The large upper-right area dominated by a black rectangle is the Canvas. Here you build and view your project. To the left of the Canvas is the Project pane, which displays all the elements in your project.

The tall, skinny component to the left of the Project pane is divided into three major panes: the File Browser, Library, and Inspector. Along the bottom of the workspace, you'll find the Timing pane, which contains the Timeline, the Audio Timeline, and the Keyframe Editor. Finally, above the Timing pane is the toolbar, which contains tools and controls for creating and editing project elements.

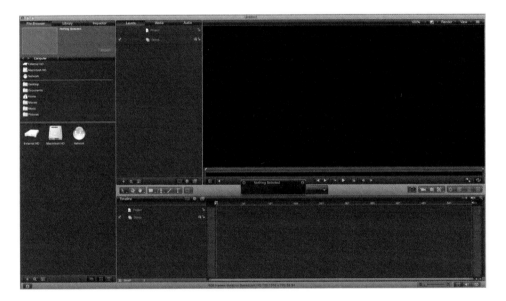

When you add any video, graphic, or text element to Motion they are called layers. The first way you'll create a layer is by bringing a video clip into your project.

In the File Browser, you'll locate, preview, and import media into your project. Media can include graphics, video, and audio files that are located on your computer or connected storage devices.

1   In the middle of the File Browser, click the Desktop icon. This section of the File Browser is called the sidebar.

The contents on your desktop are now displayed in the lower section of the File Browser, called the stack.

2   Double-click the Motion5_Book_Files folder.

3   Double-click the Media folder, and then double-click the Skier folder, which contains a single video clip, mogul_1.

4   Select the clip and look at the top of the File Browser.

In this preview area, you can preview a video clip and also find important information about the clip, including its resolution, codec, and frame rate.

Because this is the clip you want to use, you can add it to your project by simply dragging it into the Canvas or clicking the Import button.

5   Drag the clip from the File Browser stack (not from the preview area) to the Canvas but don't release the mouse button just yet.

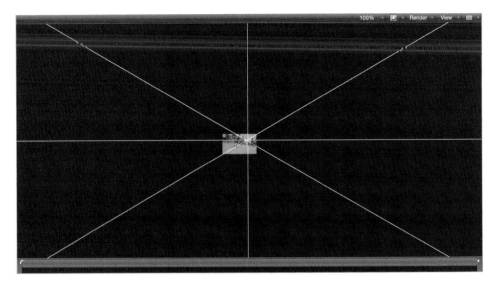

Yellow lines appear as you move the clip near the vertical and horizontal center of the Canvas. You'll see the clip *snap* to those lines as it approaches them. These lines, called dynamic guides, help you center an element in the Canvas and align multiple elements.

6   Snap the clip to the center of the Canvas and release the mouse button.

Congratulations. You've now created your first Layer in Motion.

NOTE ▶ If the dynamic guides don't appear, turn on snapping by choosing View > Snap, or pressing N.

Before you go any further, it's a good idea to save your project.

7   Choose File > Save, or press Command-S.

8   Navigate to Desktop > Motion5_Book_Files > Lessons > Lesson_01 > Student_Saves.

TIP The lower half of the Save dialog includes a menu for Collect Media. When set to Copy to Folder, Motion copies all the external video, audio, and graphics used in the project into the same folder as the saved project, making it easy to back up your project or move it to another Mac.

9 Name your project *Lesson_01_practice*, and click Save.

When you added the clip to the project, you may have noticed that a translucent gray window appeared in the center of the workspace. It's called the heads-up display, or HUD, and you'll use it later in this lesson. For now, you can turn it on and off by clicking the HUD button on the right side of the toolbar or by pressing F7.

Setting a Play Range

Now for the fun part: building your project while it plays. First, you'll set a play range to focus your efforts.

1 At the bottom of the Canvas find the transport controls. Click the Play button, or press the Spacebar, to start playback.

Motion is set to loop project playback, so at the end of the project the clip will play again from the beginning. This clip includes audio that you will not use. For now, let's mute it.

2 In the toolbar directly under the left edge of the Canvas, click the Mute button.

Notice that a few seconds of black plays after the end of the clip. This is because the clip is shorter than the overall project duration. At the bottom of the Canvas, notice that the green bar doesn't quite extend to the end of the project.

The area that contains the blue bar is titled *mogul_1*, and the green playhead above it is called the mini-Timeline. It shows the currently selected element and is handy when moving and trimming single elements in your project.

To play just a section of the video clip, you'll adjust the play range—the area that loops or repeats during playback, identified by white triangles. Changing the play range is a great way to focus on a specific part of your project.

3   As the project plays, drag the play range Out point (the rightmost white triangle) to 300 frames (5 seconds). A tooltip appears showing the new location of the Out point.

> **TIP** ► If you pause playback before moving the play range In or Out points, the playhead will jump to the new In or Out point and the Canvas will display the frame you are on, making it easier to choose a play range based on a specific frame.

At frame 300, the skier in the clip is just beginning to go out of focus, a good point at which to stop.

> **TIP** ► To switch between frame and timecode displays, click the arrow to the right of the frame counter and choose Show Timecode.

4   Review the results of the new play range, by pressing the Spacebar and then press the Spacebar again to stop playback. Press Command-S to save your work.

Transforming and Duplicating a Clip

Every element you add to a Motion project can be manipulated or *transformed*, whether it's a video clip, a graphic, or a Motion object such as a text or shape layer. Transformations include changing an element's position, scale, rotation, and other properties. Before you begin transforming an element, you must first be sure that you can see the entire frame in the Canvas.

1   In the top right of the Canvas area, the Zoom Level pop-up menu is set to 100%. Click the pop-up menu and choose Fit In Window.

The entire Canvas and frame are displayed in the Canvas area. It's important to note that the clip and the project have not changed size or resolution, only the display has changed. Now you are ready to transform the image.

> **TIP** ▶ Shift-Z is the Motion keyboard shortcut for Fit In Window, just as it is in Final Cut Pro. Using this key combination can scale the Canvas larger than 100 percent if you have a large screen. To scale to exactly 100 percent, press Option-Z.

2   In the Canvas, click the clip to select it. Notice the thin white line around the edge of the clip. This is called a bounding box and appears around any selected object.

3   Click anywhere inside the clip and drag it around. You can change the position of any selected element by dragging it.

4   Choose Edit > Undo Move, or press Command-Z, to return the clip to the center of the Canvas.

For this project, you'll use this clip as a full-screen background and then duplicate it to create a scaled-down copy for the main foreground element.

The small blue circles at the corners and midpoints of the bounding box are transform handles. You can drag them to manipulate the clip size.

> **TIP** ▶ The "x" in the center of the clip represents the element's *anchor point*, which you can reposition. You'll use anchor points in a later lesson. The handle coming off the right of the anchor point can be dragged for Z rotation.

5   Choose Edit > Duplicate, or press Command-D, to create a copy of the clip.

6   Drag the top-right transform handle down to the left.

The clip changes size nonproportionally—that is, you can make it skinny or fat—which is something you often want to avoid. Secondly, the clip doesn't stay centered as you scale. Rather, the control handle at the bottom left stays locked in place as the center of the clip moves around.

Often you'll want to scale an element proportionally *and* around its center. To do so, you can hold down modifier keys while dragging a transform handle.

7   Press Command-Z to undo the scale change.

8   Shift-drag the upper-right transform handle. The clip now scales proportionally, but the center is still moving.

9   Press Command-Z to undo.

10   Shift-Option-drag the upper-right transform handle again. The clip scales both proportionally and around its center.

11   Scale the clip down to about 70 percent of its original size. You can watch the scale display in the upper left of the Canvas as a guide.

> **TIP** The scale percentage displays in the upper-left corner of the Canvas only when you begin changing the clip's size. Other information, such as position and rotation, also displays in this area.

12 Press Command-S to save your work.

OK, so far we haven't done anything that's too compelling, but next you'll add filters to this project to make a more interesting composite.

Adding Effects

You'll now apply effects to make your project come to life. Motion has three categories of effects: filters, behaviors, and masks. You'll use at least one of each for this project. You'll also try out a powerful technique, called blend modes, that lets you change the interaction between overlapping elements. But first, let's look at a critical part of the Motion interface: the Project pane.

Hiding and Showing the Project Pane

While you can work exclusively in the Canvas, you'll eventually find it helpful to use a view that lists all the elements in your project—particularly when you want to select, rename, or reorganize them. Motion calls this view the Project pane.

1   To hide the Project pane, click the Show/Hide Project pane button to the left of the
Mute button you used earlier, or press F5.

The Project pane slides away. It is useful from time to time to hide the Project pane to
give yourself more room in the Canvas.

2   Click the Show/Hide Project pane button again to show the Project pane, or press F5.

The Project pane contains three lists. The Layers list is the one you'll use the most. It
displays the elements in your project as layers stacked inside groups.

3   In the Layers list, deselect the checkbox for the upper, foreground clip, *mogul_1 copy*.
This activation checkbox toggles the visibility of the layer in the Canvas. With the
foreground clip hidden, you can more easily focus on the background clip when adding and modifying filters.

4   In the Layers list, click the *mogul_1* layer. The selected clip highlights in the Layers list,
gets a bounding box in the Canvas, and appears in the mini-Timeline.

Stylizing with Filters

You can use filters to change the look of an element in your project. For example, you could use filters to color-correct a video clip that was too dark, turn a flat map into a sphere, or remove a green screen background to composite one clip on top of another.

You'll find the filters in the Library.

1   In the same pane as the File Browser, click Library, or press Command-2.

> **TIP** ▶ If you press Command-2 when the Library is already open, the entire pane closes. Press Command-2 to open it again.

The Library is organized like the File Browser with a preview area at the top, a sidebar in the middle, and a stack at the bottom. But rather than displaying files on your hard disk, the Library displays all the elements that are installed with Motion.

2　Select the Filters category.

Let's apply a Gamma filter to darken this background clip—that way, it won't distract the viewers' attention from the foreground.

NOTE ▸ Filter icons in your stack may not resemble the previous figure if you are viewing the Library contents as a list. To toggle between View as Icons and View as List, click the buttons in the lower-right corner of the Library.

3　Select the Color Correction folder.

4　In the Library stack, locate the Gamma filter.

5　Drag the filter onto the video in the Canvas.

Notice that the filters appear in the Layers list under the layer to which you applied it. Not much happens by default with this filter. You'll need to change the settings.

6　If the HUD is not visible, click the HUD button in the toolbar or press F7. The HUD appears displaying the Gamma parameter. Making Gamma adjustments darkens or lightens the midtones of an image.

7　Drag the Gamma slider to the left to reduce Gamma to about 0.50 and darken the background clip.

Next, let's add a retro style to this image to make it more interesting. This time you'll make your adjustment as the clip is playing.

8   Press the Spacebar to begin playing the project.

9   In the Library, select the Stylize folder, and then drag the Bad TV filter onto the Canvas. You can now adjust the Bad TV settings even as the clip is playing.

10   In the HUD, adjust Roll to 1 to remove the split screen and lower Saturate to roughly –50 to give the clip more of an old TV look.

11   In the toolbar, click the HUD button to close the HUD, or press F7.

Even though you may not remember that TV reception once looked like this, you have successfully mimicked an old TV look. You'll now turn your attention to the foreground clip.

Framing with a Mask

Masks allow you to hide parts of a layer based on a shape or a characteristic of another layer. In Motion, you can create countless complex masking effects.

For this exercise, you'll add a simple shape mask to the foreground video clip and adjust it to create a more interesting frame.

1   Stop playback and drag the playhead to the first frame of the project.

To draw a mask, it will be easier to work on a single frame of the video. The first frame is a good place to start.

2   In the Layers list, click the *mogul_1 copy* layer to select it.

3   Select the activation checkbox for the layer to make it visible in the Canvas.

4   On the left side of the toolbar, click the Rectangle Mask tool.

5   Starting above and to the left of the skier, draw a rectangle that encompasses the skier yet leaves room to the right to reveal her direction of travel. The video now appears inside this rectangle only. Notice that the mask appears in the Layers list and is selected.

You may want to adjust the size and position of the mask after you draw it. You can adjust the mask the same way that you previously transformed the video clip. You'll know when the mask is selected (as opposed to the clip) because the selection rectangle turns red.

6 With the mask selected, drag inside the mask to reposition it slightly.

7 Drag a transform handle on the bounding box to change the shape and size of the mask so it fits a bit more tightly around the skier.

Let's soften and round the edges of the mask a bit.

8 Click the HUD button to open the HUD, and increase Feather to 25 and Roundness to 20.

To distinguish the foreground clip from the background clip, you can add a drop shadow.

9 In the Layers list, select *mogul_1 copy*.

10 In the HUD, select the Drop Shadow checkbox.

11 Save your work.

12 Start playback to review your work so far.

You've given a single video clip some pizzazz by transforming it, duplicating it, and adding a few filters and a mask. Well done! You can perform one more step to more effectively composite the two images. You'll use a Blend mode to achieve a more appealing blended composite.

Compositing with a Blend Mode

Blend modes are a compositor's best friend. They alter the ways text, images, or video layers interact with each other based on their overlapping colors and/or luminance. In this exercise, you'll use a blend mode to lessen the harsh distinction between the two clips.

1   In the Layers list, select the foreground layer, *Mogul_1 copy*.

2   In the HUD, click the Blend Mode pop-up menu.

You can choose from many blend modes. In later lessons, you'll learn more about how they are organized and when certain modes are best used.

3   From the Blend Mode pop-up menu, choose Screen to brighten the two images where they overlap.

With the video clips now composited, masked, and filtered, you'll add some new elements to round out the project: animated text to describe the scene, and an animated graphic to draw attention to the text.

Adding Text

Our skier is competing in the Freestyle Moguls competition. This seems like important information that your viewers might want to know, so let's add text, format it, and position it onscreen.

1   Click in the gray area of the Canvas to deselect everything, or choose Edit > Deselect All.

2   Press the Spacebar to start playback, if necessary.

> **TIP** Depending on your hardware configuration, your playback performance may decrease as you add more elements to your project. One way to improve performance is to temporarily turn off layers. For example, as you're creating text, you really don't need to see the background **mogul_1** video—so you could turn off that layer by deselecting its activation checkbox in the Layers list.

You'll add the text while the project is playing so that you can position it interactively.

3   In the toolbar, click the Text tool.

4   Click near the center of the Canvas, a little below the masked skier, and type the skier's name, *Veronica Paulsen*.

5   Press the Esc key to return to the Select/Transform tool. The Select/Transform tool is the default tool with a pointer that looks like an arrow.

6   In the HUD, click the Font pop-up menu. Scroll down through the fonts, and choose Futura. Then from the Typeface pop-up menu, choose Condensed ExtraBold.

As you scroll, the Canvas updates in real time to show you each selected font.

7   Drag the HUD's Size slider to change the font size to 70 points.

8   Change the text color by clicking the down arrow next to the color well in the HUD and choosing a dark icy blue tone to match the cold feel of the clip.

9   Drag the text to position it against the left edge of the Canvas.

NOTE ▶ If this project were intended for broadcast, you'd need to make sure that the text is placed a safe distance away from the edges of the Canvas. By keeping your text within a safe zone, you're guaranteed that it will be visible on analog televisions. You can display safe zones from the View pop-up menu in the top right of the Canvas.

Let's animate that onscreen text to attract more attention.

Animating with Behaviors

Behaviors are a type of effect in Motion that let you animate elements with drag-and-drop simplicity. To make something move, grow, spin, wriggle, oscillate, speed up, or slow down over time, you just apply a behavior and adjust it to suit the situation.

Most behaviors can be applied to any video, still image, graphic, or text element in your project, and some are specifically designed for text. In this exercise, you'll use both types of behaviors to animate the text.

1   With the *Veronica Paulsen* text selected and the project playing, go to the Library and select the Behaviors category.

2   Select the Basic Motion folder.

3   Select the Throw behavior and watch the preview. In the preview area, you'll see a description of the behavior and an animation that shows what it does.

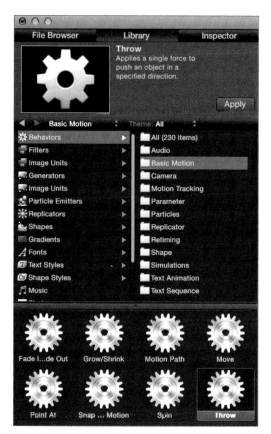

4   In the lower left of the Canvas, click the Show/Hide Project pane button to open the Project pane, or press F5, if necessary.

5   Drag the Throw behavior onto the *Veronica Paulsen* text layer in the Layers list.

6   In the HUD, drag from the center of the circle out to the right while watching the project play back.

The text moves to the right. The farther you drag out, the faster and farther the text moves across the screen.

Now you'll also hold down the Shift key to horizontally constrain the Throw direction.

7   Shift-drag the Throw direction so the tip of the arrow is just about to the middle ring in the HUD.

Only the skier's name is on the screen. You still need to add the name of the event. Instead of recreating the text font, color, and animation settings, you'll duplicate the skier's name and change the text.

8   In the Layers list, select the *Veronica Paulsen* text layer and choose Edit > Duplicate.

You now have identical text layers on top of each other. Although you can't see them in the Canvas, you can see each one in the Layers list. You'll now reposition one and change the text.

9   In the Canvas, drag the top text down to separate the two text layers.

10   Triple-click the lower text to highlight the entire name, and type *Freestyle Moguls*. Yes, you can even do this while the project is playing!

11 In the HUD, change the Typeface to Condensed Medium, and then change the text Size to 60.

12 Press the Esc key to exit the text editing mode and return to the Select tool.

13 Close the HUD.

14 In the Layers list, Command-click the *Veronica Paulsen* text layer.

15 Choose Object > Alignment > Align Right Edges.

Now let's add a behavior specifically created to animate each character in a text layer.

16 From the Library's Behaviors category, select the Text Sequence folder and double-click the Text-Basic folder.

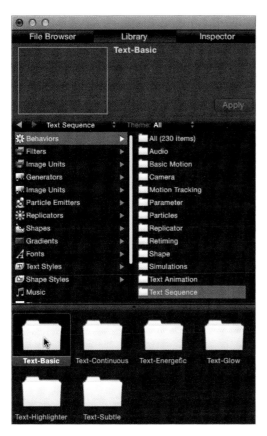

17 Drag the Fade Characters Left In behavior onto the *Freestyle Moguls* text layer in the Layers list.

18 Drag the same behavior to the *Veronica Paulsen* text layer in the Layers list.

You've now created sophisticated text animation using Basic and Text Sequence behaviors. The last step to complete your project is to add an interesting background to make the text stand out. To do that, you'll use content that is included with Motion.

Using Library Content

Although you can create your own graphics in Motion, a massive repository of graphical elements is included in the Content category of the Motion Library.

For this exercise, you'll add an animated graphic on the bottom third of the video that makes the title stand out.

1   In the Library, choose the Content category. As you can see, this folder includes over 1,300 elements.

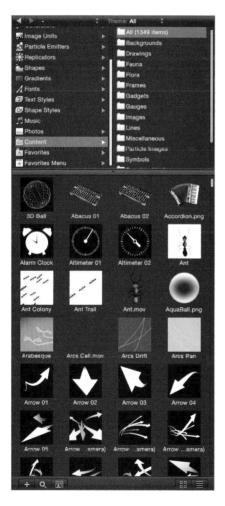

NOTE ▶ When you purchase and download Motion from the App Store, the accompanying content must be acquired as a separate download. If your Content category has no entries, check Software Update.

2   Select the Lines folder. Scroll down through the icons, select Bar 19, and watch the preview. The yellow animated strips will be a great complement to the dark blue text and the icy blue video.

TIP ▶ You can choose to view these elements as a list or as icons by clicking the appropriate button in the lower right of the Library. When viewing as icons, you can change the size of the icons by dragging the Icon Scale button to the left of the Icon View button.

3   In the preview area of the Library, click Apply.

4   Watch the project to see the new graphic you added.

The animated graphic is added to the Canvas on top of the other layers. It needs to be placed lower on the screen and arranged behind the text. Also the timing of the text animation and the yellow lines could be improved by offsetting them. All of these issues can be dealt with using the Layers list and the Timing pane.

Arranging Layers

In previous steps, you learned how to position elements spatially in the Canvas, but you haven't yet learned how to arrange the elements in front of or behind one another. You'll do that now using the Layers list to place the bars behind the text.

1   In the Layers list, drag the thumbnail frame of the *Bar_19* layer just below the Throw behavior within the *Veronica Paulsen* text layer.

TIP ▶ When moving elements in the Layers list, it's easy to drop one on top of another, thereby "nesting" layers into groups when you really wanted to change their stacking order. When inserting elements between other elements in the Layers list, be sure that a thin blue line appears where you want to insert the element. Alternatively, after placing the element, you could choose Bring to Front or Send to Back from the Object menu.

The Bar_19 graphic now animates under the text layers, but it could still be better positioned so that it doesn't obscure as much of the skier.

2   In the Canvas, drag down the Bar_19 graphic so the top of it aligns with the top of the *Veronica Paulsen* text layer.

Although that looks better, some of the skier is still obscured, so let's arrange the elements so that the skier clip is layered above the Bar_19 graphic.

3   In the Layers list, select the *mogul_1 copy* layer and drag its thumbnail frame just above the *Bar_19* graphic layer.

You now have a nicely arranged composite. The text stands out on that bright yellow graphic and the skier isn't obscured at all.

With the layers set, let's look at the timing of the elements. Currently, the text is onscreen from the very first frame of the project. It would be more effective if the text appeared after the Bar_19 graphic appeared. You can make this change in the Timing pane.

4   In the Timing pane, drag the *Freestyle Moguls* text layer to the right until the tooltip display shows an In point of 60 frames.

You've now set the *Freestyle Moguls* text to begin two seconds into your project. Let's set the skier's name to begin at one second into the project.

5   In the Timing pane, drag the *Veronica Paulsen* text layer to the right until the tooltip display shows an In point of 30 frames.

6   After you view the project a few times, press the Spacebar to stop playback.

Terrific! You created your very first Motion project and have become familiar with the Motion interface and many of its key features, including real-time playback; importing and transforming media; filters, masks, and behaviors; blend modes; Library content; and text.

Using Function Keys

You have worked briefly with the File Browser and the Library and also looked at one list in the Project pane, the Layers list.

But Motion has more lists to explore: the Inspector, two more lists in the Project pane, and an entire pane that you haven't yet opened that contains four panes of its own. Toolbar buttons are available for each of these panes and tabs, but it's much quicker to access them using their keyboard shortcuts.

> **TIP** ▶ On some keyboards, you must hold down the Fn key before pressing a function key.

1   Click the Media list.

The Media list displays all of the media—video and graphics—that is included in your project. Notice that the text and the bars graphics aren't included here because they are elements that came from the Motion Library.

2   Click the Audio list. If you have any audio in your project, you can see it, select it, and adjust it here.

3   Click the Layers list again, and select the *mogul_1 copy* layer.

4   If the HUD isn't visible, press F7.

As you've seen, the HUD gives you quick access to a few key parameters for a selected element. But it doesn't show you everything that you can change. For that, you'll use the Inspector.

5   Next to the Library, click Inspector.

6   Click the Properties pane, if necessary.

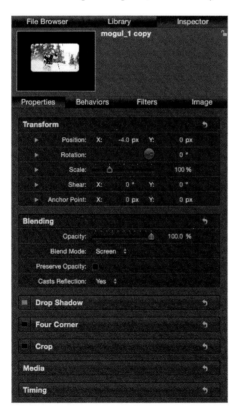

The Inspector contains four panes of its own. In the Properties pane, you can make precise adjustments and set keyframes for parameters that are common to any kind of layer. You'll work in the Properties pane in later lessons.

7   Press F2 to open the Behaviors pane. This pane is empty because no behaviors are applied to the selected layer.

8   In the Layers list, select the *Veronica Paulsen* text layer. Now the two applied behaviors appear in the Behaviors pane.

9   Press F3 to open the Filters pane, and then in the Layers list, select the *mogul_1* layer. In the Filters pane, you can adjust all the parameters for any applied filters.

10   Notice that the last pane currently reads *Image*. In the Layers list, click below all the layers to deselect everything. The pane name changes to *Object*.

11 Press F4 to bring the Object pane forward. The Object pane is context sensitive. Its name and contents change depending on what is selected.

NOTE ▶ You'll work in all these Inspector panes in later lessons.

12 Press F1 to return to the Properties pane. Notice that you can navigate to each of these four panes by pressing the function keys F1, F2, F3, and F4.

You already know that F5 opens and closes the Project pane. Leave that pane open for now.

13 Press F6 to hide the Timing pane, and then press F6 again to show it. The Timing pane contains three components: the Timeline, the Audio Timeline, and the Keyframe Editor. The Timeline component is selected by default. You'll work with the Audio Timeline and the Keyframe Editor in upcoming lessons.

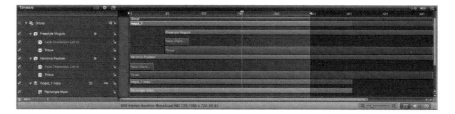

You already know that pressing F7 toggles the HUD.

14 Press F7 to hide the HUD. Click in the bottom of the Layers list to deselect everything, if necessary, and then press F8 to open Player mode.

The Player mode fills your entire monitor with the Canvas, transport controls, and toolbar. However, you can still apply changes to a project in this mode.

TIP ▶ In Player mode, you may want to press Option-Z to set your zoom level to exactly 100 percent.

15 Press F8 to exit Player mode.

16 Save your work.

Additional keyboard shortcuts allow you to go directly to each of the nine panes and to execute a variety of Motion commands. You'll explore these in later lessons. If you have a graphics tablet, you can use a special set of commands called *gestures* to navigate the interface and perform many other tasks. For more information, see the Motion Help documentation in the Help menu.

Outputting Your Projects

Your first project is done! Now the client comes calling and you need to deliver your work. So how do you get it out of Motion?

In Motion you have options—lots of 'em! If you want to output to tape, add to iTunes, watch on an Apple TV, burn to Blu-ray disc, or post to the web, you need only render your project into a movie file.

The rendering choices are located in the Share menu. The actual steps to render the different output choices are similar, so let's walk through one to get a general feel for the process.

1 Choose Share > Export Movie, or press Command-E.

For many Share options, the output format is dictated by the destination device. When you choose Export Movie, you have access to more formatting options because that option has no specific destination hardware. It's the best option to choose when you want to render a Motion project as a movie file to be used in Final Cut Pro.

> **TIP** ▶ The default export setting is called Current and is always set to ProRes 4444 format. ProRes 4444 is the best QuickTime format for exporting a movie with a transparency channel. Because Motion is a graphics application, chances are your project will have a transparency channel you will want to preserve.

2   From the Export pop-up menu, choose ProRes 422 (HQ).

Yes, I know what the preceding tip says, but this project has no alpha channel so we can save some space and time by exporting our movie in ProRes 422 (HQ) format. This format is a good choice for motion graphics without alpha channels because it provides high color fidelity.

Export "Freestyle Moguls 15" as a QuickTime movie

Vanessa Paulsen

| Options | Render | Advanced | Summary |

Export: Apple ProRes 422 (HQ)
Export a movie using the Apple ProRes 422 (HQ) codec

After export: Open with QuickTime Player

Include: Video and Audio

Duration: Entire Sequence (00:00:10:00)

Cancel   Next

The After Export pop-up menu includes several choices. By choosing the default menu selection, Open with QuickTime Player, the rendered file opens immediately after exporting it, so you can play the final file. You'll keep the default choice for this lesson.

Because the skier clip you used in this project had some irrelevant ambient audio, you'll want to include just the video in the rendered file.

3   From the Include pop-up menu, choose Video only.

Finally, you can choose to export the entire project or just a play range selection. Earlier in this lesson, the play range was set when you moved the Out point, so you'll limit this export to that section of the project.

4   From the Duration pop-up menu, choose In/Out Points, and then click the Render button.

In the Render pane, you can override the Project and Canvas settings. In this exercise, you won't modify these settings because you want a full resolution project that exactly matches what you have seen in the Canvas. The Render pane also includes 3D rendering options, which you'll learn more about in the last two lessons in this book.

5   Click the Advanced button.

Options in the Advanced pane are used only if you have purchased and installed the Compressor application. When using Compressor, you can set the Background Rendering pop-up menu to This Computer Plus to utilize other computers on your network for rendering. By clicking Send to Compressor, additional advanced compression options are available. You can learn more about Compressor from *Apple Pro Training Series: Final Cut Pro X Advanced Editing* (Peachpit Press).

NOTE ▸ If you haven't installed Compressor, a dialog will appear when you click the Send to Compressor button. The dialog will include a Buy Now button, offering you the opportunity to purchase Compressor from the Mac App store.

6 Click the Summary button.

If you are not using Compressor, the Summary pane displays a good overview of your current export settings. The Output Filename is taken from the project name, but you are able to change it after you click Next.

7 Click Next.

Export "Freestyle Moguls 16" as a QuickTime movie

Options   Render   Advanced   Summary

1 output file will be created.

Output Filename: Freestyle Moguls 16.mov
File type: QuickTime movie
Estimated size: 59.87 MB
Apple ProRes 422 (HQ), Width and Height: 1280 x 720. Frame rate: 23.976 fps

Cancel   Next

A standard Apple Save dialog opens, allowing you to choose a location for the exported file and to change the filename.

8   Click Save.

An export progress bar appears with a time estimate for completion. When using Export Movie, the rendering is performed in the foreground, preventing you from using Motion during the export process.

If you select any other Share option or you use Compressor, the exporting is performed in the background. In those cases, the Share Monitor will open a detailed view of your project's export progress.

That's it! You've exported your project to high quality ProRes format that is ready to be used in Final Cut Pro. Take the time to review what you learned in this lesson by answering the following questions.

Lesson Review

1. In the Project Browser, what must you do to create and open a new Motion project?

2. Identify the four main areas that are visible in a new project.

3. How can you precisely center a clip in the Canvas?

4. Other than in the Timing pane, in what part of the Motion interface can you change the play range or adjust a selected layer?

5. Do you have to stop playback to change the scale of a video clip?

6. How do you change the scale of a layer in the Canvas without changing its proportions?

7. Name the three kinds of effects you can add to a layer.

8. How can you change the way the pixels of one layer combine with pixels of a layer underneath?

9. Where is all the content that ships with Motion located?

10. In what part of the Motion interface can you interactively view fonts for a text layer without going to the Inspector?

11. Which keyboard shortcut opens Player mode?

12. If you choose Export Movie, can you still render in the background as long as you open the Share Monitor?

Answers

1. Select the Blank category in the sidebar and the Motion Project in the project stack, and then click Open.

2. The Canvas, File Browser, Project pane, and Timing pane

3. Drag the clip and use the dynamic guides with snapping enabled, or click the Import button in the File Browser.

4. The mini-Timeline

5. No, you can build an entire Motion project while the project is playing, although it's sometimes easier to accomplish certain tasks when the playhead is stopped.

6. Shift-drag a transform handle.

7. Filters, masks, and behaviors

8. Change the blend mode.

9. The Library

10. The heads-up display, or HUD

11. F8

12. No, Export Movie renders in the foreground unless you use Send to Compressor.

Keyboard Shortcuts

File Commands

Command-S   Save the project

Windowing Keys

F1   Open the Properties pane of the Inspector

F2   Open the Behaviors pane of the Inspector

F3   Open the Filters pane of the Inspector

F4   Open the Object pane of the Inspector (context sensitive depending on the selected object)

F5   Open and close the Project pane (which opens to its Layers list by default)

F6   Open and close the Timing pane (which opens to its Timeline component by default)

F7   Show/hide the HUD

Navigation

Option-Z   Zoom Canvas to 100 percent

Shift-Z   Set the Canvas to Fit in Window zoom mode

Play Range Commands

Spacebar   Turn playback on and off

Miscellaneous

Command-Z   Undo the previous action

2

Lesson Files	Motion5_Book_Files > Lessons > Lesson_02
Media	Motion5_Book_Files > Media > Rockumentary
Time	This lesson takes approximately 90 minutes to complete.
Goals	Apply blend modes and combine with filters
	Import layered Photoshop files
	Copy layers and filters
	Work with image sequences
	Perform Timeline edits
	Change preferences
	Make clone layers
	Transform and add masks to groups

Building a Composite

Creating motion graphics involves both compositing and animating. Before diving into animation, it's useful to have a good grasp of compositing.

To build a composite image, you combine often disparate elements to create a visually striking, integrated look that makes the final result much greater than the sum of its parts.

In this lesson, you'll build part of an opening title sequence. You'll work in the Layers list to organize your composite and in the Timeline to edit an image sequence. Finally, you'll combine blend modes, opacity changes, and filters to build textures from multiple graphical elements into a cohesive design.

Setting Up the Project

The rock group Pale Divine has asked you to create an opening title sequence for their new rockumentary project, *One—to Document the Years*. They have provided you with a handful of publicity and performance shots of the band, as well as their logo. You'll combine these images with some ink and paper graphics to create an organic, gritty look. First, let's preview the completed project.

1   In the Finder, open Motion5_Book_Files > Lessons > Lesson_02 > **Rockumentary_ Open.mov**, and play the movie file.

The movie has two distinct sections: the opening animation, with the photos and other graphics appearing to fall through space; and the rest of the movie, which contains only subtle movements.

In this lesson, you'll focus on compositing the elements that constitute the second half of the title animation.

2   Close the QuickTime Player and open Motion; or, if Motion is already open, choose File > New. In the Project Browser, make sure Blank is selected in the left column, and then click the Motion Project icon.

NOTE ▶ You will work with some of the Final Cut Pro project types in later lessons.

3   If necessary, from the Preset pop-up menu, choose Broadcast HD 720.

This HD setting matches the footage that was shot for the documentary so your title project will integrate easily into the final show.

4   Change the Duration field to 20 seconds, and press Return to open a new project.

A project duration of 20 seconds will provide enough time for the photos to animate, and to play the audio that we'll add later.

NOTE ► Pressing Return after entering a duration value will immediately open the new project. If you want to keep the Project Browser open, press Tab.

Right now, the new project's Canvas is empty. Although it appears black, Motion is just displaying that color to show that the workspace is empty. The background is actually transparent.

At the upper right of the Canvas are a series of pop-up menus: Zoom Level, Channels, Render, View and Overlay, and View Layouts. You can use these menus to change the appearance of the Canvas.

5   From the Zoom Level pop-up menu, choose Fit In Window or press Shift-Z. Now you can see the entire Canvas area.

6   From the Channels pop-up menu, choose Transparent. A gray and white checkerboard pattern appears, indicating that the background is transparent.

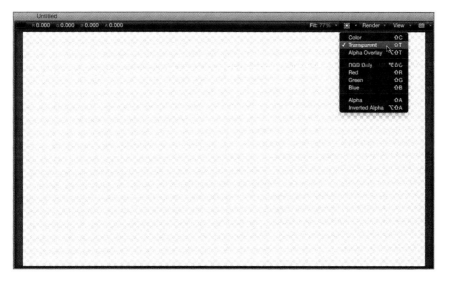

You won't want any transparency in this project. Therefore, it's a good idea to fill your background with a solid color. You can do this in the Project Properties window.

7   Choose Edit > Project Properties, or press Command-J.

The project is selected in the Layers list, and the Properties pane is displayed in the Inspector. In the Inspector, you can see project properties such as resolution, pixel aspect ratio, and frame rate. These reflect the settings you chose when you selected a project preset in the Project Browser. In this pane, you can customize that preset, or change the background.

NOTE ▶ The frame rate of a project cannot be changed once it is selected in the Project Browser.

8   From the Background pop-up menu, choose Solid. The description under the menu explains that the background will create a solid alpha channel. In other words, a black layer will exist under all the layers you add to your project.

Notice that the Canvas turns black, even though the Channels menu is still set to Transparent.

9   To save your work. choose File > Save, or press Command-S, and navigate to
     Motion5_Book_Files > Lessons > Lesson_02 > Student_Saves. Name the project
     My Rockumentary Open, and click Save.

With these initial technical considerations addressed, you can now turn your attention to
the creative process of building your composition.

Creating a Background Using the Inspector

You'll composite layers for this project, and use blend modes to make them interact. To
see the interactions between shapes and colors, it can be helpful to start from the bottom
layer and build up. Therefore, your first step should be to create a background. You'll use a
single graphic and place it in its own group to keep the project organized, and then you'll
apply a filter to modify that graphic.

1   In the Layers list, rename the default group to *Background*.

2   In the File Browser, navigate to Motion5_Book_Files > Media > Rockumentary, and
     select **radial_gradient.png**.

In the preview area, notice that the white blurred circle has no background and that the bit depth is described as "Millions of Colors+". The + (plus) symbol indicates that this graphic file includes an alpha channel, or transparency information. In other words, the graphic is composited over a transparent background.

3   Near the top of the File Browser, click Import to import **radial_gradient.png** into the *Background* group. The blurred circle appears in the Canvas over a black background. By previously setting the background to Solid, you ensured that no transparent areas will appear in the final project.

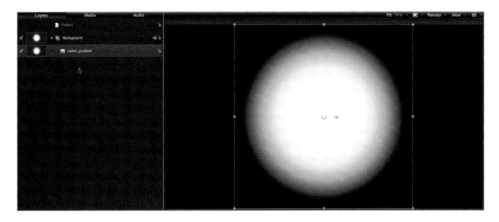

Notice that the layer's bounding box touches the top and bottom of the Canvas. By default, Motion scales down large images to fit the Canvas. This resizing can be helpful, but in this case, you will make the graphic larger to create a soft vignette effect.

NOTE ▶ To change the scaling behavior, choose Motion > Preferences, and click the Project icon. Then from the Large Stills pop-up menu, choose "Scale to Canvas Size" or "Do Nothing."

While you could directly transform the layer's scale in the Canvas, there's a better option to use when you want to make precise adjustments, or when you want to change parameters that aren't available in the Canvas or the HUD (heads-up display). For those situations, you'll use the Inspector.

4   Click the Inspector pane, and if necessary, select the Properties pane.

As discussed in the previous lesson, the Inspector includes four panes of its own: Properties, Behaviors, Filters, and Object—a contextual pane that changes depending on the type of layer selected. Currently, the Object pane is named *Image*.

The Properties pane contains all the layer parameters you can change directly in the Canvas—such as position, rotation, and scale—as well as parameters such as anchor point, blend mode, drop shadow, and crop. The parameters in the Properties pane apply to almost any type of layer: graphic, video, text, or other Motion objects. Changes made in the Canvas are reflected in the Properties pane and vice versa.

5   In the Canvas, drag the *radial_gradient* layer to change its position. Notice that the Inspector's Position parameter changes as you drag the layer.

6   Restore the layer to its previous position by choosing Edit > Undo Move, or pressing
     Command-Z.

You can change values in the Inspector using the sliders, dials, and value fields.

7   To try the multiple ways to change the Scale parameter, drag the Scale slider, click the
     value field and drag left and right or up and down, and type a numerical value into
     the value field. After each change, press Command-Z to undo the change.

Dragging directly in the value field is often the quickest way to make a change, and
frequently allows you to set a value that can't be achieved using the slider. For example,
the Scale slider goes only to 400%, but you can drag or type a higher value in the value
field.

TIP ▶ Shift-dragging in a value field changes the parameter ten times faster than
just dragging, which is great when you want to make an extreme change in the layer
scale or quickly move the layer far away. Option-dragging changes the parameter 100
times more slowly and is great for fine-tuning values.

Sometimes you'll want to reset all the basic properties of a layer at once. Rather than
typing a value in several value fields, you can click the Reset buttons—the hooked
arrows along the right side of the Inspector—to quickly reset groups of parameters.

8   Notice that the Scale value for the layer is currently 70.31%. Next to the Transform
     group of parameters, click the Reset button. All the Transform parameters are reset to
     their default values, so Scale is now 100%.

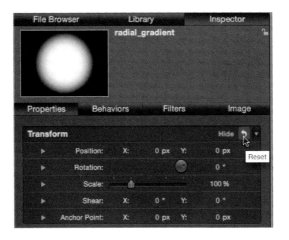

However, it's still not large enough for the vignette effect.

9   In the Scale value field, type *140* and press Return. Now the gradient fills most of the screen, leaving dark edges.

A filter can give the layer some color. In Lesson 1, you previewed filters in the Library before applying them to a layer, but you can also use a shortcut method to apply filters.

10   In the toolbar below the Canvas, click the Add Filter pop-up menu and choose Color Correction > Colorize. The filter appears underneath the layer it is applied to, and the white color in the Canvas changes to a pale off-white.

In the Inspector, the Filters pane automatically comes forward. The HUD contains some of the parameters that can be found in the Inspector. (If the HUD is not visible, press F7.)

While the HUD usually contains just a subset of the parameters for a selected layer or effect, the Inspector contains every adjustable parameter. In this case, you can use the Inspector to input specific RGB values.

The Colorize filter changes the dark and light areas of an image or video clip to colors that you specify by using the Remap Black To and Remap White To color swatches.

11 In the Inspector, next to the Remap White To parameter, click the disclosure triangle. In the data fields, type *0.63* for Red, *0.35* for Green, and *0.06* for Blue.

NOTE ▶ Motion employs an RGB scale of 0 to 1, with 0 using none of the color channel and 1 using its full value. You may have seen a range of 0 to 255 used in other applications. That range is based on an 8-bit color space, in which each color channel has 256 possible values. Because Motion works in either 16- or 32-bit space, its 0 to 1 scale works for any bit depth.

The background group is now complete. Next, you'll add the title elements, which will appear on top of the composition.

Using Photoshop Files

Instead of building this project strictly from the bottom up, you'll now add the very top elements. Why? Because the elements that sit on top of all the other layers are the titles and graphics, which can serve as guides as you composite the elements beneath them. You can think of this top group as a template that helps you align the entire composition.

The title elements were created in Photoshop using multiple layers and blend modes. Motion provides several options for using these Photoshop elements.

> **NOTE** ▸ You do not need Photoshop installed on your system to use Photoshop (.psd) files in Motion.

1   With the Colorize filter selected, from the Object menu, choose New Group.

Notice that the new group is created inside the *Background* group. Groups are always added just above the selected layer or effect. However, in this case, you want the new group to be placed outside and above the *Background* group.

2   Drag the new group above the *Background* group, wait for the position indicator and the + (plus sign) symbol to appear, and then release the mouse button.

The new group is now located above the *Background* group. Make sure that the position indicator is visible before releasing the mouse button. If the *Background* group has a white outline, it means you'll be dragging the selected group back inside the *Background* group.

TIP ▶ If nothing is selected when you create a new group, it is automatically placed at the top of the Layers list.

3   Rename the new group *Title*. Immediately naming new groups based on their intended contents will help keep your project organized.

4   Click the *Background* group disclosure triangle to collapse the group. Closing groups you aren't currently working with reduces Layers list clutter and helps focus your attention.

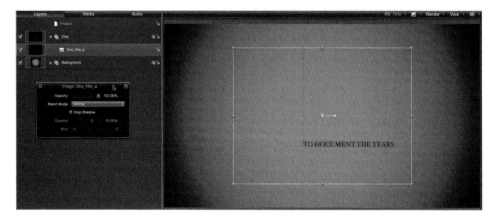

5   Press Command-1 to reveal the File Browser, and select One_title_a.psd.

The preview description tells you that this is a Photoshop file. The + (plus) next to "Millions of Colors" tells you that it has transparency. This Photoshop file has a few other properties that aren't listed: It comprises three layers, each with a blend mode applied.

NOTE ▶ Blend modes are also referred to as *blending modes, composite modes,* and *transfer modes.*

6   With the *Title* group selected, click the Import button in the File Browser. The file appears as a single layer in the Layers list, and all its elements appear in the Canvas.

Motion's default behavior is to combine all Photoshop layers into a single image. Although this result is often useful, it has two disadvantages. First, any applied blend modes won't pass through to other layers in Motion; second, you cannot transform or animate the individual Photoshop layers. While you won't animate layers in this lesson, you *will* want to keep the blend modes intact. Fortunately, Motion provides an alternative to combining Photoshop layers.

7　Press Command-Z to undo the media import.

8　From the File Browser, drag `One_title_a.psd` to the *Title* group, but don't release the mouse button.

A drop menu appears. You can choose Import Merged Layers (the default), or Import All Layers; or you can select a specific layer to import. The layer names in the drop menu match the layer names in the Photoshop file.

9　Move the hooked arrow over Import All Layers and release the mouse button. A new group with the name of the Photoshop file appears within the *Title* group, and each Photoshop layer appears as a separate layer within that group.

Because you already created a group for these layers, you don't need the *One_title_a* group. In fact, this group is not allowing the blend modes applied to its layers to pass through to the background layer. Therefore, let's move all the layers out of that group and delete the group.

NOTE ▶ When you import a layered .psd file into Motion, the group containing all the layers is set to "fixed resolution" by default. When a group is set to fixed resolution, blend modes applied to layers within the group aren't passed through to the groups beneath it. You can turn off this default in the Group pane of the Inspector.

10 To select all the layers, click the uppermost *lines* layer, and then Shift-click the lowest layer, *title_back*.

11 Drag all the layers from the *One_title_a* group into the *Title* group, and release the mouse button when a white outline appears around the target group.

12 Select and delete the now-empty *One_title_a* group.

TIP ▶ An empty group doesn't have a disclosure triangle next to its name.

These elements are too small for this HD project. To scale them up, you can scale the group containing them.

13 Select the *Title* group, press F1 to reveal the Properties Inspector, and change the Scale value to 180%.

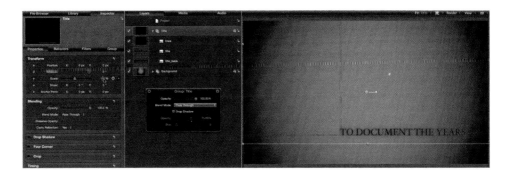

The text in the Canvas now has a red glow because the blend modes are enabled. How can you see the blend modes applied to each layer? One method is to use the HUD.

14 Select the uppermost *lines* layer, and if the HUD is not already visible, press F7. The HUD indicates a blend mode of Linear Light.

TIP ▶ Blend modes for an individual layer can also be seen (and changed) in a shortcut menu by Control-clicking (or right-clicking) the layer in the Layers list.

You could click each layer to inspect its blend mode, but there is a way to see the blend modes of all layers at once.

15 Choose View > Layers Columns > Blend Mode. The blend mode for each layer now appears on the layer itself.

NOTE ▶ To see the full blend mode names, you may need to adjust the Project pane width by dragging the small vertical line along the right edge of the pane.

NOTE ▶ Certain Photoshop effects and elements—such as layer effects, layer masks, adjustment layers, paths, and shapes—will not appear in Motion unless the layers are first rasterized or converted to Smart Objects in Photoshop.

You've completed the two outer layers of your composition "sandwich"—a background and the title. You'll now turn your attention to the "meat" of the project, the graphics, to give your composition mood and texture.

Compositing with Blend Modes and Filters

With the top elements in place, let's return to the bottom-up construction process and add graphics that will give your composition texture, color variation, and depth.

For source material, you'll use still images of ink and ripped paper. You'll scale, rotate, and position these images to complement or frame the title elements and the photographs that will appear on top. Finally, you'll employ duplicates, blend modes, and filters to make these layers work together with the other layers in the project.

This is a creative, interpretive process, so feel free to deviate from the recommendations in this exercise and come up with your own unique look.

1   Close the *Title* group. You are finished with this group.

2   Select the *Background* group, and press Command-Shift-N to create a new group, which is placed above the selected group and sandwiched between the two current groups.

3 Name the new group, *Graphics Under*. This group will contain all the graphics underneath the band pictures that you will add later.

4 From the File Browser, drag `brayer_03a.png` to the *Graphics Under* group. The image appears in the Canvas.

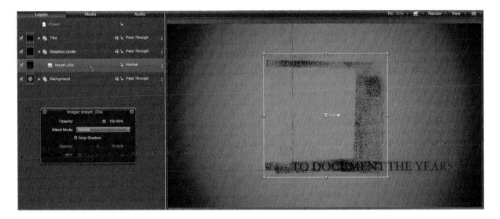

NOTE ▶ Because this image is already smaller than the project, it isn't scaled down to fit.

A *brayer* is a hand roller used to spread ink for making prints. This image, like several others in the File Browser, is derived from the extra ink that is rolled onto a backing sheet after the print has been removed. It's organic, grungy, and real—a nice design element.

5 In the Canvas, drag the handle extending from the anchor point in the center of the bounding box to rotate the image 90 degrees counterclockwise, Shift-drag a

bounding box handle to scale it up to about 125%, and position it at the bottom right of the frame underneath the title text.

TIP Because exact values aren't necessary here, manipulating the layer directly in the Canvas is faster than using the Inspector. Holding down the Shift key while rotating a layer will constrain the rotation to 45-degree increments, and will constrain scale changes to remain proportional to the original size.

6 Drag **brayer_03b.png** directly onto the *Graphics Under* group. When dragged onto a group, layers are added above any existing layers.

7 Keep its current rotation and scale, and position the layer at the top left of the frame.

8   Choose Edit > Duplicate, or press Command-D, to make a copy of this layer. Then scale down, rotate, and reposition the copy near the red vertical line.

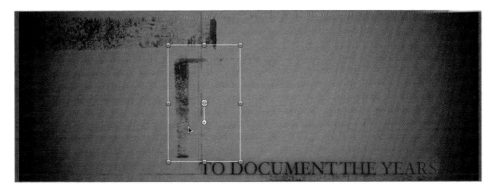

TIP If the yellow dynamic guides appear as you drag, press N to turn off snapping.

9   Add **brayer_06a.png**, to the *Graphics Under* group, rotate it 90 degrees clockwise, and then scale and reposition it to roughly fill the upper-right square formed by the red lines. It's OK if it obscures the text. You'll fix that in the next few steps.

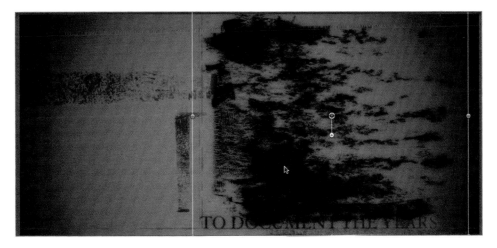

10 Click the Blend Mode pop-up menu for the *brayer_06a* layer to display all the available blend modes.

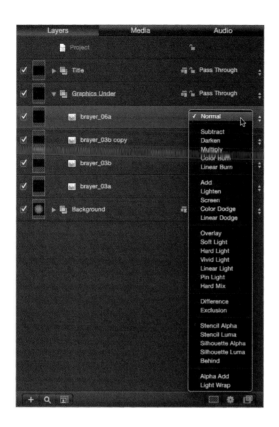

As you learned in Lesson 1, each blend mode performs a mathematical operation that combines the pixels of the selected layer or group with the pixels of the underlying layer. The default blend mode, Normal, displays just the pixels of the selected layer and obscures anything underneath.

The best way to determine a blend mode's impact is to try it out. Blend modes are organized into logical groups delineated by separator bars, and there are some general rules that often (but not always) apply to the groups:

▶   The first group of five blend modes, starting with Subtract, will generally darken the resulting image. Of these, Multiply is probably the most commonly used mode.

▶   The second group of five modes, starting with Add, will generally lighten the resulting image. Of these, Add and Screen are probably the most commonly used modes.

▶   The third group of seven modes will generally do both: make the light pixels lighter and the dark pixels darker to increase overall contrast. The first of these modes, Overlay, is probably the most commonly used.

The rest of the blend modes have more specialized functions.

Sometimes a blend mode's effect is too strong, too weak, or not quite what you expected. You can apply a filter to change the impact of a blend mode, and you can adjust the opacity of a layer to moderate the intensity of a blend mode.

11 Choose the Linear Light blend mode. The image stays black because this blend mode affects only those pixels that aren't completely black or white. To see the effect of this blend mode, you'll add a filter.

12 In the toolbar, click the Add Filter pop-up menu and choose Color Correction > Colorize.

This is the same filter you previously applied to the background gradient.

13 In the HUD, click the disclosure triangle next to the "Remap Black To" color well and sample a dark yellow to give the graphic a brownish-orange tint. Then select the *brayer_06a* layer, and in the HUD, lower Opacity to about 20%.

The combination of a blend mode and the Colorize filter allows a great deal of creative control. You'll use this same blend mode and filter combination, with a few adjustments, in another part of the composition.

14 Select the *brayer_06a* layer. Press Command-D to duplicate the layer, and then in the Canvas, rotate it 180 degrees and reposition it to cover the leftmost rectangle. Feel free to scale it non-proportionally (without holding down the Shift key) to fit the rectangle.

When you duplicate a layer with effects applied, the effects are duplicated as well.

15 On the copied layer, select the Colorize filter and remap black to a light gray. Select the layer and increase its Opacity to about 50%. Save your work.

By transforming a layer and changing the filter parameters, you can reuse elements multiple times in the same composition.

Completing the Underlying Graphics

To finish the graphics that will display underneath the images and text, you'll add a few more layers and apply both blend modes and filters.

As you complete these steps, feel free to experiment with the transformations, blend modes, and filter adjustments to create your own look.

1   From the File Browser, drag the **brayer_05a.png** file to the *Graphics Under* group.

2   Change the scale and position of the layer so that it covers the *brayer_06a copy* layer at the upper left of the Canvas.

This layer will add more texture to the composition. You'll apply a blend mode to brighten it and make the title you place on it stand out. Rather than applying the Colorize filter from the Add Filter pop-up menu, you can copy one of the existing filters.

3   Option-drag the Colorize filter from the *brayer_06a copy* layer onto the *brayer_05a* layer. Option-dragging any selected layer, group, or effect copies it to the new location.

4   In the HUD, change the blend mode of the *brayer_05a* layer to Linear Light, and change the Colorize filter's Remap Black To parameter to a darker gray so that the image doesn't appear too bright.

To accent the vertical line separating the brayer graphics, you'll use another graphic.

5   Drag the `brayer_05b.png` file to the same group.

6   Rotate, scale, and position the layer to cover the vertical red line. You can see how the title elements you've already added allow you to position these underlying graphics.

7   Option-drag a Colorize filter from any other layer to this new layer.

8   Change the layer's blend mode to Multiply to darken the combined graphics.

9   In the HUD, remap black to a red so that the graphic is a dark reddish brown. The Multiply blend mode in combination with the filter blends the graphic with the elements beneath it.

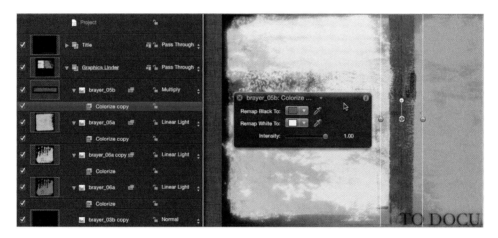

To finish, you'll add a graphic to highlight the title.

10   Drag **torn_vellum_strip.psd** to the *Graphics Under* group, wait a moment for the drop menu to appear, and choose Import Merged Layers. This is a multilayered Photoshop file, but it has no blend modes applied, so you can bring it into the composition as a single file.

> **TIP** If you know you want to import a layered .psd file as a single merged layer, you don't need to wait for the drop menu to appear as it will be imported as merged by default.

11   Press F1 to reveal the Properties Inspector, and next to the Transform group, click the Reset button (hooked arrow) to reset the scale of the graphic to 100%. Because the

graphic is larger than the Canvas, it was automatically scaled down, but it will work better at full size.

12 Reposition the graphic underneath the line of text, and lower its Opacity in the HUD to about 25%. The lower opacity reveals the black brayer graphic underneath but makes the torn strip look a bit dingy.

13 Choose Edit > Duplicate, or press Command-D, to copy the layer.

14 Change the blend mode of the copy to Overlay, and decrease the Opacity to about 20%. These changes brighten the strip but still allow the lower graphics to show through.

Good work! You've built a richly textured background that creates a mood, leads the eye to the title element, and leaves open spaces for the band pictures and logo.

Editing in Motion

So far, you have built a static composite that does not change over time. Every layer lasts for the full project duration. In the next exercise, you'll add a series of photographs that will change as the project plays.

To add layers that start and stop at specific points in a project, let's explore the editing options in Motion, including composite edits, overwrite edits, and sequential edits.

Working with Image Sequences

First, you'll look at the photos that you'll edit into the composition.

1   Press Command-1 to open the File Browser. Select vid_pix_[###].jpg:1:20, and play it in the preview area.

This file appears as a single icon in the stack and plays like a movie that contains a series of one-frame images. It is described as a JPEG sequence. A collection of still images with sequentially numbered filenames will appear in the File Browser by default as a single image sequence. You can use this image sequence as you would use any other QuickTime movie in Motion.

Sometimes you'll want to work with a series of images as an image sequence, but at other times you'll want to work with the images individually. Motion lets you do both.

2   At the bottom of the File Browser, the "Show image sequences as collapsed" button toggles how image sequences are viewed. By default, the button is enabled. Click the button to expand the image sequence. The individual images now appear in the stack. There are 20 images, which is why *1:20* appeared at the end of the sequence name.

TIP ▶ Digital cameras frequently save files with sequential numbers, so if you are looking for digital photos in the File Browser and see only one image, it may actually represent multiple images collapsed as an image sequence.

For this project, you want to work with the individual images. Before adding those images to the project, you will create a group to contain them.

3   Close the *Graphics Under* group. Then select that group, create a new group above it, and name the new group, *Stills*.

You'll composite the photos on top of everything you've created so far except for the title graphics.

There are 20 photos, and the project is 20 seconds long. So let's keep things simple and have each photo play one after the other for one second each. You have several options for editing the photos into the project.

4   With the Stills group selected and the playhead still at the beginning of the composi-
     tion, select **vid_pix_001.jpg** and click the Import button.

The layer appears in the Layers list; the graphic appears in the Canvas; and in the
mini-Timeline, the blue bar representing the graphic extends for the length of the
project.

By default, elements that you add to a composition will start at the playhead position
and end at the end of the composition (except for video clips, which will end based
on their durations). This behavior was effective for all the background elements you
previously used, but in this case, you want each picture to last just one second. One
way to achieve this is to trim each layer to the correct duration and location in time.
For the first photo, you want to set the Out point of the clip at one second.

5   In the mini-Timeline, position the pointer over the very end of the *vid_pix_001* bar so
     that it changes to a trim pointer.

6   Drag left until the tooltip indicates a duration of 1:00. The layer now lasts only one
     second, starting at the beginning of the project.

NOTE ▸ If the timing display at the bottom of the Canvas is showing frames, click the
arrow to the right of the frame counter, and choose Timecode.

TIP ▶ You can also trim a clip's Out point by moving the playhead to the point at which you want to make the trim (at one second, in this case) and choosing Mark > Mark Out, or pressing O.

Normally, when you import an element into a project, it is composited on top of the existing layers without changing those layers in any way. But you can choose other editing options when you are working in the Timeline.

Editing in the Timeline

You can perform many editing operations in the mini-Timeline: trimming In and Out points, moving layers in time, and even slipping video clips. But when you want to see how layers and effects relate to each other over time—or to access to additional editing options—you'll want to work in the Timeline.

1   Press Command-Z to undo the previous trimming operation.

2   If necessary, press F6 to open the Timing pane. In the left side of the Timeline, close all open groups except for the *Stills* group.

In the Timeline, you can simultaneously see the duration of multiple layers. The left side shows the groups and layers, exactly like the Layers list in the Project pane. The right section contains bars to indicate the duration of each layer. Currently, every layer lasts for the full duration of the project, including the *vid_pix_001* layer.

To perform editing, you can drag clips directly into the Timeline.

3   From the File Browser, drag vid_pix_002.jpg to just above the *vid_pix_001* layer in the Timeline. Watch the tooltip and move the image horizontally until the tooltip reads 1:00, and then hold the pointer in place but don't release the mouse button.

NOTE ▶ It is critical to position the pointer just above the layer, not below. If you position the pointer below the layer, different options will appear in the drop menu.

The tooltip indicates that the clip will start at 1:00. The horizontal black line above the *vid_pix_001* layer indicates that the clip will be placed above this layer.

The drop menu offers three edit choices: Composite (the default), Insert, and Overwrite.

4   Position the pointer over Overwrite and release the mouse button. The new layer overwrites the existing layer, trimming it to one second.

NOTE ▶ An insert edit would split the *vid_pix_001* layer into two layers, with the second half on a new layer and its In point pushed forward in the Timeline to start after the Out point of the *vid_pix_002* layer.

This overwrite edit is clearly more efficient than manually trimming each layer. You could add all the images this way, dragging the next image to 2:00, overwriting the next photo, and so on. But because you know that you want every photo to last for one second, you can tell Motion to automatically set their durations.

5 Choose Motion > Preferences, or press Command-, (comma), and click the Project button at the top of the window.

You use the Preferences window to change the Motion default settings.

6 In the Still Images & Layers section, set Default Layer Duration to "Use custom duration." From the pop-up menu, choose Seconds, and in the value field enter *1.0*.

You may later want to restore the Default Layer Duration to "Use project duration", but for now this option will make the editing process much more efficient.

NOTE ▶ Changes you make to preferences remain in effect for all projects, so it's a good habit to review them before you create a new project or update an older project.

7 Close the Preferences window.

8 From the File Browser, drag `vid_pix_003.jpg` to 2:00 in the Timeline, just above the *vid_pix_002* layer, and in the drop menu, choose Overwrite.

The new layer comes in already trimmed to 1:00. The overwrite edit divided the lower *vid_pix_002* layer into two sections, and you don't need the second section.

9 Select and delete the *vid_pix_002 1* layer.

With all layers set to last just one second, you could now drag each photo to the end of the previous photo layer and use the default composite edit to edit the rest of the pictures into the sequence. But another edit type is perfect for adding a sequential set of images: the sequential edit.

10 At the bottom of the File Browser, click the List View button to see the files displayed as a list. This view will make it easier to select all the files in order.

11 If necessary, click the Name column header to sort the files in ascending order by name; then Shift-click `vid_pix_004.jpg` and Shift-click `vid_pix_020.jpg` to select the remaining 17 photos (or drag to select them).

12 Drag the photos from the File Browser to the Timeline, and snap them above the Out point of the *vid_pix_003* layer at 3:00. When the drop menu appears, notice that a new option is available: Sequential.

NOTE ▸ If you have trouble snapping to the Out point of the layer, make sure you chose View > Snap to enable snapping.

13 Choose Sequential. All the selected images are laid into the Timeline one after the other, creating a staircase of clips that will play sequentially.

TIP ▸ The sequential edit works with any collection of files, not just image sequences.

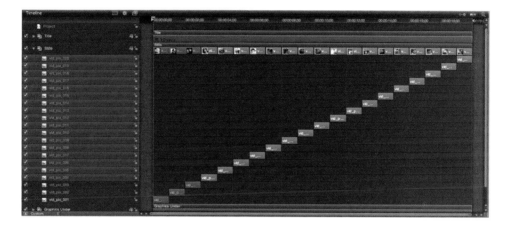

The files will be added in the order in which you selected them in the File Browser. If you want to play them in a different order, you can Command-click each file to select them in the order you desire.

14 Click in the Timeline to make it active, then choose Edit > Deselect All. Save your work, and then play the project.

The photos now play in order, each lasting for one second. With the editing complete, you'll turn your attention to making the images blend with the other elements.

Applying Masks and Using Clones

The series of photographs look like they have been slapped on top of the other layers, with some in color and some in black and white. You will now combine masks, clones, and blend modes to integrate the images into the composition.

1 Stop playback. Return the playhead to the first frame, and close the *Stills* group in the Timeline.

2   Close the *Stills* group in the Layers list and then select it. By transforming and apply-
    ing effects to the group, you'll affect all the layers within the group at once.

3   In the Canvas, scale the group to about 110%, and reposition it to fit roughly in the
    upper-right rectangle. Make sure to hold down Shift as you scale to maintain the
    image proportions. You will use a mask to blend the edges of the images into the
    background.

    TIP ▸ If snapping is making it difficult to position the group, press N to turn it off.

4   In the toolbar, place your pointer over the Rectangle Mask tool and hold down the
    mouse button to display a list of tools. Then, choose the Circle Mask tool.

5   With the *Stills* group still selected, Shift-Option-drag a mask from the center of the
    photo in the Canvas and make it large enough to encompass the drummer.

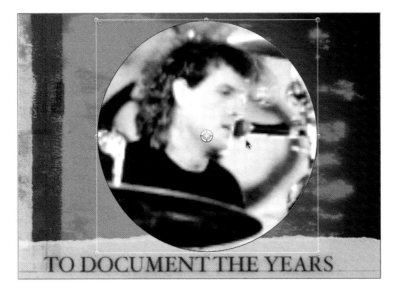

> **TIP** ▸ The same modifier keys that work when transforming layers—Shift to constrain proportions and Option to scale around the anchor point—also work with masks.

6   In the HUD, increase the Feather amount all the way to 100. That's still not enough feathering. Remember, if you can't get the value you want within the HUD, try the Inspector.

7   Press F4 to reveal the fourth pane of the Inspector. This is the context-sensitive pane that changes its name depending on the selected element. It is currently called Mask.

8   Increase the Feather value to about 200. The increased feathering may reveal the original edges of the photo.

> **NOTE** ▸ Not all parameters can be increased beyond the values available in the HUD or using the slider in the Inspector.

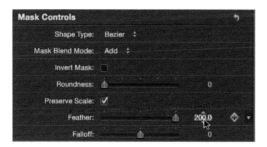

9   In the Canvas, adjust the scale and position of the mask as necessary.

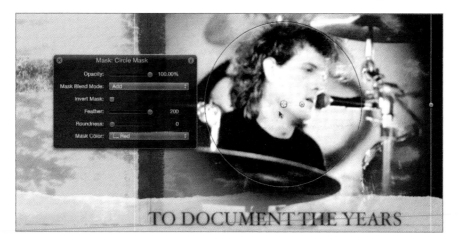

To further integrate the photos into the overall look of the project, you'll copy them and add some filters to the copies.

Previously you copied layers by duplicating them. Motion provides an alternative to duplicating called *cloning*. By cloning a layer or a group, you use less memory. In addition, changes made to certain properties of the source layers will be passed to the clones.

10 Close and select the *Stills* group.

11 Choose Object > Make Clone Layer, or press K. A clone layer appears in a new group above the *Stills* group. The clone, an exact copy of the *Stills* group, sits on top of the group and covers it.

12 Change the blend mode of the clone layer to Linear Light. The result doesn't quite match the look of the rest of the composition. You'll colorize the clone and blur it to blend it in.

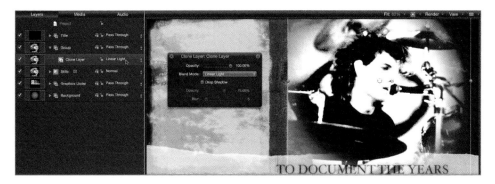

13 Click the Add Filter pop-up menu and choose Color Correction > Colorize.

14 Remap black to a dark gray, and white to a light brown.

15 Click the Add Filter pop-up menu and choose Blur > Gaussian Blur. A Gaussian Blur filter softens an image by averaging each pixel with its neighboring pixels.

16 Increase the Amount parameter to about 20.

17 Save your work, and then play through the project. You can reposition the clone layer or individual photos in the *Stills* group within the circle mask to suit yourself.

TIP ▶ When using photos in which people face the edge of the Canvas, consider adding a Flop filter from the Distortion category. Just make sure that there isn't any text in the image, as it will be reversed.

Excellent! Your last step is to add the graphics on top of the photos.

Importing Motion Projects

The graphics that you'll add on top of the photos include the band's logo, an additional title element ("*One*"), graphics that represent the years covered in the rockumentary (1984 to 1992), and one more ink-based element to add a bit more grunge and tie everything together. Blend modes, colorize filters, and blur filters will help integrate these elements.

Because you have already worked with the techniques that created these elements, we've "prebaked" them for your convenience. That is, they have been saved as a Motion project that you can just drop into the current project. But first, as usual, you will need to organize the Layers list to make room for the new guests.

1 Rename the group containing the clone layer to *Graphics and Stills*. This group will contain all the elements that are not in the *Title* group on the very top or in the *Background* group on the very bottom.

2 Drag the *Stills* group on top of the *Graphics and Stills* group.

The *Stills* group is now on top of the *Clone Layer*, but it needs to be underneath for the clone to blend with it.

3   Choose Object > Send to Back, or press Command-Shift-[(left bracket). The *Stills* group moves to the bottom of the *Graphics and Stills* group, and the composition once more looks correct in the Canvas.

> **TIP** ▶ Choosing a menu command or pressing a keyboard shortcut to move layers or groups within a group can be easier than dragging them. For example, when dragging, it's possible to accidentally drag one group into another group.

4   Close the *Clone Layer* layer to hide the filters, and drag the *Graphics Under* group on top of the *Graphics and Stills* group. Then press Command-Shift-[(left bracket) to move the *Graphics Under* group to the bottom of the *Graphics and Stills* group.

5   Open the File Browser, and switch to icon view. Click the "Show image sequences as collapsed" button to consolidate the images (so you can see the other files in this folder), and locate Graphics Over.

This file has a Motion application icon because it represents a group of layers from a Motion project that was saved by dragging the group from a project to the File Browser.

6   With the playhead located at the first frame of the project, drag the **Graphics Over** file to the *Graphics and Stills* group. A new group, *Graphics Over*, appears at the top of the *Graphics and Stills* group.

7   Open the *Graphics Over* group and all its layers. The layers in this group have blend modes and filters applied to help composite them into the project.

TIP ▶ Depending on your screen size and resolution, you may not be able to see all the layers without scrolling the Layers list. You can change the height of layers and groups in the Layers list by positioning the pointer between any two layers, waiting for it to change to a resize pointer, and dragging upward or downward.

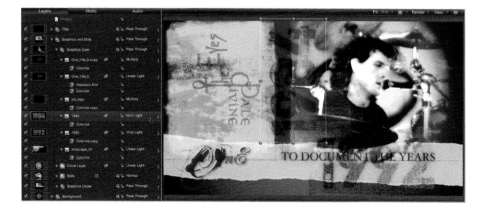

8   Select and deselect the activation checkboxes next to the layers and filters in the *Graphics Over* group to see how they have been composited in the Canvas. Once again, feel free to change the position, scale, and rotation of layers, and to try different blend modes and filter settings to customize the look.

9   Play through the project, and make any final adjustments to individual photos.

Applying a Flop filter makes the musician face the center of the Canvas instead of looking offscreen.

10   Press Command-, (comma) to open Motion Preferences. In the Project pane, change the Default Layer Duration back to "Use project duration."

11   Close all open groups in the Timeline and the Layers list, and save your work.

Congratulations. You now have a solid grasp of many of the compositing options in Motion using transformations, blend modes, opacity adjustments, and filters to create an integrated look. Along the way, you've learned how to edit in the Timeline, use clones and masks, and work with the Layers list—all critical skills for compositing motion graphics.

Lesson Review

1.   How can you ensure that transparent areas of your project will appear black?

2.   You are using the HUD to change the brightness of a filter, but even at the maximum setting, it's not bright enough. Where can you enter a higher value?

3.   Name two blend modes that will generally result in a lighter image.

4. Identify two ways to modify the impact of a blend mode.

5. When you want to make a copy of a layer or group, what is an alternative to duplicating?

6. Identify the three options for importing a multilayered Photoshop file.

7. A client gives you 50 digital photos to use in a Motion project. You put them in a folder on your desktop, but when you look in that folder using the File Browser in Motion, all you see is a single icon. What's going on, and what can you do to see all the photos?

8. Name three types of edits you can perform in Motion.

Answers

1. Choose Edit > Project Properties and set Background to Solid.

2. In the Inspector

3. Add, Lighten, Screen, Color Dodge, or Linear Dodge

4. Lower the opacity of the layer, duplicate the layer, or add a colorize filter.

5. Use Make Clone Layer, which is similar to duplicating, but uses less memory, and the clone layer inherits certain properties of the original.

6. As merged layers, as all layers, or by selecting an individual layer

7. The photos are numbered sequentially and appear by default in the File Browser as a collapsed image sequence. Click the "Show image sequences as collapsed" button to see the individual files.

8. Composite, overwrite, insert, sequential

Keyboard Shortcuts

Command-1	Reveal the File Browser
Command-2	Reveal the Library
Command-3	Reveal the Inspector
Command-D	Duplicate the selected layers(s) or group(s)
Command-J	Reveal project properties
Command-Shift-N	Create a new group

Keyboard Shortcuts

Command-, **(comma)**	Open Preferences
Command-[**(left bracket)**	Send the selected layer back (down)
Command-] **(right bracket)**	Move the selected layer forward (up)
Command-Shift-[**(left bracket)**	Send the selected layer to the back (bottom of the group)
Command-Shift-] **(right bracket)**	Bring the selected layer to the front (top of the group)
Option-drag	Create a copy in the Canvas, Layers list, or Timeline
K	Clone a group or layer

Animation

3

Lesson Files	Motion5_Book_Files > Lessons > Lesson_03
Media	Motion5_Book_Files > Media > Rockumentary
	Motion5_Book_Files > Media > Stage
Time	This lesson takes approximately 60 minutes to complete.
Goals	Create animation using Basic Motion behaviors
	Adjust, copy, and trim behaviors
	Use Simulation behaviors
	Apply Parameter behaviors
	Clone animated groups
	Compare animation using behaviors and keyframes

Creating Animation with Behaviors

Motion has a unique method for putting the "motion" in motion graphics: using *behaviors*. So what are behaviors? They are an *effect*, like a filter or a mask, that you can apply to a layer or group of layers. They allow you to create animation *procedurally*—that is, they contain a set of instructions that describe how to make an element move, or spin, or fade, so you don't have to create the animation manually with keyframes.

Motion includes a huge variety of behaviors to animate graphics, video, shapes, particle systems, and text; stabilize footage; track objects; simulate gravity; and even animate cameras to fly around in 3D space.

In this lesson, you will use Basic Motion and Simulation behaviors to animate the first half of the opening title for your Rockumentary project. After that, you will explore Parameter behaviors in a new project.

Adding Basic Motion Behaviors

When you want to float a layer across the screen, rotate it, or fade it into view, you should reach for a Basic Motion behavior. These behaviors create animation using simple drag-and-drop techniques, and they even work in 3D. In the upcoming exercises, you'll use several Basic Motion behaviors to make graphics appear to tumble through space.

First, let's play the final Rockumentary animation again to preview what you'll create in this lesson; then we'll examine the partially completed project, and add the first behavior.

1   In the Finder, open Motion5_Book_Files > Lessons > Lesson_03 > Rockumentary_ Open.mov, and play it.

You want to illustrate the touring years of the rock group Pale Divine by creating a cascade of dates and images. In the first 15 seconds of the title, you can animate dates and photos to fade in, spin back into space, and fade out.

2   In the Finder, open Motion5_Book_Files > Lessons > Lesson_03 > Rockumentary Behaviors Start. Save a working copy of the project to the Lesson_03 > Student_Saves folder. You can leave the QuickTime movie open for reference if you like.

3   In the Layers list, click the disclosure triangles to view all groups and layers.

> **TIP** You can drag up between any two layers or groups to resize all the layers and see more of them without scrolling.

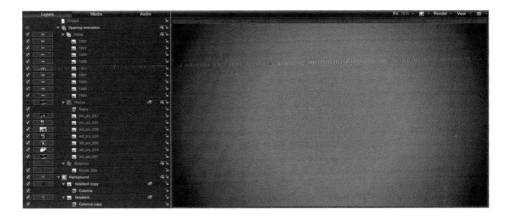

There are two top-level groups: The *Background* group contains two still-image layers with filters and blend modes applied to create an aged, vignetted background look; and the *Opening animation* group contains a group of dates, a group of photos, and a group with a brayer image. The icons for all but one of the layers in the *Opening animation* group are black and white because they don't exist at the current playhead location. The *Photos* and *Graphics* groups are dimmed because they are disabled.

4   If necessary, choose Window > Video Timeline to reveal the Timeline below the Canvas. In the Timeline, open the *Opening Animation, Dates,* and *Photos* groups. If necessary, drag the zoom slider to see the full project.

TIP You can increase the height of the Timing pane by dragging up between the Timing pane and the toolbar. You can also resize the layers and groups by dragging between any two of them, but they won't get as small as they will in the Layers list.

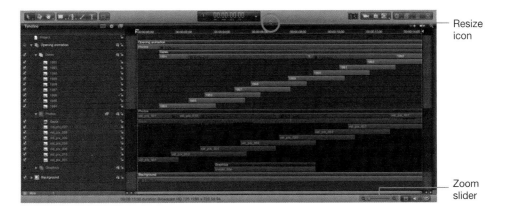

Resize
icon

Zoom
slider

The *Dates* and *Photos* layers are staggered in a staircase-like pattern to introduce one after the other. The layer bars in the *Photos* group are dimmed because the group's visibility is turned off, enabling you to focus on the dates.

5   Close the *Background, Graphics,* and *Photos* groups in both the Timeline and the Layers list. Press the Spacebar to play the project, and then click each of the layers in the *Dates* group.

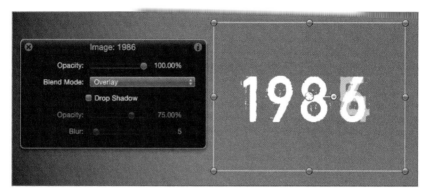

The HUD shows that each of the layers has the Overlay Blend Mode applied.

NOTE ▶ If the HUD isn't visible, press F7 or choose it in the toolbar.

Now that you have a feel for the project's structure, you will animate the dates. First, you will set a play range around one layer.

6   Stop playback, select the bottom *1984* layer, and press Shift-I to move the playhead to the layer's In point.

7   Choose Mark > Mark Play Range In or press Command-Option-I.

8   Press Shift-O to move the playhead to the layer's Out point, press Command-Option-O to set a play range Out point, and then press the Spacebar to play the play range.

NOTE ▶ At the far right of the transport controls below the Canvas, make sure that Loop Playback is turned on.

The next two layers, *1985* and *1986*, overlap the *1984* layer, which makes them pop onscreen in a distracting way.

9   During playback, turn off the visibility of the *1985* and *1986* layers. You are now set up to animate the *1984* layer by adding several Basic Motion behaviors.

10 Press Command-2 to open the Library. Select Behaviors, and then select the Basic Motion folder. The folder contains eight behaviors.

11 Select the Grow/Shrink behavior. The preview area shows an animation of the behavior in action, along with a written description. You can use this behavior to create the illusion that the layer is falling "back" in space.

12 Drag the Grow/Shrink behavior onto the *1984* layer in either the Timeline or the Layers list.

Behaviors appear under the layer they are applied to, just like a filter or a mask. In the mini-Timeline, a purple bar representing the behavior matches the duration of the layer between the play range's In and Out points. In the HUD, a graphical interface allows you to manipulate the behavior. In the Canvas, nothing appears to happen, even though the project is playing. Many behaviors must be adjusted to create animation.

13 In the HUD, drag inward on a corner of the square. The layer shrinks over the duration of the behavior, appearing to fall back in space.

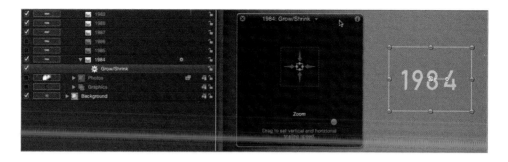

TIP Be sure to drag from a corner. If you drag an edge handle, the layer will scale nonproportionally.

14 Save your work.

It's a good start, but the animation could use more pizzazz. Luckily, it's easy to add multiple behaviors to the same layer.

Stacking Behaviors

You can add multiple behaviors to a layer, and Motion will combine their effects. In this exercise, you apply two additional behaviors: one behavior to make the layer fade into view and then disappear, and another behavior to make the layer tumble as it falls away.

1 From the Library, drag the Fade In/Fade Out behavior onto the *1984* layer.

2 Drag in the HUD to increase the Fade In duration to 30 frames.

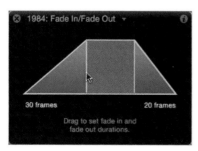

To make the layer tumble, you would use the Spin behavior. Rather than return to the Library, this time you'll use the toolbar to apply the behavior.

3   In the toolbar, click the Add Behavior pop-up menu, and choose Basic Motion >
     Spin. The Spin behavior appears underneath the *1984* layer, stacked on top of the
     other behaviors.

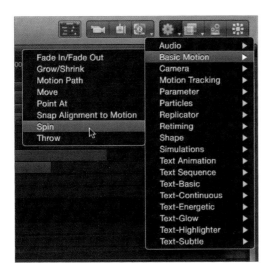

TIP ▶ While the Library lets you preview behaviors as you select them, you may
find it faster to select behaviors from the toolbar.

4   In the HUD, drag around the edge of the circle clockwise 360 degrees. An arrow indi-
     cates the direction and amount of rotation.

The layer now spins around its anchor point, but it is only rotating flat to the screen.
It would be more interesting if the layer tilted (like a laptop computer screen) and
swung (like a door).

5   In the HUD, drag the sphere containing the 3D arrows. The layer now rotates on all
     three axes as it shrinks.

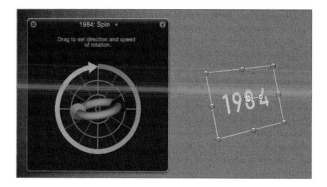

With three behaviors applied to this layer, you can adjust each of them in the context
of the completed animation while playing the project, quickly switching between the
behaviors in the HUD. Or, use the Inspector to apply more precise adjustments.

6   Press D to select the next behavior, the Fade In/Fade Out behavior, and adjust it as
     desired in the HUD.

Pressing D repeatedly cycles through each layer and each of the behaviors and filters
applied to it, allowing you to quickly make changes in the HUD.

7   Press F2 to open the second pane of the Inspector: the Behaviors pane. Here, you can
     precisely adjust all of a behavior's parameters, some of which are not available in the HUD.

8   In the Spin behavior section, from the Axis pop-up menu, choose Y. The layer now swings around its vertical y-axis only.

9   Return the Axis pop-up menu to Custom, and adjust the Latitude and Longitude parameters to your liking.

10 Stop playback and save your work.

Your first date layer animation with behaviors is complete. You'll animate the other dates by copying some of these behaviors and applying new ones.

Using Basic Motion Behaviors in 3D

In later lessons, you'll use more of the 3D features in Motion, but for now let's get a general feel for them. In 3D space, you can change a layer's rotation and position along all three axes: the horizontal, or x-axis; the vertical, or y-axis; and the depth, or z-axis (the axis pointing straight in and out of the screen).

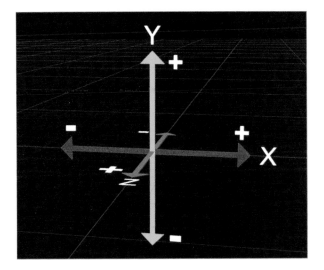

Every layer in a Motion project can be rotated and positioned along the x, y, and z axes without turning on the 3D features—such as 3D groups, 3D tools, views, and cameras—that you will use in later lessons.

You already animated the *1984* layer in 3D by rotating it on all three axes. But it's not really moving "back" in space, it's just shrinking in size. Instead of using the Grow/Shrink behavior to simulate this 3D movement, you can make the layer move back in z-space using the Throw or Motion Path behavior. Let's try each to see what it can do.

1   Turn on the *1985* layer, select it, and set a play range around it by dragging the play range In and Out points in the mini-Timeline, or by pressing the keyboard shortcuts you used earlier: Command-Option-I and Command-Option-O.

> **TIP** ▸ If you Shift-drag the play range indicators, they will snap to the layer's In and Out points.

2   Turn off the *1984* and *1987* layers so that they won't distract you, and start playback.

3   In the toolbar, click the Add Behavior pop-up menu and choose Basic Motion > Throw.

4   In the HUD, drag the zoom slider to about a third of the way from the left, and then, starting at the center of the circle, drag out in any direction.

> **TIP** ▸ To throw a layer vertically or horizontally only, Shift-drag from the HUD center.

The date graphic moves in the Canvas, with a red line indicating the direction and length of travel. The zoom slider in the HUD determines how far you can move. By default, the behavior moves the layer only horizontally and/or vertically along the x and/or y axes. But what about the z-axis?

5   In the HUD, click the 3D button and drag the zoom slider near the right edge of its range. Drag in the sphere to move the 3D arrow until it points away from you.

After you enable 3D for the behavior, you can throw a layer in any direction in 3D space. To make it fly directly away from you, it's easiest to use the Inspector.

6   If the Behaviors pane isn't selected, press F2. Click the Throw Velocity disclosure triangle, then set the X and Y values to 0, and the Z value to –1000. The Throw Velocity determines how many pixels the object will move over the duration of the behavior. These settings will throw the date graphic 1,000 pixels "away" from you in Z-space.

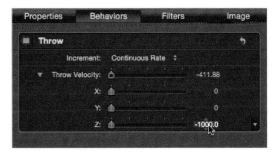

To make the layer spin and fade, you can copy those two behaviors from the *1984* layer. You need to modify the copied Spin behavior so that the animation doesn't look exactly the same for each layer.

7   In the Layers list, under the *1984* layer, select both the Spin and Fade In/Fade Out behaviors. Then Option-drag them onto the *1985* layer.

The behaviors are copied to the *1985* layer and exactly fill the play range in the mini-Timeline and Timeline, which means that they match the location and duration of the *1985* layer.

NOTE ▶ When you copy a behavior from one layer to another, the behavior automatically starts at the beginning of the target layer. However, the behavior's duration is not changed, so it may need to be trimmed to match the Out point of the target layer. In this case, all the layers have the same duration, so no trimming is necessary.

The HUD indicates that multiple objects are selected.

8   Click the Spin copy behavior, and in the HUD, adjust it to vary the tumbling animation from the *1984* layer.

The Throw behavior is great for animating a layer in a specific direction at a specific speed, but if you want a layer to change direction or orient itself in the direction in which it's moving, the Motion Path behavior is a better option. You can experiment with this behavior on the next date layer.

9   Turn on and select the *1986* layer, set a play range around it, and turn off the *1985* and *1988* layers.

10   Click the Add Behavior pop-up menu, choose Basic Motion > Motion Path, and start playback. The *1986* layer slides off the screen along a red motion path line.

11   Command-Spacebar-drag left to change the zoom level on the Canvas so that you can see both ends of the motion path line.

NOTE ▶ If Spotlight opens when you press Command-Spacebar, choose Apple > System Preferences. Click the Spotlight icon, and turn off the menu keyboard short-cut, or change it to a different key combination.

TIP ▶ After changing the zoom level with a Command-Spacebar-drag, you can move the Canvas around to re-center it by holding down the Spacebar until the pointer changes to a Hand tool, and then dragging the hand in the Canvas.

The red dots at each end of the motion path line are *control points*. You can reposition them and add more points to create a customized, curving path.

12 Move the leftmost control point off the left side of the Canvas; then Option-click the motion path line to add more control points, moving them and adjusting the Bezier handles to create a curving, looping path.

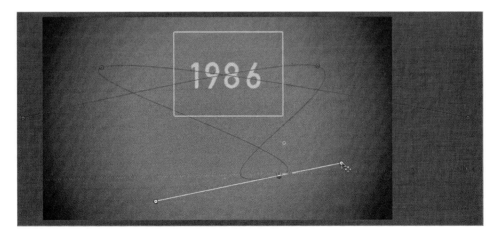

The layer moves along the path at a constant speed, no matter how many twists and turns it contains, but it doesn't rotate. To point the date graphic in its direction of travel, let's use another behavior.

13 Click the Add Behavior pop-up menu in the toolbar and choose Basic Motion > Snap Alignment to Motion. The layer now turns as it follows the path.

The Motion Path behavior is very flexible. For this project, you don't need many twists and turns. All you really need are the two original control points. And you don't need to align the movement to the motion path, because that would conflict with the Spin behavior that you will add shortly.

14 Delete the "Snap Alignment to Motion" behavior, select the Motion Path behavior, and in the Behaviors pane of the Inspector, click the hooked arrow to reset the behavior to its default values.

You can set specific values for each control point in X, Y, and Z in the Inspector.

15 Stop playback. In the Behaviors Inspector, click the Control Points disclosure triangle, and enter *0, 0, 0* for Point 1 and *0, 0, –5000* for Point 2. The layer will now fly straight back in z-space 5,000 pixels along the motion path. To make it spin and fade, you can copy those behaviors from the first layer.

> **TIP** ▶ Press Shift-Z to return the Canvas to Fit in Window, or press Option-Z to scale it to exactly 100 percent.

16 From the *1984* layer, Option-drag the Spin and Fade In/Fade Out behaviors to the *1986* layer. Then adjust the Spin behavior so that the animation doesn't look the same as the other two layers.

You used three different methods to animate three layers to fade, spin, and fall back in 3D space. To animate the rest of the date graphics, let's copy those behaviors to the remaining layers.

17 Option-drag the three behaviors from any of the layers you worked with to each of the date layers that haven't yet been animated. Then turn on the appropriate layers, set play ranges, and modify the Spin behavior of each.

18 Turn on all layers in the *Dates* group, press Option-X to reset the play range, play the animation, and adjust it as desired.

19 Stop playback, move the playhead to the start of the project, close the *Dates* group, and save your work.

Great job! You used several of the Basic Motion behaviors to animate the dates falling in space. Next, you'll turn your attention to animating the photos using another behavior-based technique.

Using Simulation Behaviors

Motion graphics animators often try to mimic real-world movements, such as an object accelerating as it starts to move, or slowing to a stop. Simulation behaviors are great for imitating motion caused by inertia, gravity, and other natural forces.

To animate the photos falling back into z-space, you will apply an Attractor behavior to an invisible layer. The layer will act like a black hole that attracts passing meteors.

1 Turn off the *Dates* group, and then turn on, select, and open the *Photos* group. The photos are much larger than the Canvas, so they will look as if they are falling into the scene very close to your view.

To make the Attractor behavior work in 3D in this group, you must first make the group a 3D group.

2 Choose Object > 3D Group.

3D groups allow the layers contained within them to be composited based on their positions in Z-space, rather than their stacking order in the Layers list. Furthermore, certain behaviors will work only in three dimensions if the group containing them is a 3D group.

Rather than applying a behavior to each layer to move it back in z-space, you will place a shape layer where you want the photos to move, and you'll use one behavior to animate them all toward that shape layer.

3 In the toolbar, choose the Rectangle tool.

4   With the playhead at the start of the project, drag in the Canvas to create a rectangle of any size. You won't see the rectangle in the final animation, so the size doesn't matter. However, you do want to place it in the center of the Canvas and 5,000 pixels back on the z-axis, much like the end of the motion path in the previous exercise.

5   Press Esc or Shift-S to return to the Select/Transform tool, and then press F1 to open the Properties Inspector. Click the disclosure triangle next to the Position parameter and set the Position values to *0, 0, –5000*.

The rectangle should get much smaller as it jumps back in z-space. Now you can apply the behavior to attract the photos.

6   Turn off the rectangle's visibility. Press Command-2 to open the Library, and in the Behaviors folder, select the Simulations folder. Click to preview a few of the behaviors.

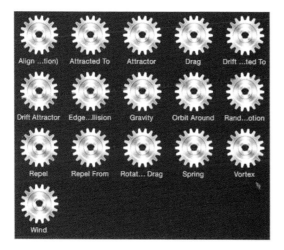

7   Drag the Attractor behavior onto the *Rectangle* layer and start playback. The pictures change from one to the next, but they don't move. By default, the Attractor does not work in z-space.

8   In the Include section of the HUD, click the Z button. There is still no change because the Influence parameter is set to 1,000 pixels by default, and the rectangle is 5,000 pixels away from the photos. The Influence parameters establish a radius around the

layer. Any objects within the radius are affected by the behavior, while objects outside the radius are not.

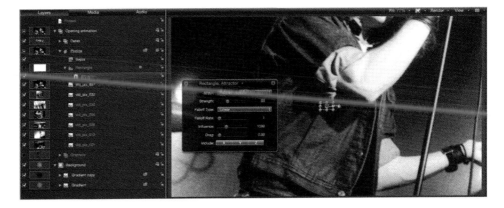

9   Drag the Influence slider all the way to the right. You'll find that the value stops at an insufficient 4,000 pixels. When the HUD won't let you set the value you want, try the Inspector.

10   Press F2 to open the Behaviors pane of the Inspector, and set the Influence value to 6,000 for good measure. Now, the pictures move back in z-space, but not very quickly.

11   Increase the Strength value to about 200.

The animation is starting to look better, but it would be more interesting if each photo started from a different position. To do this, you will first create some working room around the Canvas, and you'll then use a feature that lets you see layers outside the Canvas.

12   Stop playback, press Home, and select the first photo layer *vid_pix_001*. Then Command-Spacebar-drag left to create a lot of extra space around the Canvas— enough to easily see the bounding box of the first photo. By default, objects outside the Canvas are invisible, and you can see only the bounding box of a selected object.

13   Choose View > Show Full View Area, or press Shift-V so that layers outside the Canvas will be visible, but at a lower opacity.

14 Select and drag each layer in to a different location away from the center of the Canvas. When you are finished, Shift-click all the layers in the Layers list, and you'll see all of their bounding boxes and red motion paths.

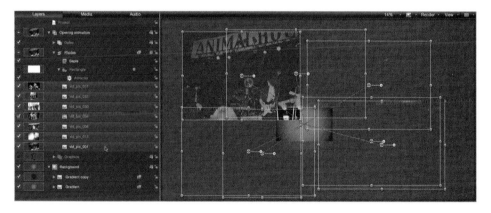

NOTE ▶ You will see an image outside the Canvas only for layers at the current playhead location.

15 Press Shift-Command-A to deselect all, press Shift-Z to fit the Canvas to the window, play the project to check the animation, and save your work.

By applying a Simulation behavior to a "dummy" shape layer, you made one behavior do the work of many. Now you can make the layers fade and spin by copying the behaviors from the *Dates* group. But the photo layers have a different duration than the date layers, so some trimming will be in order.

Trimming and Applying Behaviors to Multiple Layers

In this exercise, you'll use the Timeline to check and trim the durations of copied behaviors.

1   Move the playhead to the start of the project.

2   In the Layers list, open the *Dates* group. Open the *1984* layer, Shift-select the Spin and Fade In/Fade Out behaviors, and press Command-C to copy them. Select the *vid_pix_001* layer and press Command-V to paste the behaviors onto it. Close the *Dates* group in the Layers list.

3   In the Timeline, also close the *Dates* group. If necessary, scroll down to the *vid_pix_001* layer and open it. The behaviors begin at the start of the layer bar, but they are too short.

4   Select the *vid_pix_001* layer and press Shift-O to move the playhead to the layer's Out point.

5   Select both behaviors, and press O to trim their Out points to the playhead.

All the photo layers have the same duration, so you could now copy these two behaviors to those layers with no further trimming. However, you won't always have layers of equal duration, so let's use a different method that will automatically match every behavior to a layer's length.

6   In the Timeline, Shift-click the top and bottom layers to select all the remaining photo layers that do not have the Fade and Spin behaviors applied.

7   Click the Add Behavior pop-up menu, and choose Basic Motion > Fade In/Fade Out. The behavior is applied to all the selected layers and matches the length of each. It would do so even if the layers had different durations. Because this is a new behavior, you need to modify it to match the others.

8   In the Timeline, Command-click each of the six new Fade In/Fade Out behaviors.

TIP ▶ You could also select the behaviors in the Layers list. Command-clicking allows you to make a noncontiguous selection of the behaviors by skipping the layers and just selecting the behaviors applied to each layer. Shift-clicking includes the layers in the selection and the next step would not be possible.

9   In the HUD, increase the Fade In value to 30 frames. The HUD title, Multiple Selection, tells you that this adjustment will affect all the selected behaviors at once. Now you'll add the Spin behavior.

10   Command-click all the photo layers except the first to select the layers without selecting the behaviors applied to them. Then click the Add Behavior pop-up menu, and choose Basic Motion > Spin.

11   Select each Spin behavior one at a time, and in the HUD, give each a unique Spin Rate, Latitude angle, and Longitude angle.

As a final step, you can animate the brayer graphic in the *Graphics* group.

12   In the Timeline, close the *Photos* group. Activate and open the *Graphics* group. Open the *Dates* group, and then open the *1984* layer. Select and copy the Fade In/Fade Out and Grow/Shrink behaviors, and then paste them to the *brayer_03e* layer. This layer doesn't need to spin, but you may want to change its starting scale, position, and rotation.

13   With both behaviors still selected, Shift-drag the Out points to the right until they snap to the end of the *brayer_03e* layer.

14   Close all the groups in the Timeline and Layers list. Press Shift-V to turn off the full view area, and play the project.

You now have a nice animation of falling dates and photos, with one brayer graphic that foreshadows the additional graphic elements you'll add in the next lesson.

15 Make any final adjustments you choose. For example, you might want to increase the size of the date graphics by increasing the Scale of the *Dates* group, and change their starting positions. Save your work.

You used a variety of Basic Motion and Simulation behaviors to create animation; and learned several ways to add, adjust, copy, and trim those behaviors. To conclude this lesson, we'll use a different project to explore another type of behavior—the Parameter behavior.

Applying Parameter Behaviors

Parameter behaviors are powerful little critters that you add to your project using a different method than the behaviors you've applied so far. You create movement by applying Parameter behaviors to a specific parameter you want to animate.

In this exercise, you will use several Parameter behaviors to animate a set of gears that appear to open the curtains of a stage. You'll learn how to apply and adjust Parameter behaviors, clone groups of animated layers, and combine Parameter behaviors.

You can choose the parameter you want to animate either before or after you apply the Parameter behavior. Let's experiment with both methods.

1   Close any open projects. In the Finder, open Motion5_Book_Files > Lessons > Lesson_03 > Parameter Behaviors Start, and save a working copy to the Student_Saves folder. If necessary, open both groups in the Layers list.

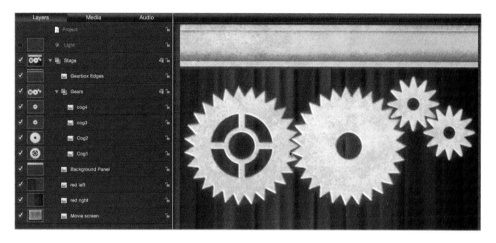

The project contains two groups: the root-level *Stage* group, which contains several layers; and within the *Stage* group, the *Gears* group, which contains the four cogs you see in the Canvas. There is also a *Light* layer, which is disabled. Currently, nothing in the scene is animated.

The first task is to rotate the left-hand gear. Your initial inclination might be to apply a Spin behavior from the Basic Motion category to rotate the cog. That would certainly work, but applying a Parameter behavior is another option.

2   Press Command-2 to open the Library, select Behaviors, and then select the Parameter folder.

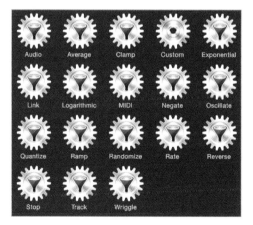

The 18 behaviors in this folder are unique because you apply them to a specific parameter of a layer, effect, or group. The Rate parameter behavior will change the value of a selected parameter at a constant rate, which is perfect for rotating the gear. One way to apply a Parameter behavior is to add it to an object, and then choose which parameter to animate.

3   Start playback, and then drag the Rate Parameter behavior from the Library to the *Cog1* layer in the Layers list. Nothing happens, because you need to tell the behavior which parameter you want to animate.

4   In the HUD, from the To pop-up menu, choose Properties > Transform > Rotation > Z.

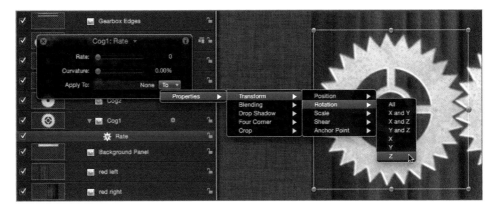

5   Drag the Rate slider to about –50. The cog now rotates at a constant rate of speed.

NOTE ▶ In Motion, negative rotation values create clockwise rotation.

Another way to apply a Parameter behavior is to first decide which parameter to animate, and then choose the appropriate behavior. Let's use this approach to animate the second large gear layer, *Cog2*, with a different Parameter behavior: the Link behavior.

6   Select the *Cog2* layer, and press F1 to open the Properties Inspector. You want to rotate the *Cog2* layer, too, so click the Animation menu for Rotation (the small downward arrow to the right) and choose Add Parameter Behavior > Link. The shortcut menu contains the Parameter behaviors you saw in the Library.

NOTE ▶ The list does not include the Track and Custom Parameter behaviors, which are used in more specialized circumstances.

You could choose Rate again and manually try to match the speed of the first cog. However, by applying the Link Parameter behavior, you can connect the animation of one layer to the animation of another.

The HUD indicates that the parameter is applied to the rotation of the layer, but you still need to tell it what source object to use.

7   Drag the *Cog1* layer into the Source Object well in the HUD.

TIP Be sure to hold down the mouse button as you drag the layer to the well. If you click the *Cog1* layer and release the mouse button, you will select the layer, and the Link behavior will no longer appear in the HUD. If that happens, reselect the Link behavior and try again.

TIP You can also drag a source object directly onto the Link behavior in the Layers list.

The *Cog2* layer now rotates, exactly matching the rate of the *Cog1* layer. But this isn't quite right. The cog should spin in the opposite direction. The Scale parameter determines how the linked layer animates in relation to the source layer. A value of 1 animates it in the same direction at the same speed. A value of 0 stops the animation, and a value of –1 reverses the animation yet maintains the same speed. The Scale slider in the HUD goes down only to 0, but we can change that value in the Inspector.

8   In the Behaviors Inspector, in the Scale value field, type *–1.* (minus one period) and press Enter. The *Cog2* layer now rotates in the opposite direction, and its teeth mesh perfectly with *Cog1*.

The same Link behavior can be used to animate the two smaller cogs.

9   In the Layers list, Option-drag the Link behavior from the *Cog2* layer to the *cog3* layer.

10 Select the Link copy behavior, and in the Behaviors pane, set the Scale value to 2.25. This cog needs to rotate in the same direction as the first cog, and because it's smaller, it also needs to rotate more quickly – 2.25 times faster – to mesh with the Cog2 gear.

11 Option-drag the Link copy behavior from the *cog3* layer to the *cog4* layer; and select the copy. In the Behaviors pane, change the Scale value to –2.25. All the cogs now animate nicely together.

12 Turn off the Rate behavior applied to the *Cog1* layer by deselecting its activation checkbox. All the cogs stop turning because they are linked to the *Cog1* layer.

13 Turn the Rate behavior on, stop playback, press Home, and save your work.

With the base animation completed, you will fill the area above the curtains with gears by using clones.

Cloning a Group

To create more animated gears, you will copy the *Gears* group. You could duplicate the group; but by creating clones, changes made to the original group will pass through to the clones, which will come in handy later. First, however, you'll scale and reposition the cogs to fit into the gold bar at the top of the curtains.

1 Close and select the *Gears* group. Then, in the Canvas, scale the group down to about 28% to fit in the gold bar, and move it to the left.

TIP ▶ Shift-drag a bounding box handle to scale the box proportionately. If the dynamic guides make it difficult to precisely scale and/or position the group, press N to turn off snapping.

Now, let's clone this group to place more gears along the gold bar.

2 Choose Object > Make Clone Layer, or press K.

NOTE ▶ Make sure the playhead is at the start of the project or is moving when you create the clone; otherwise, the clone layer's In point will start at the playhead location.

3 In the Canvas, drag the *Clone Layer* to the right of the original, and line up the layers so that the teeth of the cogs appear to mesh with the original.

TIP ▶ Change the zoom level of the Canvas if you want to get a closer look at the gears as you position the clone layer. Do so by pressing Command-Spacebar and dragging right from the location you want to see more closely. When you finish, press Shift-Z to fit the Canvas back into the window.

4   Press K to make a clone of *Clone Layer*, and position *Clone Layer 1* to the right of the other cogs.

TIP ▶ You may want to turn off the visibility of the layer's bounding box in the Canvas to see the cog teeth more clearly. From the View and Overlay pop-up menu, choose Show Overlays, or press Command-/ (slash). Remember to turn on the overlays again when you are done.

5   Press K to clone *Clone Layer 1*, and position *Clone Layer 2* at the far right. It's OK if it goes off the screen. You now have a fully assembled gearbox.

TIP ▶ You can nudge the position of selected layers or groups by holding down the Command key and tapping the Left or Right Arrow keys. The distance the layer moves each time you tap an arrow key depends on your zoom level. When you are zoomed in closer, each tap of the arrow key nudges the layer a shorter distance.

6   Press the Spacebar to start playback. All the cogs rotate and mesh together nicely.

7   Open the *Gears* group. Open the *Cog1* layer and turn off the Rate behavior. All the gears stop.

If you had duplicated the *Gears* group rather than cloning it, each duplicate would have its own Rate behavior, and you'd need to turn off each of them to stop the animation. With clones, changes you make to the source of the clones pass through to all of them.

8   Turn on the Rate behavior and save your work.

Now you can make it look as if the cogs are opening the curtains.

Combining Behaviors and Adding a Light

To animate the opening curtains, you will first link them to each other, and then link their positions to the rotation of the very first *Cog1* layer—the source of all the animation so far. And because you want the curtains to open and come to a stop, you'll add a Stop Parameter behavior to the *Cog1* layer to stop the rotation at a specific point in time.

1   Select the *red right* layer; press F1 to go to the Properties Inspector; and, if necessary, click the Position disclosure triangle to reveal the individual X, Y, and Z position parameters.

You want to link the right curtain's horizontal or X position to the same parameter of the left curtain, but move it in the opposite direction.

2   From the Animation menu for the Position X parameter, choose Add Parameter Behavior > Link.

3   Drag the *red left* layer from the Layers list to the Source Object well in the Behaviors pane, and then set the Scale value to −1.

4   Select the *red left* layer, and in the Canvas, drag the layer around; then undo.

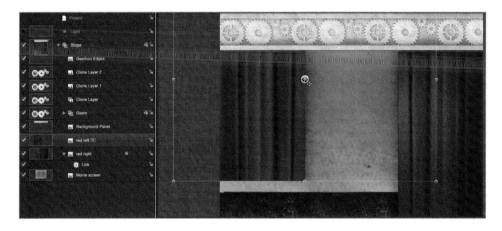

As the left curtain moves left, the right curtain moves right and vice versa; but moving the left curtain up or down has no affect on the right curtain because only the horizontal (X) position is linked.

To make the left curtain move, you will link its position to the rotation of the *Cog1* layer. You can also Control-click the name of a parameter to access a menu of parameter behaviors.

5   With the *red left* layer still selected, go to the Properties Inspector. Control-click (or right-click) the X under Position, and choose Add Parameter Behavior > Link.

6   Open the Gears group and drag the *Cog1* layer from the Layers list to the Source Object well in the HUD.

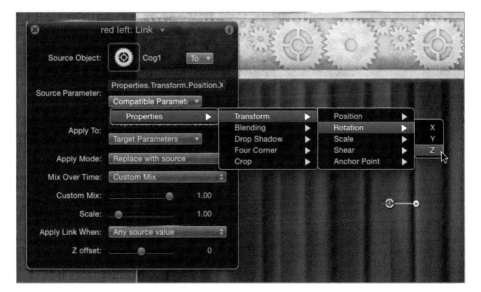

Motion assumes that you want to link the position of the left curtain to the position of the *Cog1* layer, as it says in the Source Parameter box. But you want the *rotation* of the cog to drive the *position* of the curtain.

7   From the Compatible Parameters pop-up menu, choose Properties > Transform > Rotation > Z. The curtains now open as the project plays, but they do so too quickly.

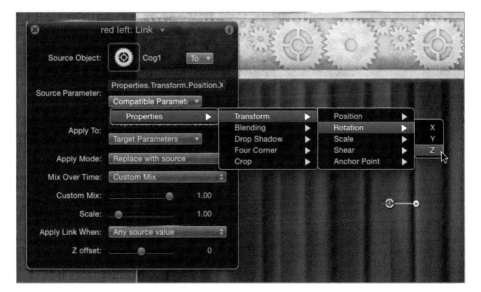

8   In the Behaviors Inspector, watch the animation in the Canvas as you Option-drag left in the Scale value field to set it to about 0.4.

> **TIP** ▶ When you Option-drag in a value field, the rate of change "gears down" to one-hundredth the normal speed, making it much easier to make small value changes; Shift-dragging makes the value change ten times faster.

It's not bad, but the animation would work better if the gears and curtains came to a stop before the curtains moved all the way out of view. We'll use another Parameter behavior to make them stop.

9   Stop playback and move the playhead to 5:00. At this point, the curtains are open but still visible.

10 Select the *Cog1* layer. In the Properties Inspector, Control-click the word *Rotation*, and from the shortcut menu, choose Add Parameter Behavior > Stop. The new Parameter behavior appears in the mini-Timeline with its In point at the playhead.

11 Resume playback. The curtains open and suddenly come to a stop at 5:00.

The stop is a bit abrupt, but let's leave it for now. In the next lesson, you'll learn how to use keyframes to create different kinds of movement. For example, you could make the gears and curtains slow down before they came to a stop.

As a final touch to this project, you can enable the light and make the screen flicker like an old-fashioned movie projector.

12 Select the activation checkbox for the Light layer. Nothing happens because lights affect only 3D groups.

> **NOTE** ▶ If you accidentally select the Light layer when you turn it on, the default Select/Transform tool changes to the Adjust 3D Transform tool, and new red, green, and blue arrows appear in the Canvas. We'll work with this tool and these controls in later lessons. For now, press Shift-S to return to the default selection tool.

13 Select the Stage group, and choose 3D group from the Object menu. The light now affects the scene. You'll explore other types of lights and how to manipulate them in a later lesson.

Let's finish by making the screen flicker using a final Parameter behavior. If the parameter you want to animate is listed in the HUD, you can apply a parameter behavior to it within the HUD..

14 Select the *Movie screen* layer, and in the HUD, Control-click the word *Opacity*. From the shortcut menu, choose Add Parameter Behavior > Wriggle. The Wriggle parameter behavior applies random changes to the value of the selected parameter, but the changes are not as extreme as with the Randomize parameter behavior.

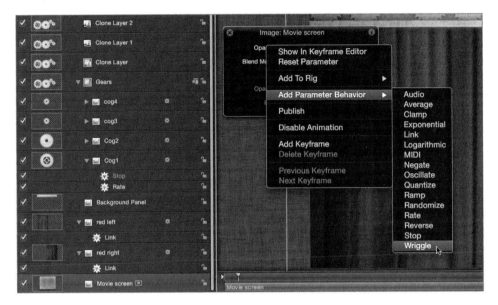

15 In the Behaviors Inspector, set the Amount to 50%, the Apply Mode to Subtract, and adjust the Frequency and Noisiness sliders to suit yourself. Subtract will subtract random values from the Opacity of the light, which is set to 100% by default. Close all the groups and save your work.

Great work. You applied many types of behaviors in two separate projects, duplicated and trimmed behaviors, worked with clones, and explored some 3D concepts.

Lesson Review

1. Name three of the Basic Motion behaviors.

2. You applied a Motion Path behavior and added control points to create a curved path. How can you make the layer turn as it moves along the path?

3. If you copy a behavior from one layer to another, will it always match the duration of the target layer?

4. How do you trim the Out point of a behavior to match the layer to which it's applied?

5. What types of behaviors mimic physical phenomena such as gravity, inertia, and random movement?

6. You added a Grow/Shrink behavior to a layer and would like to adjust it using the onscreen controls. What happens if you drag one of the blue edge handles?

7. Why would you change a group from a 2D group to a 3D group?

8. Describe two ways to apply a Parameter behavior.

9. What's one difference between duplicating a layer and cloning a layer?

Answers

1. Grow/Shrink, Fade In/Fade Out, Throw, Spin, Motion Path, and Snap Alignment to Motion are all Basic Motion behaviors.

2. Add the "Snap Alignment to Motion" behavior from the Basic Motion category.

3. No, the copied behavior will match the In point of the target layer but its duration won't change from the original. So, if the target layer is longer or shorter than the source layer, the Out point of the behavior must be trimmed to match it.

4. Select a layer in the Timeline and press Shift-O to move the playhead to the layer's Out point. Then press O to trim the Out point of the behavior to the playhead. Or drag the right edge of the behavior, holding down the Shift key to snap to other layers.

5. Simulation behaviors

6. Dragging an edge handle will scale the layer up or down non-proportionally over time.

7. You want to composite the layers in the group based on their positions in z-space rather than the stacking order in the Layers list. Also, certain behaviors will work in 3D only if the group containing them is a 3D group. Finally, lights do not affect 2D groups.

8. Drag a Parameter behavior from the Library to a layer, and then select the target parameter in the HUD or Behaviors Inspector. Alternatively, first choose the target parameter you want to animate and then in the Inspector, click the Animation menu for that parameter and choose Add Parameter Behavior.

9. A duplicated layer is independent of the original; a clone will change when you change certain aspects of the original—for example, changing the animation of the original.

Keyboard Shortcuts

D	Cycle HUD forward
Shift-D	Cycle HUD backward
Shift-V	Turn the full view area on and off
Command-Option-I	Set a play range In point
Command-Option-O	Set a play range Out point
Command-Arrow	Nudge the selected layer in the direction of the arrow
Shift-Command-Arrow	Nudge in a larger increment in the direction of the arrow

4

Lesson Files	Motion5_Book_Files > Lessons > Lesson_04
Media	Motion5_Book_Files > Media > Stage
	Motion5_Book_Files > Media > Rockumentary
Time	This lesson takes approximately 60 minutes to complete.
Goals	Record keyframes
	Set keyframes manually
	Use the Keyframe Editor
	Change keyframe interpolation and adjust keyframe curves
	Add, move, and change the values of keyframes on a curve
	Set keyframes for multiple layers simultaneously
	Change keyframe timing in the Timeline
	Choose keyframe curves for editing in the Keyframe Editor

Animating with Keyframes

In the previous lesson, behaviors allowed you to create animation *procedurally*—you applied a behavior that contained a set of instructions for making the layer animate. Setting keyframes is a way to *articulate* an animation—that is, manually identify exactly what, when, and how you want to animate.

The term *keyframes*, or *key frames*, originates from traditional hand-animation techniques in which a senior artist would draw "key" poses of a character and turn over those images to a junior artist, who would draw the in-between frames to create smooth character animation from one keyframe to the next.

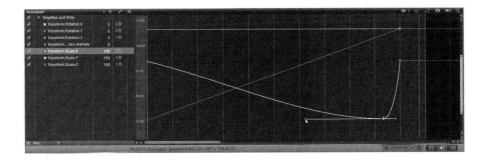

In Motion, keyframes work much the same way: You are the senior artist, creating your composition and identifying the frames you want to establish as keyframes; and the computer acts as the junior artist, creating in-between frames of animation through a process called *interpolation*.

Whether you should choose to animate using keyframes or behaviors is not always a clear-cut decision; but as a rule of thumb, if you want repeated, continuous motion— such as a graphic drifting across the screen, a pendulum swinging, or a neon sign blinking— use behaviors. If you want animation that starts, stops, and changes direction at specific points in time, use keyframes.

In this lesson, you'll open the stage project and animate the curtains using keyframes to compare that method to animating with behaviors. You'll also experiment with interpolation types and adjusting keyframe Bezier handles. We'll then set and adjust keyframes in the Rockumentary project to animate multiple layers to form a composition.

Recording Keyframes

The easiest way to set keyframes is to turn on recording. When recording is turned on, every change you make to any keyframeable parameter will be recorded as a keyframe at the playhead location, locking in the new value at that point in time. In this exercise, you will use recording to set a keyframe for the rotation value of the first cog, which will cause the curtains to part.

1   Open Motion5_Book_Files > Lessons > Lesson_04 > **Keyframes Start**, and save the project to the Student_Saves folder.

   This is the stage project you worked with in the previous lesson. The position of the curtains is linked to the *Cog1* layer with the Link behavior, as is the rotation of all the other cog layers. But the *Cog1* layer is not currently animated. You can test the animation by rotating the *Cog1* layer.

2   Open the *Stage* and *Gears* groups, select the *Cog1* layer, and in the Canvas, drag the rotation handle.

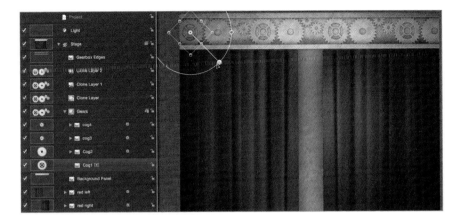

Rotating the *Cog1 layer* clockwise turns the other cogs and opens the curtains. In the previous lesson, you animated the rotation of this layer using a Rate behavior and stopped the rotation with a Stop behavior. The result was a rather abrupt ending. Here, you'll animate the rotation by recording keyframes.

3   Press Command-Z to undo the rotation, and at the bottom of the Canvas, click the Record button. The button turns red to let you know that recording is enabled.

4   Press F1 to open the Properties Inspector.

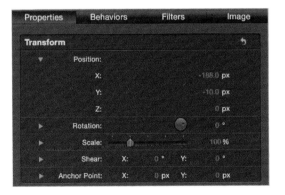

The value fields for all parameters are now red, another warning sign that recording is enabled. If you change any red parameter, it won't change for the whole project; it will change only at the playhead position. Let's see how this works.

5   In the timing display in the toolbar, type 5. (5 period) and then press Return (or Enter) to move the playhead to the frame at five seconds. This is the frame where you want the curtains to stop opening.

NOTE ▶ If the timing display is set to frames, you can move the playhead to 5 seconds by clicking the downward-facing arrow, and choosing Show Timecode. Then, type 5 (five period) to move the playhead to 5:00.

TIP ▶ You don't have to double-click in the timing display to enter a number. As long as a value field in the Inspector isn't active when you start typing, Motion assumes that you want to move the playhead and will automatically enter the number in the timing display.

6   In the Properties Inspector, drag left in the Rotation value field to about −300 degrees as you watch the curtains open in the Canvas.

A yellow diamond appears to the right of the value field to indicate that a keyframe for this parameter has been set at the current playhead location.

7   Play the project. The curtains animate open until 5:00, and then stop.

8   Stop playback on any frame other than 5:00 or 0:00. The yellow diamond for Rotation is now gray. A gray diamond indicates that at least one keyframe for this parameter exists, but not at the current playhead location.

9   Move the playhead to the start of the project. The diamond turns yellow again, indicating that a keyframe exists at the playhead. But wait a minute. You only set a keyframe at 5:00, not at 0:00. Why is there a keyframe here, too?

A single keyframe will not create animation; it locks the value of the keyframed parameter at a point in time, but the parameter will have that same value at all other points in time. *To animate with keyframes, you need to have at least two keyframes with different values.*

When you use recording to set keyframes, Motion assumes that you want the value to change over time, so it automatically sets a keyframe with the original value at the beginning of the layer you are animating. Remember that recording will *always* perform this action, although sometimes you may not want a keyframe at the beginning of the layer.

By default, when recording is enabled, any other changes you make to the *Cog1* layer, such as adjusting its position or scale, will set keyframes for that parameter as well. Sometimes, you'll want to make an overall adjustment to a parameter without setting a keyframe, yet you'd still like to add keyframes to a parameter you've already animated.

10 Double-click the Record button. The Recording Options dialog opens. One of the options in this dialog is to "Record keyframes on animated parameters only."

11 Select "Record keyframes on animated parameters only" and click OK. If necessary, click the Record button, or press A, to turn on recording

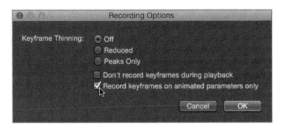

NOTE ▶ When recording is turned on, opening and closing the Recording Options dialog turns off recording, so you may need to turn recording on again.

Now only the Rotation value field is red, indicating that keyframes will be applied only to changes to this parameter. Changes to other parameters will change the value for all points in time.

12 Change the Position Y value for the *Cog1* layer, and play the project. The *Cog1* layer and all its clones are in new locations, but their positions don't change over time as they would with keyframes.

13 Press Command-Z to undo the position change. Double-click the Record button, deselect the "Record keyframes on animated parameters only" checkbox, and click OK. You are returned to the default setting. If necessary, click the Record button to turn off recording.

You've now animated the *Cog1* layer and the curtains linked to it using keyframes. But the resulting animation is very similar to the animation in the last lesson: The curtain movement still comes to an abrupt stop at 5:00. You can make the curtains slow to a smoother stop by using keyframe interpolation.

Changing Keyframe Interpolation

When you recorded a keyframe for the cog rotation value of –300 degrees at 5:00, Motion automatically set a keyframe at the start of the layer with the original value, 0 degrees.

Therefore, the layer needs to change from 0 degrees at 0:00 to –300 degrees at 5:00. To get from 0 to –300 over the course of five seconds, Motion calculates, or *interpolates*, the value over time between the starting and ending values. You can change the type of interpolation in several ways using the Keyframe Editor.

1   Choose Window > Keyframe Editor. A new window appears below the Timeline. Drag the divider up to make more room.

> **TIP** ▶ Pressing Command-8 will also open the Keyframe Editor.

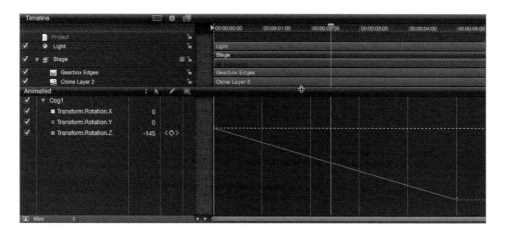

The animated parameter for the *Cog1* layer, Transform.Rotation.Z, appears on the left side of the window along with the other two Rotation parameters. Next to it is the value of the parameter at the current frame (–145) and a hollow diamond, indicating that keyframes exist for this parameter but not at the playhead position.

NOTE ► Depending on your playhead location, the value for the Transform. Rotation.Z parameter may differ from the preceding figure.

NOTE ► By default, the Keyframe Editor displays all animated parameters for selected layers or groups, as indicated by the presence of the word *Animated* in the Show Curve Set pop-up menu in the Keyframe Editor. Motion will include all "channels" for the parameter (for example, x, y, and z) even if not all the channels are animated.

On the right side of the window, a pink line connects two diamonds. The diamonds are the keyframes, and the line is the *keyframe curve*. The curve is straight because the default interpolation for rotation is linear, meaning that the rotation value changes at a constant rate. You can change the interpolation in the Animation pop-up menu, which appears as a downward facing arrow in the parameter column to the right of the keyframe icon when you place your pointer over it.

NOTE ► The Animation pop-up menu in the Keyframe Editor is similar to the Animation pop-up menu in the Inspector, but it contains more options.

2   Start playback, and from the Animation pop-up menu, choose Interpolation. The submenu includes four interpolation options: Constant, Linear, Bezier, and Continuous.

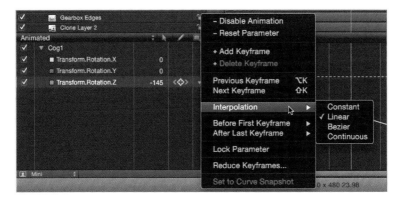

3   Choose Bezier.

Bezier interpolation creates smoother, more real-world animation by imitating the effect of inertia: Objects with mass take some time to get up to speed and to slow to a stop. Instead of a constant rate of change, the rate of change starts low, increases over time, and then decreases again.

The curve starts out flat, gets steeper in the middle, and then flattens out at the end. The curtains now start opening slowly, speed up, and then slow to a smooth stop, creating more realistic animation.

4 Experiment with the other interpolation options. Constant maintains the keyframe value until the next keyframe, when the value changes instantaneously.

Continuous is similar to Bezier in that it creates a smooth ramping into and out of keyframes. It's easier to create smooth motion with Continuous interpolation; however, the curve cannot be adjusted as with Bezier interpolation.

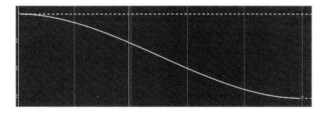

TIP You can also change the interpolation of individual keyframes along a curve by Control-clicking (or right-clicking) a keyframe and choosing an interpolation type. Using this technique you'll have access to five additional interpolation options: Ease In, Ease Out, Ease Both, Exponential, and Logarithmic.

5 Return the interpolation type to Bezier. Bezier interpolation gives you the most creative flexibility to fine-tune your animation. You can use it to speed up the time it takes the curtains to open and make them come to an even slower stop.

6   Click the keyframe at 5:00 to select it, and then drag the Bezier handle to the left to make it longer and flatten out the curve coming into the keyframe.

> **NOTE** ▶ If you do not see a bezier handle extending from the keyframe when you select it, Command-drag left on the keyframe to create one.

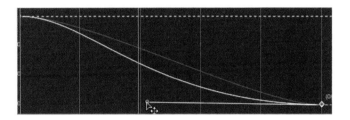

> **TIP** ▶ Be careful not to pull the Bezier handle down, or the curve may dip below the keyframe value and the curtains will start to close again before opening fully.

7   Click the keyframe at 0:00. Adjust the Bezier handle to create a steeper curve and, therefore, faster initial movement. Play the project to see the results of your changes.

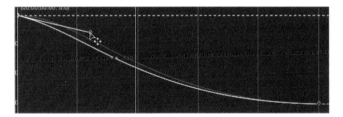

Currently, the animation starts at 0:00 because keyframe recording automatically added a keyframe at the start of the layer. But what if you want the curtains to stay closed for the first second to build a little suspense? Setting keyframes manually gives you the most creative control.

Setting Keyframes Manually

In addition to recording keyframes, you can manually set keyframes, whether or not recording is enabled. Manually setting keyframes is a great solution when you want to lock in an existing value at the current frame. (Recording requires you to change the value to create a keyframe.)

In this exercise, you'd like the curtains to stay closed for the first second. In other words, you want the rotation of the *Cog1* layer to remain at 0 degrees from 0:00 to 1:00, and *then* start to change. So, let's delete the current keyframe at 0:00 and create a new one at 1:00.

NOTE ▶ Deleting the first keyframe isn't strictly necessary, but knowing how to do it is useful.

1   In the Keyframe Editor, select the keyframe at 0:00. Then press Delete to remove it.

Only the keyframe at 5:00 remains, and the flat dotted line indicates that there is no animation because only one keyframe exists, and at least two keyframes with different values are required to create animation. The Rotation value at the keyframe of −300 is the same for the entire layer, and the curtains remain open. You want them to be closed at 1:00.

2   In the timing display, type *1.* (1 period), and press Return to move the playhead to 1:00.

3   In the Keyframe Editor, from the Animation pop-up menu, choose Add Keyframe. When adding keyframes manually, you must *first* add the keyframe, and *then* change the value. If you change the value first, you change the value of the parameter for the full duration of the layer, not just at the playhead.

TIP ▶ After you set a keyframe and moved the playhead, you can press Control-K to set a keyframe for that same parameter, or choose Object > Add Keyframe. In this case, the menu would read Object > Add Rotation Keyframe.

4   Double-click the value field for Transform.Rotation.Z, type *0*, and press Return.

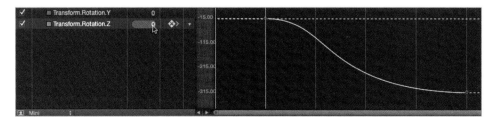

5   If necessary, at the top right of the Keyframe Editor, click the "Fit Visible Curves in Window" button to see the full curve.

6   Play the project. The curtains stay closed for the first second, and then they animate open from 1:00 to 5:00.

7   You can adjust the Bezier handles on each keyframe to suit yourself. You can also add and adjust keyframes directly on a curve.

8   Double-click anywhere along the curve to add a keyframe.

9   Drag the keyframe up or down to change its value. Shift-drag up or down to constrain the pointer to vertical movement and avoid dragging left or right, which would change the keyframe's timing. As you drag, the numbers that appear in parentheses indicate the timecode of the keyframe location and the value of the keyframe, in that order.

10 Double-click the keyframe to enter a specific value for the parameter at this frame. Play the project.

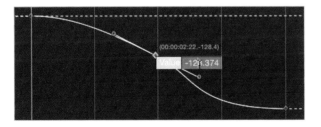

By adding keyframes, you can radically alter the animation. For this project, two keyframes will suffice.

11 Stop playback, delete any extra keyframes, save your work, and close the project.

TIP ▶ You can delete multiple keyframes by dragging a selection rectangle around them and pressing Delete.

You've now explored the basics of creating keyframes by recording them or setting them manually for a single parameter on a single layer. Next, you'll explore techniques for applying and adjusting the keyframes of multiple parameters on multiple layers.

NOTE ▶ For more information on keyframe interpolation, refer to the Motion 5 Help document available from the Help menu.

Using Keyframes on Multiple Parameters and Layers

Because keyframes are so precise and flexible, they are often used to animate multiple layers to move, spin, or blur at a specific point in time. In this exercise, we'll return to the Rockumentary project and animate all the title elements to fall into place and form the final composition. Motion lets you quickly set keyframes for parameters on multiple layers, and it also lets you choose which keyframes appear for editing in the Keyframe Editor.

Keyframing Multiple Layers

The first step is to add keyframes that will lock in place all the layers that are to be animated.

1   Open Motion5_Book_Files > Lessons > Lesson_04 > **Rockumentary Keyframes Start**. Save it to the Student_Saves folder, and if necessary, open the Project pane.

In previous lessons, you created the second half of this project, the composite image of the title elements with the sequence of photos. You also animated the initial photos and dates "falling" through space. Now we'll concentrate on the middle part of the project: animating the title elements into position. Unlike the photos and dates that fell away with continuous movement, these layers need to fall and then stop in a specific arrangement, which happens to be a great task for keyframes.

NOTE ► This project does not include the opening sequence of falling dates and pictures, but starts with the title elements you will animate into position.

As with many motion graphics projects, it will be easiest to approach this task in reverse. You'll first set keyframes that lock each layer into its final position, and then set keyframes at the start of the project to spread out the layers in z-space, completely offscreen.

Let's take a look at the layers we'll animate.

2   In the Layers list, open the *Graphics Over* and *Graphics Under* groups, and adjust the layer heights in the Layers list as necessary to fit everything into the view. These layers will start offscreen and then animate onscreen by "falling" into place.

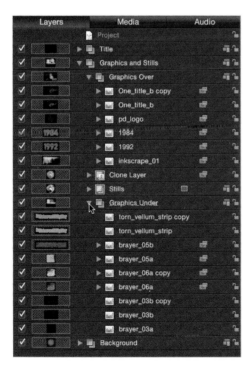

3   Set the timing display to Show Timecode, and move the playhead to 5:00.

At 5:00, you want all the layers to have landed in their final positions, so you will set a keyframe here to lock them in place on this frame. Rather than individually setting a position keyframe for each layer, you can set a keyframe for multiple layers at the same time.

4   Shift-click the first and last layers in the *Graphics Over* group to select them all, press F1 to reveal the Properties Inspector, and open the Position parameter.

The value fields for Position x, y, and z contain dashes because you have selected multiple layers, each with a different position value. But you can still set a keyframe for all of them at once.

5   From the Animation pop-up menu for the Position Z parameter, choose Add Keyframe. An orange diamond appears in the Animation pop-up menu, indicating that a keyframe exists at the current playhead position.

6   In the Layers list, click each layer individually in the *Graphics Over* group to select just that layer and examine its Position values.

Each layer has a keyframe for Position Z. Now let's create the same keyframes for the layers in the *Graphics Under* group, this time using a shortcut.

7   Select all the layers in the *Graphics Under* group; then, in the Properties pane, click the gray diamond with the + (plus) symbol that appears when you move the pointer over the Animation pop-up menu for Position Z. With a single click, you add a keyframe to this parameter for all the selected layers.

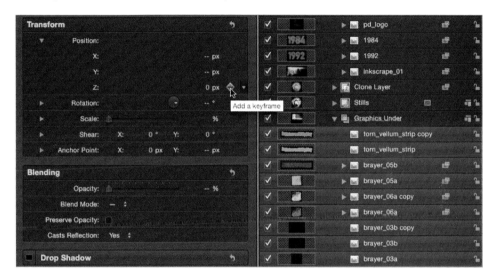

With the layers safely locked in place in their final "assembled" positions, you can now go to the beginning of the project and move the layers away in z-space. Because you are setting keyframes manually, you must *first* set the keyframe, and *then* change the value for each layer.

8   Move the playhead to the start of the project.

9   With all the layers in the *Graphics Under* group still selected, Command-click each of the layers in the *Graphics Over* group to add them to the selection.

10 In the Properties pane, click the gray diamond to the left of the Position Z Animation pop-up menu to add a keyframe to all the selected layers.

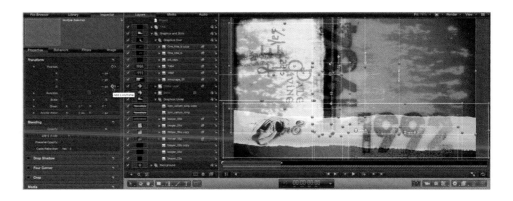

NOTE ▶ Because at least one keyframe has already been set for this parameter (but none at the current playhead location), the gray diamond turns orange when you move the pointer over it.

Now that a keyframe is set at 0:00, when you change the Z-position of each layer at this frame, it will change only at this frame, and animate back to its final position by the next keyframe at 5:00.

Each layer now has two keyframes; but if you play the project, nothing is animating because the keyframes for each layer have the same value. With the beginning and ending keyframes in place, you can start animating.

Animating Layers and Groups with Keyframes

To animate the layer positions, you'll give each layer a new Position Z value on the first frame. Then, you'll animate the rotation of the group containing the layers to add a nice spin to the overall animation as the layers assemble themselves.

1   With the playhead at the first frame of the project, select the lowest layer in the *Graphics Under* group. In the Inspector, drag right in the Position Z value field to set it to about 1,000 pixels, enough to make the layer disappear off the edge of the Canvas.

2   Continue up the group, selecting the next *brayer* layers individually, and setting a Position Z value for each one at around 1,000 to 2,000 pixels, until each one is off-screen. Give each layer a different Position Z value to spread them out.

3   When you get to the two *vellum* layers, Shift-click each to select it, and then change both their values at the same time so that they will stay together as they move.

4   Continue to the layers in the *Graphics Over* group, selecting each layer in the group and changing its initial Position Z value to move it off the screen. When you are done, you should see nothing but the background image in the Canvas.

5   Play the project. The layers all move into position and come to a soft landing. Why don't they stop abruptly like the curtains in the last exercise?

6   Select all the animated layers in the two groups, press Command-8 to open the Keyframe Editor, and drag up on the divider to make the window taller.

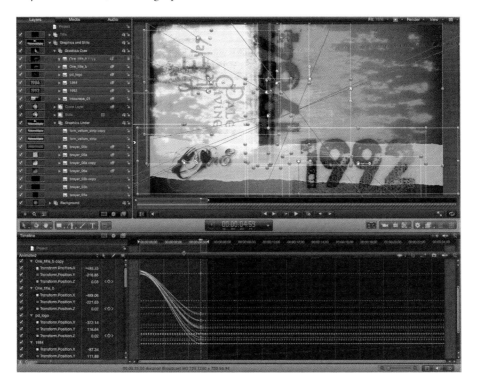

The red motion paths in the Canvas are straight lines that indicate the path of travel. The orange keyframe curves in the Keyframe Editor indicate how the speed of each layer changes over time. They are curved because the default interpolation for the Position parameters is Bezier (most other parameters have a default interpolation of Linear).

It's nice that the layers already come to smooth landings, but you can take the animation a step further by rotating the layers into position. You can achieve this action by animating the group containing all layers.

To rotate the group containing all the layers, let's work backward from its final value. You want to move the playhead to 5:00, the same frame as the other keyframes. Rather than entering a time value, you can jump the playhead directly to a keyframe.

7   In the Properties pane, click the Animation pop-up menu for Position Z and choose Next Keyframe, or press Shift-K.

NOTE ▸ The keyboard shortcuts for jumping to keyframes are Shift-K for the next keyframe and Option-K for the previous keyframe of the selected layer(s). You can also click the small arrows on either side of the keyframe icon to move to the next or previous keyframe for that parameter.

8   Select the *Graphics and Stills* group, and in the Properties pane, set a keyframe for the Rotation parameter of the group by clicking the gray diamond next to the Animation pop-up menu.

9   Move the playhead to the start of the project, set an initial keyframe for the rotation of the group, and then set the Rotation value to –90 degrees. Notice the straight sloped line for the Rotation parameter in the Keyframe Editor, indicating a linear interpolation.

   NOTE ▶ If you don't see the keyframe curve for the rotation parameter in the Keyframe Editor, click the bar above the list of parameters, and from the pop-up menu, choose Animated.

   NOTE ▶ If any layers now appear on the screen at the start of the project due to the rotation, select them and increase their Position Z values to move them completely offscreen.

10   Play the project.

All the layers now rotate as they fall into position. However, they all come in at pretty much the same time, and land without much punch. You'll now work in both the Keyframe Editor and the Timing pane to liven things up.

Working with Multiple Keyframe Curves

You'd like all the layers to suddenly snap into final position. Rather than adding keyframes to each layer's Position Z property, you can achieve this effect using just one keyframe on the group. Then, in the Timing pane, you can adjust the timing of keyframes on individual layers to create more of a cascading effect as the layers fall into place.

1   Stop playback, and with the *Graphics and Stills* group still selected, press Shift-K to move the playhead to the ending keyframe for the rotation of the group.

2   In the Keyframe Editor, frame the curve by dragging left on the right side of the zoom slider at the bottom of the window.

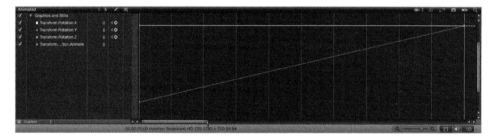

Currently, only rotation is animated for this group. We will now animate the Scale parameter over the last ten frames of the project.

3   In the Properties pane, add a keyframe for Scale at 5:00.

4   Type *–20* and press Return to move the playhead back 20 frames.

5   Add a keyframe for Scale at the playhead position, and set the value to 70%. The scale now changes from 70% to 100% over the last ten frames, but it's scaled at 70% for the entire project before the last ten frames.

6   Go to the first frame, set a keyframe, and set the Scale value to 100%. Play the project. Now the layers scale down slowly from 100% to 70% and then quickly scale up to 100% at the end. But they do so too smoothly.

7   In the Properties pane, from the Animation pop-up menu for Scale, choose Show in Keyframe Editor. Now just the curve for Scale appears.

8   In the Keyframe Editor, drag a selection rectangle to select the middle Scale X, Y, and Z keyframes that are stacked on top of each other, and then Control-click and choose Interpolation > Bezier from the shortcut menu. Then drag out the right Bezier handle to make a steeper curve up into the final keyframe.

   NOTE ▸ If you just click the keyframe to select it, only Transform.Scale.X is selected and not Y and Z, which are directly underneath it. Dragging a selection rectangle around keyframes that are stacked selects them all.

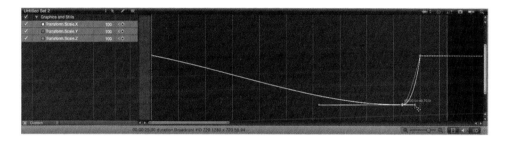

   Play the project. The layers now scale down and then pop back up and appear to snap onto the screen.

   Your final step is to stagger the keyframes on the layers so that they don't all appear at once. When you want to change the timing of keyframes, using the Timeline rather than the Keyframe Editor is frequently easiest.

9   Open the *Graphics Over* and *Graphics Under* groups, and drag the top of the Timeline up to make the window much taller. Drag down on the divider bar for the Keyframe Editor to make room for the Timeline layers.

10 If it's not already active, click the Show/Hide Keyframes button at the top right of the Timeline to display the keyframes under each layer bar.

   NOTE ▸ It's not necessary to reopen the Keyframe Editor for the next steps, but it's helpful to see how changing keyframes in the Timeline also changes them in the Keyframe Editor.

There are three reasons why it can be easier to change the timing of keyframes in the Timeline rather than the Keyframe Editor:

▶ You can see the relationships of keyframes applied to multiple layers.

▶ Each keyframe at a given frame is actually a "bundle," representing all keyframes at that point in time for a group or layer, so it's easy to select and move all of them.

▶ You can't accidentally drag a keyframe up or down, which would change its value.

Here, you want to stagger the introduction of each layer in time by moving the first keyframe a different amount for each layer.

11 Select the second-to-last layer in the *Graphics Under* group, *brayer_03b*.

The keyframes appear under each layer. You don't have to select a layer to select its keyframes, but doing so enables you to clearly see which keyframes are related to that layer.

NOTE ▶ If you don't see the keyframes in the Timeline, click the Show/Hide Keyframes button at the top right of the Timeline window.

12 Drag the first keyframe to the right a small amount.

The animation for this layer will now start a little later than the layer below it.

13 In the *brayer_03b copy* layer, move the first keyframe to the right a little bit more than the first keyframe in the *brayer_03b* layer.

14 Move the first keyframe for each of the layers in the *Graphics Under* group to a different point in time. When you reach the upper *vellum* layer, Shift-drag to snap it to the lower *vellum* layer. As you Shift-drag, thin vertical lines appear on the layer bar, representing all possible snapping points.

15 Repeat the process for the layers in the *Graphics Over* group, staggering the keyframes. Then play the project and adjust the keyframe locations to your liking. The layers now drop into the scene at different times, but they all end in their final positions at 5:00.

For a final touch, you can animate the strips of vellum to spread out just before they land.

Animating Crop with Keyframes

To make the strip of vellum appear to open up, let's animate its Crop parameter. Because the graphic comprises two layers, we will animate them in tandem.

1 Stop playback, drag down on the top bar of the Timing pane to return it to its original size, and move the playhead to the start of the project.

2 In the Layers list, Shift-select the *torn_vellum_strip* and *torn_vellum_strip copy* layers, and press Shift-K twice to move the playhead to the second keyframe at 5:00. In the Properties Inspector, a solid diamond appears in the Position Z Animation menu, confirming that the playhead is parked on a keyframe.

3   In the Properties Inspector, select the Crop checkbox, and click the word Show to display the Crop parameters. Click the gray diamond next to the Animation pop-up menu for the Left and Right parameters to set keyframes.

Once again, you are working backward, first locking the final crop values. Now you'll back up in time and crop the layers.

4   Drag the playhead back to a point where the layers are still rotated, at about 4:00.

5   Set keyframes for the Crop Left and Crop Right parameters, and then increase their values so that the crop lines cross in the middle and make the layers disappear, at just over 700 pixels each.

6   Play the project.

    It looks good, but let's say you'd like to modify the keyframe interpolation.

7   Press Command-8 to open the Keyframe Editor, and then from the Show Curve Set pop-up menu located above the list of parameters, choose Animated.

The Keyframe Editor shows the curves for all animated properties—in this case, Position and Crop. That's great, but sometimes you want to focus on just one or two curves.

TIP ▶ The Show Curve Set pop-up menu also allows you to reveal keyframe curves for specific parameters—such as Position, Rotation, and Scale—of the selected layers.

8 In the Properties pane, from the Animation pop-up menu next to the Crop Left parameter, choose Show in Keyframe Editor.

9 Do the same for the Crop Right parameter. Now only those two keyframe curves appear in the Keyframe Editor. Now you can focus on these curves without being distracted by other animated parameters of the selected layers.

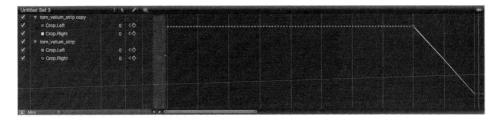

TIP ▶ You can choose Show in Keyframe Editor for parameters from different layers or groups to add them to the Keyframe Editor. It's a great way to match the timing of multiple objects without cluttering the window with other curves.

10 Shorten and reposition the zoom slider to center the curves and make them larger.

11 Command-click the names of each parameter to select them all, and then use the Animation pop-up menu in the Keyframe Editor to change the curve interpolation to Bezier for all four curves at once.

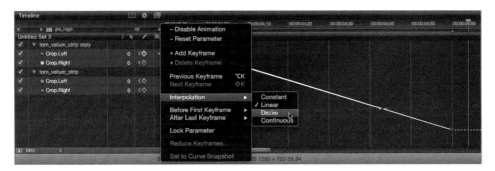

12 Drag a selection rectangle around the starting set of keyframes that are stacked on top of each other to select them all and use the Bezier handles to adjust the curves to your liking. Repeat this action for the ending keyframes.

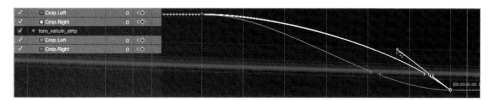

13 Save your work.

You now have a good understanding of recording keyframes and setting them manually, changing interpolation and adjusting Bezier curves, and adding and adjusting multiple keyframes at the same time.

Lesson Review

1. How does Motion let you know that recording is enabled?
2. Which parameters of a layer or group are keyframed when recording is turned on and their values are changed?
3. How many keyframes do you need to create animation?
4. The position of a video is keyframed at 1:00 and 5:00, but it does not move. Why?
5. How do you open the Keyframe Editor?
6. How do you change the interpolation for a keyframe curve?
7. How can you set the interpolation for a keyframe to Logarithmic?
8. You want to set a keyframe at 3:15 for the scale of three layers that are each in different groups. How can you set it for all of them at once?
9. When you set a keyframe with recording enabled at a frame that is not at the beginning of a layer, what does Motion do automatically?
10. When setting keyframes manually, which do you do first—set the keyframe or change the value—and why?
11. What parameters can be keyframed?

Answers

1. The Record button turns red, and all keyframeable value fields in the Inspector turn red.

2. All keyframeable parameters will be keyframed by default if you change their values with recording enabled. You can change the recording options by double-clicking the Record button and selecting the checkbox to record keyframes on animated parameters only.

3. To animate with keyframes, you need to have at least two keyframes with different values.

4. Because the keyframes have the same value.

5. Choose Window > Keyframe Editor or press Command-8.

6. In the Keyframe Editor, from the Animation pop-up menu, choose Interpolation. The submenu includes four interpolation options: Constant, Linear, Bezier, and Continuous. You can also Control-click a keyframe or a curve in the Keyframe Editor.

7. In the Keyframe Editor, you can change the interpolation of individual keyframes along a curve by Control-clicking a keyframe and choosing an interpolation type. This technique provides access to five additional interpolation options: Ease In, Ease Out, Ease Both, Exponential, and Bezier.

8. Command-click each of the layers to select them. Then click the Animation pop-up menu in the Properties Inspector for Scale and choose Add Keyframe, or click the keyframe icon.

9. Motion automatically sets a keyframe at the beginning of a layer if recording is enabled when you change the value of a parameter at any other point in time.

10. Always set the keyframe first and then change the value when setting keyframes manually; otherwise, the value will change for the entire duration of the layer, not just at the keyframe.

11. Any parameter of any layer, group, or effect that has an Animation pop-up menu in the Inspector.

Keyboard Shortcuts

A	Toggle recording on and off
Control-K	Add a keyframe for the last animated property
Command-8	Open the Keyframe Editor
Shift-K	Move to the next keyframe
Option-K	Move to the previous keyframe

Motion Graphics Design

5

Lesson Files	Motion5_Book_Files > Lessons > Lesson_05
Media	Motion5_Book_Files > Media > Mountain Gorilla > gorilla face.ai
Time	This lesson takes approximately 90 minutes to complete.
Goals	Draw shapes
	Create and modify gradients
	Apply generators
	Search the Library
	Mask with images
	Use Shape behaviors
	Import vector graphics
	Work with paint strokes

Creating Content with Shapes, Generators, and Paint Strokes

Often in a motion graphics project, you have little or no content in hand, so you need to create almost everything from scratch. This is where Motion shines. In addition to the massive amount of material in the Content folder of the Library, Motion allows you to create an amazing variety of graphic design elements using shapes, generators, and paint strokes.

Shapes are open or closed splines you create using several different tools and animate with their own special behaviors. *Generators* are elements that create patterns—some very simple, some quite intricate. And *paint strokes* are a type of shape to which you can apply a dizzying array of shape styles to create beautiful effects.

In this lesson you'll use a wide range of Motion tools and elements to design an opening graphic to a documentary. You'll import graphics from other applications and optimize them for improved performance or higher quality.

Drawing Shapes

Shapes are diverse and versatile elements in Motion, and they can range from rectangles, circles, and lines to free-form shapes and free-hand paint strokes. The Library also contains dozens of shape styles.

You are going to build the opening graphics to a documentary on the plight of the critically endangered mountain gorilla. You'll start by creating a simple shape with a gradient color fill.

1   If you have an open project, close it. Then create a new project using the Broadcast HD 720 preset.

2   Press Shift-Z to view the entire Canvas. Then in the toolbar, choose the Rectangle tool.

3   From the upper-right corner of the Canvas, drag down to the left to create a rectangle that covers a third of the entire screen.

Notice that when the pointer is located over the Canvas, it changes to a crosshair, which indicates that the Rectangle tool is still selected. To manipulate the rectangle you've just drawn, you need to return to the Select/Transform tool.

4   Press the Esc key to exit the Rectangle tool.

> **TIP** ▶ On the Canvas, you can move layers in small increments by holding down Command and repeatedly pressing the Arrow keys.

The default white fill looks a little bland, so let's fill it with a gradient.

5   Press F4 to open the Shape pane of the Inspector. Change the Fill Mode to Gradient, and click the disclosure triangle next to the Gradient parameter.

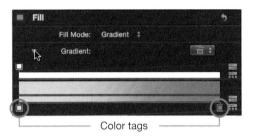

This action opens the gradient editor. The small squares at either end of the colored bar are color tags you can use to set the colors of the gradient. You can add an unlimited number of color tags here, move and delete them, and adjust the opacity of the gradient in the top white bar, the opacity bar.

6   Click the light blue color tag on the left to select it, and then click the disclosure triangle next to the color well and select a medium to dark teal color.

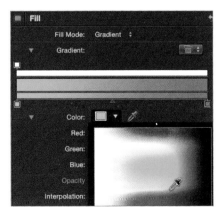

TIP ▶ You can add additional color tags anywhere along the gradient bar by clicking where you want to add the tag. To remove a color tag, drag it off the gradient bar and it will disappear in a puff of smoke.

7   Click the dark blue color tag on the right to select it. Then click the disclosure triangle next to the color well and select a dark navy blue color.

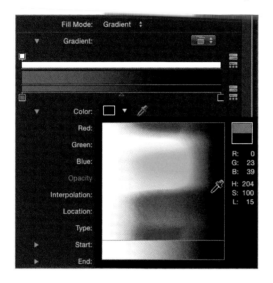

On the right side of the gradient bar, you'll find identical icon groups for the gradient's opacity and color. The top buttons in both groups reverse the direction of the gradient. The bottom button in both groups evenly distributes any tags you add between the start and ending tags. Let's reverse the colors so the darker navy blue appears at the top of the rectangle.

8   Click the Reverse Tags icon next to the color gradient bar. The gradient colors reverse direction in the bar and in the Canvas.

You can also assign colors to gradients and other modifications in the Canvas.

9   In the Canvas, Control-click (or right-click) the rectangle, and from the shortcut menu, choose Edit Gradient. A vertical line appears to indicate the gradient's direction and spread length. The color tags to the left of the line display the gradient colors, and the single white box on the right shows its opacity.

10 To increase the spread of colors, drag the bottom triangle down to the bottom of the Canvas. The range of colors in the gradient is now widened.

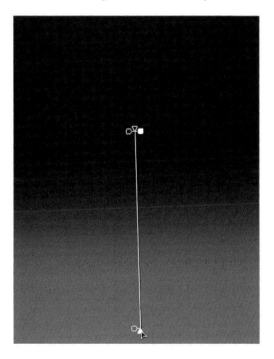

11 To return to the Select/Transform tool, Control-click the rectangle in the Canvas, and from the shortcut menu, choose Transform.

There is now a nice gradient rectangle on the right and an empty area on the left, so let's create a moody background there worthy of our mountain gorilla story.

Creating a Background with a Generator

Using the generators in Motion, you can create something out of nothing. Some generators animate by default, while you can animate others using keyframes or behaviors.

In this exercise, you use an animated generator to create a cloudy background for your project.

1   Move the playhead to the start of the project, if necessary.

2   In the Layers list, double-click Group and name it *Sidebar*. Then close the *Sidebar* group and click beneath it to deselect everything. Click the Add (+) button to create a new group.

3   Choose Object > Send to Back, or press Command-[(left bracket) to move the new group below the *Sidebar* group, and then rename the group to *Background*.

TIP   If an element in the *Sidebar* group is selected when you create a new group, the new group is created above the selected element *inside* the *Sidebar* group. If this happens, drag the new group down and to the left to move it out of the group; or press Command-Z to undo, and try again with no element selected in the *Sidebar* group.

4   Press Command-2 to open the Library, and select the Generators category. The Library contains 24 generators, four of which are text generators.

5   Select a few generators to inspect them in the preview area. Then select the Clouds generator, and click Apply to place the generator in the *Background* group and centered in the Canvas.

6   Click in the empty gray area of the Layers list to deselect everything. Then press the Spacebar to play the animation.

     The clouds are self-animated, but let's change some things.

7   Select the Clouds layer, and press F4 to open the Generator Inspector, if necessary.

8   Drag the Horizontal scale all the way to the right, and then drag the Speed slider to about 0.20. This gives the clouds a softer, less stormy look.

Remember, you're building an opening graphic for a documentary about mountain gorillas, so let's give the clouds a jungle-like appearance by changing their colors.

9   Click the Gradient arrow to open the gradient controls. This time you'll select the gradient colors using a different method.

10 To the left of the gradient bar, click the black color tag.

11 Click the eyedropper next to the color well, and then click the dark navy blue color at the top of the gradient rectangle you created earlier in the Canvas.

The clouds now have a nice blue tone. For the next color, you'll apply a more precise color selection technique.

12 Click the white color tag on the right of the gradient bar, and then click the color well to open the Mac OS X Colors window.

13 Click the Sliders button at the top of the Colors window, and from the pop-up menu, choose RGB Sliders.

14 Drag the sliders to set Red to 60, Green to 90, and Blue to 20. Then close the Colors window, and press the Spacebar to stop playback.

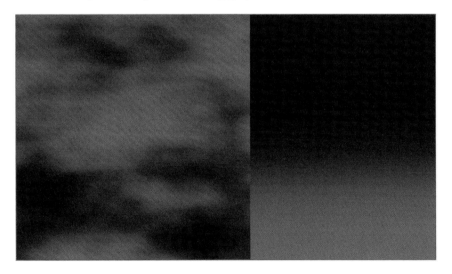

You now have a smoldering, murky background animation that is perfect for our mysterious and endangered mountain gorillas.

15 This is a great point to save your work. Choose File > Save. Name the project *Murky Gorillas* and save your work in the Lesson_05 > Student_Saves folder. You now have a saved project to use to if you make a major mistake.

Searching for Content

Generators are just one type of content that Motion allows you to add to your projects. The Motion Library is full of content types, but can you really find something in the Library that is suitable for a project about mountain gorillas? The easiest way to answer that question is to search the Library.

1   Press Command-2 to open the Library pane.

2   Select the Content > All category.

3   At the bottom of the Library pane, click the Search button (the magnifying glass icon) to open the Search field. You'll search for a graphic of the Earth to help you point out where these gorillas live.

4   In the Search field, type *earth*.

    The Library includes a few Earth-related graphics. You'll add the black-and-white Earth image because it will more easily allow you to change its colors.

5   Position the playhead at the start of the project, if necessary.

6   In the Library, click the Earth Transparent element.

7 You want to add the element to the *Sidebar* group. So, first select the *Sidebar* group in the Layers list, and then click Apply at the top of the Library.

8 Press the Spacebar to watch the Earth spin in your project.

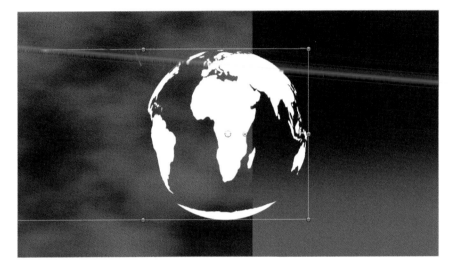

The Earth is already animated, which is both good and bad. It's good because you don't have to figure out how to animate it, but it's bad because you now have to figure out how to make it stop on Africa.

Modifying Animated Content

Sometimes you can easily modify animated content in Motion, and at other times animation changes can be complex and take a long time to figure out. Are you ready for a moderate challenge?

1 Press the Spacebar to stop playback. First, position the Earth in your project.

2 Shift-drag one of the bounding box handles on the Earth to scale it to roughly 65%. Remember to watch the Scale display in the upper-left corner of the Canvas to help set the scale precisely.

3 Position the Earth element in the upper half of the gradient rectangle. Don't place it right up against the top edge. Leave a little room at the top because you'll add text there in the next lesson.

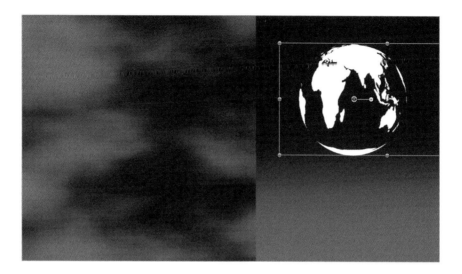

Now you're ready to tackle the animation. Let's locate the keyframes by selecting the elements inside the *Earth Transparent* group to see if keyframes appear in the Keyframe Editor.

4   Choose Window > Keyframe Editor, or press Command-8, to open the Keyframe Editor. Then, choose Window > Video Timeline, or press Command-7, to hide the Video Timeline.

Nothing is displayed in the Keyframe Editor because no keyframes are placed on the *Earth Transparent* group. Let's drill down into the group to find those keyframes.

5   In the Layers list, click the *Earth Transparent* group's disclosure triangle to reveal its contents, and then reveal the contents of the Earth Transparent image.

6   Click the Earth Transparent image, click the Sphere, and finally click the Rotate Earth behavior until you see keyframes in the Keyframe Editor.

There, you found keyframes on the Rotate Earth behavior. Two keyframed parameters appear in the parameter list to the left. These parameters also have two keyframes, which somehow repeat through the entire project, indicated by the dotted saw tooth lines. This is achieved using a Repeat function in Motion. Using this function, you can place the initial keyframes and then Motion will repeat that animation for the length of the layer. In this case, you want to stop that repetitive animation and have the Earth stop on Africa.

7   To stop the repetitive Position X animation, from the Animation menu located in the far-right column of the parameter list, choose After Last Keyframe > Constant

Now the Position X graph ramps to the first keyframe and remains constant. A straight line in the graph indicates that the parameter value is not changing.

8   To stop the repetitive Center X animation, from the Animation menu, once again choose After Last Keyframe > Constant

9   In the transport controls under the Canvas, click the "Play from Start" button to review the animation. Press the Spacebar to stop playback.

The Earth now rotates once and stops. That is near perfect. The spinning Earth even stops exactly on Africa. Still, the animation could be improved by smoothly slowing to its final position, rather than making an abrupt stop.

10 In the Keyframe Editor, Control-click the Position X keyframe, and from the shortcut menu, choose Ease In. Then, do the same for the Center X keyframe.

11 In the transport controls under the Canvas, click the "Play from Start" button to review the animation. Press the Spacebar to stop playback.

Now you have a nice smooth Earth animation that slows to a stop with Africa showing. You will now turn your attention to the Earth's appearance.

TIP ▶ You got lucky on this animation. The rotation just happens to stop correctly on Africa. If this project were about Gibbons in Indonesia then you wouldn't be so lucky. In that case, you would adjust the Center X and Position X keyframes so that the earth landed correctly.

Masking with Images

In previous lessons, you masked elements using the Mask tool in the toolbar. However, you have other ways to mask images using the alpha, luminance, or color channels of a video clip, photo, or graphic. The technique of using image channels as a mask is called an image mask, which can be added to any element or group in a project. You'll use an image mask here to change the color on the white Earth graphic.

1   Press Command-7 to open the Timing pane, and then press Command-8 to close the Keyframe Editor.

2   Press the Home key, or drag the playhead to the start of the project.

3   In the Layers list, select the *Sidebar* group to make sure the new shape you draw is created at the top level of that group.

4   Make sure the Line tool is chosen, and from the pop-up menu, choose Rectangle.

You are going to draw a rectangle to cover the Earth. You'll then set the color of the rectangle to recolor the white areas of the globe.

5   In the Canvas, draw a rectangle to cover the Earth.

6 Press the Esc key to switch from the Rectangle tool to the Select/Transform tool.

7 Press Command-3 to open the Inspector.

8 Click the eyedropper next to the Fill Color, and in the Canvas, click a green area of the clouds.

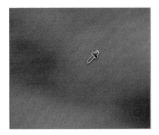

The rectangle now matches the green color used in the Clouds generator. Next, you'll create an image mask on the rectangle and fill it with the Earth element.

9 In the Layers list, Control-click the *Rectangle 1* layer, and from the shortcut menu, choose Add Image Mask.

A new *Image Mask* layer is created directly under the *Rectangle 1* layer. In the Inspector, the image mask includes a drop well for a mask source. To assign the source used as the mask, you can either drag an image into the Mask Source drop well, or you can drag the image directly on top of the *Image Mask* layer in the Layers list.

10 Drag the *Earth Transparent* group onto the *Image Mask* layer in the Layers list.

The green rectangle is now masked based on the transparency or the alpha channel of the *Earth Transparent* layer. But it looks very flat. You can easily give this a more spherical appearance by applying a gradient to the rectangle.

> **TIP** ▶ If the mask image you use does not have an alpha channel, in the Source Channel menu in the Inspector, you can choose to use the Luminance channel or a color channel.

11 In the Layers list, select the *Rectangle 1* layer.

12 In the Inspector, change the Fill mode pop-up to Gradient. Then open the gradient editor and select the blue color tag to the right.

13 Click the eyedropper next to the color well, and in the Canvas, click a green area of the clouds in the Canvas.

This gradient is linear from top to bottom, but to get a rounder appearance on the Earth, the white color should act more like a highlight. You can do that in the Inspector by switching from a linear gradient to a radial gradient.

14 From the Type pop-up menu in the Inspector, choose Radial.

Our Earth is now in place and has a great three-dimensional appearance. You can now focus on filling up the right side of your project with a gorilla graphic.

Importing Vector Graphics

At some point in your motion graphics career, you will need to use artwork created in a vector-based drawing application such as Adobe Illustrator and saved in a format such as AI (Illustrator) or PDF (Portable Document Format). The vector nature of this artwork means that you can scale it as large as you like without losing its resolution. You'll import a vector drawing of a gorilla to add to your project.

1   Close the *Sidebar* and *Background* groups. Click in an empty area of the Layers list to deselect everything. Then click the Add (+) button to create a new group above the two existing groups, and rename it *Gorilla*.

2   Make sure the playhead is at the start of the project.

   After the gorilla graphic that you create fades up, it will last the entire length of the project.

3   Press Command-1 to open the File Browser. Navigate to Motion5_Book_Files > Media > Mountain Gorilla, and select **gorilla face.ai**.

4 Click Import to place the file into the *Gorilla* group at the playhead location, and then roughly center it over the cloudy green background.

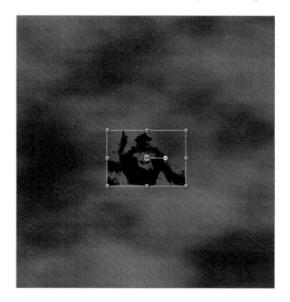

At 100% size, the logo is very small. This is a mountain gorilla, the largest of the apes! You need to dramatically increase the size of this layer.

5   Shift-Option-drag a control handle on the *Gorilla* layer's bounding box and increase the scale until the sides of the bounding box reach the edges of the cloudy green background.

The face appears blurry, as if this layer were a bitmap rather than a vector image. This is because, by default, imported vector files are set to *fixed resolution* to maximize performance. You can change this setting by selecting the underlying media for the layer instead of the layer itself.

6   In the Project pane, click the Media list to see all the files you imported into a project.

7   Select the `gorilla face.ai` file, and then press F4 to open the context-sensitive Object pane in the Inspector, which now is also named Media. The Media pane of the Inspector contains settings for the source media file.

8   Deselect the Fixed Resolution checkbox. The *gorilla face* layer now looks crisp and clear, even at this very large scale.

> **TIP ▶** If you are not scaling imported vector files over 100%, you needn't deselect the Fixed Resolution checkbox. Leaving it selected will optimize playback performance and render speed.

9   Press Command-4 to open the Layers list, and select the *gorilla face* layer.

The graphic is sharp, but you can see the edges of the graphic document. You'll create an oval-shaped mask to obscure the sharp edges of the gorilla graphic.

10   In the toolbar, from the mask tools pop-up menu, choose Circle Mask.

11   Option-drag out from the center of the gorilla's face to the left edge of the frame, and then drag down until the oval shape just meets the top and bottom of the gorilla graphic.

12 In the Inspector, adjust the Feather parameter to 15 to soften the edges of the oval mask.

Finally, you'll add a simple Fade behavior to fade in the gorilla graphic at the start of the project.

13 Press Command-2 to open the Library, and select the Behaviors category.

Hey! Nothing shows up. Where did all the behaviors go? You didn't clear the Search field after you added the Earth content. This can happen often and it's a good situation to be aware of.

14 To the right of the Search field, click the Clear button (X) to clear the *earth* search. Suddenly, all your behaviors are back.

15 Select the Basic Motion behavior category, and drag the Fade In/Out behavior onto the *gorilla face* layer in the Layers list.

16 In the toolbar, click the HUD button, or press F7. Drag the right edge of the fade graphic until it reads 0 frames, and then close the HUD.

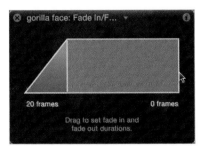

17 In the transport controls, click the "Play from Start" button to view the entire project. Click the Pause button to stop.

> **TIP** Occasionally, pressing the Spacebar to start and stop playback may not work because the window focus is in the Library. Click an empty space in the Layers list to reactivate the Spacebar for the Canvas.

This project is really shaping up. It needs more dramatic impact, which you can add by using a bit more color and animation.

Working with Paint Strokes

Almost any shape that has an outline but no fill is a *paint stroke*. However, paint strokes have much, much more to offer, including a Paint Stroke tool and a huge variety of presets, called *shape styles*, with which to paint.

In this exercise, you'll create paint stroke elements in two ways: a simple airbrush line that better defines the two halves of the layout, and a freehand paint stroke to bring a more organic touch.

1 In the Layers list, select the *Sidebar* group because this is the group you want to contain the first paint stroke. Make sure the playhead is at the start of the project.

2 With the pointer over the Rectangle tool in the toolbar, click and hold down the mouse button. From the shape tools pop-up menu, choose the Line tool.

3 To draw a line, drag from the upper-left corner of the rectangle to the lower-left corner. The result is a white line that acts as a border between the two sides of your design.

> **TIP** Holding down Shift while drawing with the Line tool constrains the line horizontally and vertically.

4   Press Esc, and then press Command-3 to open the Inspector.

The Inspector now shows the controls for the line, which are the same shape controls used for the rectangle. The rectangle also used the fill controls, but the line uses only the outline controls as noted by the blue box next the Outline heading.

5   Click the Outline's color well disclosure triangle and select a mustard yellow color for the line.

Shapes have other advanced controls in the Inspector, but most of them are available only when you change the Brush Type to Airbrush or use an image as a brush.

6   From the Brush Type pop-up menu, choose Airbrush.

In the Canvas, the line gets a bit softer when you choose the Airbrush type. A few other subtle changes also happen. Two additional active panes, Stroke and Advanced, appear in the Inspector. Let's taper the line a bit more using the stroke controls.

7   At the top of the Inspector, click the Stroke pane.

We could spend an entire book exploring these shape tools, but for now let's just vary the width of the airbrush over the length of the stroke.

8   Click the disclosure arrow next to Width Over Stroke to reveal the graph control.

A green line is flat across the graph, indicating that the width of the line is constant from start to end. By adding control points and changing their vertical positions, you can vary the width of the airbrush line.

9   Drag down the control point on the left edge of the green line to a width of approximately 50.00 as shown by the numbers to the left of the graph.

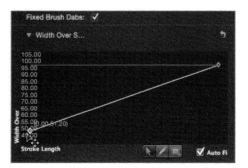

Notice that the line in the Canvas is now thinner at the top and thicker down the bottom. By adding new points on the graph line you can alter the thickness anywhere along a stroke's length.

10 Double-click, or Option-click, in the center of the line to add a control point and drag it up to a width of roughly 100.00, using the numbers to the left of the graph as your guide.

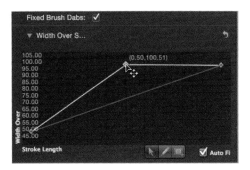

11 Drag down the control point on the right edge of the green line to match the value of the first control point to create a tapered paint stroke line.

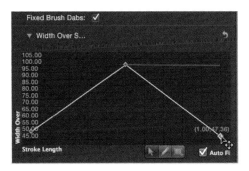

TIP ▶ You can make the transition between points smoother by Control-clicking a point, and from the shortcut menu, choosing Interpolation > Continuous.

The airbrush is the simplest paint stroke. You'll animate it in the next section, but let's first draw a more advanced paint stroke using the more flexible Paint Stroke tool.

12 Close all the open groups in the Layers list, and select the *Background* group so the new paint stroke will be placed in that group.

13 Position the playhead at 3:19 (or 200 frames) because you want this paint stroke to appear onscreen one-third of the way into the project.

14 In the toolbar, choose the Paint Stroke tool.

The Paint Stroke tool works much like a brush, pen, or pencil because it allows you to draw in a free-form manner (although you can change its shape at any time.) Before using the tool, you can choose what media you will paint with, much as you would choose a color from a palette. But instead of choosing a color, you can choose an image or even a movie as your paint medium.

15 Open the HUD and click the Shape Style pop-up menu to browse through the categories.

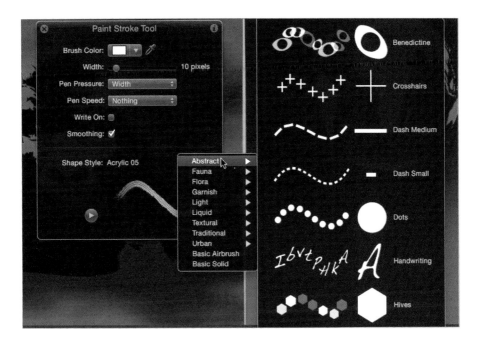

Each shape style is an image or a short movie. When you paint, you create a trail consisting of many copies of the image or movie. Each of those copies is called a *dab*. When the dabs are sufficiently close together, they form a continuous stroke. To try this out, you will use a shape style from the Traditional category.

16 Choose Traditional > Sable 03 Buildup.

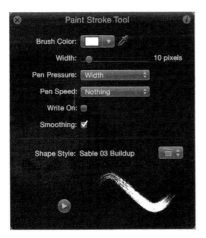

17 Draw a paint stroke that starts at the left edge of the Canvas just below the gorilla and extends to the gradient rectangle. This paint stroke reveals text you will create and animate in the next lesson.

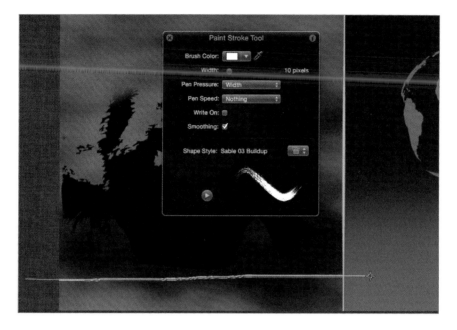

NOTE ▶ Don't worry about being too exact with paint strokes. Although they look like fixed strokes, they are still Bezier-based paths that can be edited by Control-clicking and choosing Edit Points from the shortcut menu.

18 Close the HUD. In the transport controls, click the "Play from Start" button to watch the project. Press the Spacebar to stop.

The paint stroke is a bit small, and it just pops on. Let's fix the color of the stroke and then the width.

19 Position the playhead toward the end of the project where you can see the entire paint stroke in the Canvas.

20 Click the disclosure triangle next to the brush color and select a vibrant crimson red.

> **TIP** ▶ You can change a shape style after you have drawn it by choosing a new style from the Shape Style pop-up menu in the Inspector.

21 Drag the width slider to 75 to create a much thicker paint stroke.

Using Shape Behaviors

Shapes and paint strokes can be animated by applying any of the keyframing techniques or behaviors you've already used, but Motion also has a special category of behaviors just for animating shapes.

1 Press Command-2 to open the Library. Select Behaviors, and then select the Shape folder.

2 Drag the Write On behavior from the Library to the *Line* layer in the *Sidebar* group of the Layers list.

3 Click in the gray empty space at the bottom of the Layers list to deselect the line, and then click the "Play from Start" button in the transport controls. Do not stop the playback.

The Write On behavior animates the line from top to bottom, but it does so too slowly. You can increase the behavior's speed by changing its Duration in the Timing pane or the mini-Timeline.

4 In the Layers list, select the Write On behavior.

5 In the mini-Timeline, drag the right end of the Write On behavior to 3:19, just to where the paint stroke appears onscreen.

The line now moves at a much brisker pace. Now add the Write On behavior to the paint stroke.

6 Drag the Write On behavior from the Library to the *Sable 03 Buildup* layer in the Layers list.

7   This animation is also too slow, so in the mini-Timeline drag the right end of the Write On behavior until its Duration is at 1:40. Use the tooltip as a guide.

That's peppy! In the next lesson, however, you'll use this paint stroke to reveal text, so you not only need it to paint on, you also need it to paint off the screen.

8   Press Command-3 to open the Inspector for the *Sable 03 Buildup* Write On behavior.

9   From the Shape Outline menu, choose Draw and Erase.

The paint stroke now paints on and off the screen. You have one more method to create a painterly effect that offers a lot more control using a standard Bezier tool.

Using the Bezier Tool

Unlike the Paint Stroke tool, which automatically places a lot of control points along a freehand-drawn path, the Bezier tool lets you place each control point manually to create a very precise path. Using the Bezier tool, you can create a more refined path for drawing shapes or paint strokes.

1   Make sure playback is stopped, select the Sidebar group, and position the playhead at 4:59.

2   In the toolbar, choose the Bezier tool.

> **NOTE ▸** The B-Spline tool, located underneath the Bezier tool, is sometimes a better option for creating totally smooth paths. You'll use the B-Spline tool later in this lesson.

3   In the Canvas, click to create an arcing path that starts at the top of the Earth and goes around its left side. End the path off the screen to the right.

If you drag as you click, the path will curve through the control point rather than making a sharp turn. At the moment, you are just roughing in the arc to establish the timing. You'll fix the path later in this exercise.

4   After setting the last control point, press Return to finish the shape. The shape is created as a closed, filled shape, but for the purpose of this project you need to display it as an outline.

5   In the Shape pane of the Inspector, disable the fill by clicking the blue icon next to the Fill name. When it is disabled, the color fill disappears and leaves just the outline.

You now have a Bezier-shaped path you can easily turn into a paint stroke. Instead of choosing the shape style from a list as you did when using the Paint Stroke tool, you'll apply the shape style by dragging it from the Library.

6   Press Command-2 to open the Library pane. Choose Shape Styles > Light > Light Tail 07. Drag it over the *Bezier* layer in the Layers list, and wait briefly to and drop it on "Copy Style to Shape" in the pop-up menu.

7   Press the Spacebar to play the new Light Tail paint stroke, and then stop playback.

The Light Tail paint stroke is a shape style that is automatically animated. You didn't need to add a Write On behavior. It still needs some adjustments, but you can make those adjustments more quickly if you just play back the part of the project containing the light tail and not the entire project.

NOTE ▸ To determine if a shape style is animated before you apply it, select it in the Library and watch the preview. If it animates in the Library preview window, then it will autoanimate when you apply it.

8   Position the playhead toward the end of the project, where the light tail has gone off the Canvas (roughly at 8:00). Press Command-Option-O to set a play range Out point at the playhead.

9   Press Shift-I to move the playhead to the *Bezier* layer's In point, and then press Command-Option-I to set a play range In point at the playhead.

10 Press the Spacebar to begin playback.

As you learned earlier, paint strokes have an incredible number of parameters you can adjust. Let's try a few.

11 In the Inspector adjust the Width to around 40, and then click the Geometry pane.

The paint stroke is a little less smooth than you might like. In the Geometry pane, you can smooth the shape and more easily adjust the points.

12 Change the Shape Type to B-Spline.

With just that small menu change, the paint stroke already looks much improved. That's because B-Splines are sweet! B-Splines should be your preferred drawing tools for masks and paint strokes because they are much easier to modify than Bezier shapes and the results are always smooth.

B-Splines are also easier to manipulate because they don't use tangent handles like Bezier shapes. Instead, the control point *influences* the curve by pulling it in any direction. By default the curve is always smooth, although you can create sharp angles if you need to.

TIP ▸ Command-dragging a control point on any B-Spline shape will produce a sharper angle at that point.

13 Stop playback, and double-click the shape to reveal the control points. Drag the control points of the B-Spline to create an arc that goes along the left edge of the Earth graphic.

14 Press Option-X to reset the play range. Review the project and save your work.

You covered a large amount of ground in this lesson, learning the essential design tools found in Motion and how to import design elements created elsewhere. The relative benefits of creating all your elements in Motion versus importing vector graphics created in other programs is for you to decide. You can increase performance by using imported elements, but as you'll learn in the next lesson, a wealth of animation features accompanies the Motion design tools. In the end, a healthy combination of imported graphics and Motion-designed elements work best.

Lesson Review

1. How many color tags can you add to a shape's gradient in the Inspector?
2. How do you reverse the direction of a gradient?
3. Where do you change the fill for a shape such as a rectangle?
4. How do you create an image mask?
5. True or false: A source image for an image mask must contain an alpha channel.
6. You've added a vector graphic in the Illustrator or PDF format but when you resize it, it looks blurry. How can you fix this?

7. How do you create a generator?

8. If you select a category in the Library and it is empty, what might be the first thing to check?

9. How does the Paint Stroke tool differ from the Bezier tool?

10. How can you increase the speed of a Shape behavior?

11. Describe two ways to apply a shape style preset to a paint stroke.

12. What behavior can you use to animate the appearance and/or disappearance of a paint stroke from the first control point to the last?

Answers

1. There is no limit.

2. Click the Reverse Tags icon next to the color gradient bar.

3. With the layer selected, press F4 to open the Shape pane of the Inspector, and choose the appropriate option from the Fill Mode pop-up menu.

4. In the Layers list, Control-click the appropriate layer, and choose Add Image Mask from the shortcut menu. Drag an image into the Mask Source drop well.

5. False. An image mask can use an alpha channel, luminance channel, or a color channel.

6. Switch to the Media List in the Project pane to select the AI or PDF file. Then view the Media pane in the Inspector and deselect the Fixed Resolution checkbox.

7. Press Command-2 to open the Library, and select the Generators category. Select a generator, and click Apply.

8. Check to make sure the Search field is empty at the bottom of the Library.

9. The Paint Stroke tool is a freehand tool. The Bezier tool lets you place each control point as you draw by clicking in the Canvas.

10. You can increase a behavior's speed by shortening its duration in the Timing pane or the mini-Timeline.

11. Choose a shape style from the HUD pop-up menu, or drag it from the Shape Style category in the Library onto the paint stroke layer.

12. The Write On behavior

Keyboard Shortcuts

B	Select the Bezier tool/B-Spline tool
C	Select the Circle tool
P	Select the Paint Stroke tool
R	Select the Rectangle tool
Shift-S	Select the Select/Transform tool
Esc	Exit the Rectangle, Circle, or Line tool
Shift-Home	Move the playhead to the play range In point
Shift-End	Move the playhead to the play range Out point
Command-4	Open the Layers list

6

Lesson Files	Motion5_Book_Files > Lessons > Lesson_06 > Lesson_06_Start
Media	Motion5_Book_Files > Media > Mountain Gorilla > gorilla face.ai
Time	This lesson takes approximately 60 minutes to complete.
Goals	Create, format, and style text layers
	Save and apply text style presets
	Format glyphs
	Animate text with text behaviors
	Customize the Sequence Text behavior
	Save text animation favorites
	Animate text on a path
	Work with motion blur

Creating Text Effects

Text and motion graphics were made for each other. When you integrate video, audio, motion graphics, and animated text into a presentation, you have a powerful vehicle for entertaining, educating, and persuading your audience.

The text engine in Motion is powerful and flexible. Using the text behaviors along with formatting, styling, and animation tools, you can create dynamic, engaging, and unique text treatments to complement your motion graphics.

In this lesson, you will develop an animated text for your Mountain Gorilla project.

Creating, Formatting, and Styling Text Layers

The first step is to place your text at the appropriate time using project markers, and in the appropriate space relative to the background. After entering text using the Text tool, you will adjust its format and style in the HUD and the Inspector. You'll work with an updated Mountain Gorilla project similar to the one you finished in Lesson 5.

1   Open Lessons > Lesson 06 > Lesson_06_Start and save it to the Student_Saves folder.

2   If the playhead is not already at the start of the project, press Home (or if your keyboard lacks a Home key, press Fn-Left Arrow). Then press Command-Option-Right Arrow to move the playhead to the first marker at 00:29.

Let's place the main text at this marker.

TIP ▶ You can add your own marker by selecting a layer and pressing M. If no layer is selected, the marker is added to the Timeline Ruler.

3   In the Layers list, select the *Sidebar* group. Click the New Group (+) button to create a new group, and name it *Text*. The *Text* group is created above the *Sidebar* group. To create a text layer, use the Text tool.

4   Press Shift-Z to view the entire Canvas. In the toolbar, select the Text tool, or press T.

5   Click just above the gorilla's head, and type *Mountain*. Press Return, and on the next line type *Gorillas*.

NOTE ▶ Your text font may appear differently than the font used in the following figure depending on the most recent font you used in a Motion project. The screen shot is best used to get a rough idea of the placement of the text and not its appearance.

6   Press Esc to return to the Select/Transform tool.

With the title typed, you can format the text to better fit the space provided and to match the style of your graphic.

7   Open the HUD, if necessary, and drag the Size slider to 75 points. From the Font pop-up menu, choose Trebuchet MS Bold, and under the font name, click the Center Alignment button.

> **TIP** ▸ If you drag through the list of fonts, the text in the Canvas will update the font in real time, so that you can see exactly how each font looks in your project.

It's a good idea to turn on the safe zones to help place the text.

8 From the "View and Overlay" pop-up menu at the top right of the Canvas, choose Safe Zones, or press the ' (apostrophe) key.

The outer blue rectangle represents the action-safe area, and all critical action should happen within it. The inner blue rectangle represents the title-safe area, and critical text shouldn't extend outside it.

NOTE ▶ Although the safe zones were designed for broadcast television viewing, they ensure that you don't crowd the edge of the frame no matter which delivery system or display device your audience is using.

9 In the Canvas, drag the text while watching the dynamic guides, and center the text over the gorilla's head within the title-safe area.

You can continue to modify the text format and style in the HUD, but to access even more parameters, use the Inspector.

10 Close the HUD and press F4 to open the fourth pane of the Inspector, which is now the Text pane. The Text pane contains a large number of parameters in three panes: Format, Style, and Layout.

The Format pane contains many of the parameters also found in the HUD, such as the font family, typeface, size, and tracking.

11 In the Format pane, change the line spacing to –15 to bring the two text lines closer together. Then, change the tracking to roughly 25% to spread the characters farther apart. Lastly, at the bottom of the Inspector, select the All Caps checkbox to convert your text to capital letters.

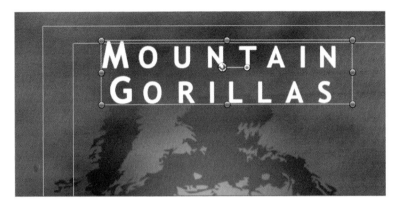

12 In the Inspector, click the Style pane.

In the Style pane, you can customize four attributes of a text layer: Face, Outline, Glow, and Drop Shadow. Each attribute has a similar group of adjustable parameters. The text color is pure white by default, so it doesn't quite match the jungle colors you're after in this project.

13 Click the Face color eyedropper icon, and then click the yellow line coming down to the right of the text to apply that color to the text layer.

TIP You can also change the text color using the color well in the HUD.

An outline could help distinguish this text from the background.

14 Select the Outline checkbox, click the arrow next to the color well, and select black. Increase the Width to 2.

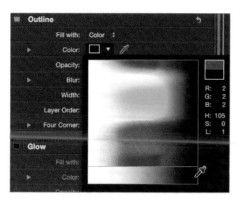

That more clearly sets off the text, but a soft, subtle drop shadow would add some depth.

15 Select the Drop Shadow checkbox. Change Opacity to 80% and Blur to 2.

You can often improve the appearance and readability of text by adjusting the distance between individual characters, a technique called *kerning*. Some letters in *Gorillas* look a little too far apart relative to the others, but you can fix that.

16 Double-click the text in the Canvas to select it, and then click once between the *o* and *r* of the word *Gorillas* to place the insertion point.

17 Press Control-Left Arrow a few times to reduce the space between the letters.

NOTE ▸ If you are using Mac OS X Lion, be sure to disable all Mission Control keyboard shortcuts located in the Keyboard System Preferences to enable Control-Arrow shortcuts in Motion.

18 Press the Left and Right Arrow keys to move the pointer between the other characters, and adjust the kerning as you see fit. Press Esc to exit the Text tool, reposition the text layer as necessary, and save your work.

The main text for the project is now positioned and formatted so you can move on to the next text layer. Don't worry if this text isn't perfect. In Motion you can change the format, style, and layout of text at any stage of your project.

Saving Text Style Presets

You want to create several other text layers for this project. Rather than building each layer from scratch, you can save your modified text as a style preset, and then apply that preset to other text layers.

1   With the *Mountain Gorillas* text layer still selected, click the Style Preset pop-up menu that currently displays the title NORMAL.

In this menu, you can select one of the preset text styles from the Motion Library or save your own style. When saving a style, you have the option to save only the Format parameters (including Font, Size, and Tracking) or only the Style parameters (including Face, Outline, Glow, and Drop Shadow); or you can save all the parameters from both the Format and Style panes.

2   Choose Save Style Attributes. The Save Preset To Library dialog appears. Type *Trebuchet Yellow Outline and Shadow* and click Save.

The new custom preset now appears in the Style Preset pop-up menu and in the Text Styles section of the Library. Let's prepare for the next text layer and see how you can apply the new style.

3   In the Timeline, press Command-Option-Right Arrow to move the playhead to the second marker, at 3:59. This is the point where the red paint stroke is fully onscreen and the next line of text should appear.

4   In the Layers list, select the Background Group, and press T to choose the Text tool. Click directly over the red paint stroke, and type *A Species in Danger*.

Motion applies formatting identical to the most recent time you used the text tool, so the font, size, and color are the same, but the style is not. Furthermore, this text layer needs to be centered.

5   Press Esc to exit the Text tool. In the Format pane of the Inspector, click the Center Alignment button, and reposition this text layer so that it fits within the red paint stroke, centered under the gorilla.

6   Press Command-2 to open the Library. Select the Text Styles category, and locate the *Trebuchet Yellow Outline and Shadow* preset style you saved. The small human silhouette at the bottom right of the icon indicates that the preset was created by a user and is not part of the original Motion Library.

7   In the Layers list or the Canvas, drag the text style preset onto the text layer.

8   To make the red paint stroke reveal the text, drag the *A Species in Danger* text layer below the *Paint Stroke* layer in the Layers list.

Saving styles can help you quickly reuse great-looking text parameter combinations you may have created for previous projects. The Style settings take up very little storage space so it's worth creating lots of them and giving them names that will make them easy to find in the future.

Modifying a Single Character

So far, you've formatted entire text layers, assigning the same size and color to each letter in the text. You can also make those changes to individual text characters, or *glyphs*, using the Transform Glyph tool.

1   In the Timeline, press Command-Option-Right Arrow to move the playhead to the third marker.

By now, you know how to type text, so we'll save you the steps. For this exercise, the text was already created but disabled in the *Sidebar* group. You'll enable the text layer and then change an individual glyph.

2   In the Layers list, open the *Sidebar* group and select the activation checkbox to view the text layer *The Gorilla Group Fund*.

You will redesign the fund's text so that it stands out a bit more in your project. Using the Transform Glyph tool, you'll resize a letter *G* so it can be used for both *Gorilla* and *Group*. Let's start by deleting one of the current letter *G*s.

3   In the Layers list, select *The Gorilla Group Fund* text, and then double-click the text in the Canvas to activate the Text tool.

4   Click between the letters *G* and *O* of *Gorilla*, and then press Delete. To push the remaining letters in the word roughly back into place, press the Spacebar and then press the Esc key.

Because you will work within a small area of the Canvas, you may want to zoom into that work area.

5   Press Command-Spacebar, and then drag the *Gorilla Group* text to the right to zoom into it. Next, Spacebar-drag in the Canvas to center the text you'll work on.

TIP If you press Command-Spacebar and the Spotlight search window opens, hold the Spacebar first then hold the Command key.

6   Control-click (or right-click) the *Gorilla Group Fund* text, and from the shortcut
     menu, choose Transform Glyph.

     TIP ► You can also choose the Transform Glyph tool by clicking the Select/
     Transform tool in the toolbar and choosing Transform Glyph from the pop-up menu.

     A bounding box surrounds a glyph in the text layer, which you can use to change its
     scale, rotation, and position as well as its color, outline, glow, and drop shadow.

     NOTE ► Although you can change the style parameters for an individual glyph, you
     cannot assign a saved style to an individual glyph.

     The selected glyph has onscreen controls for position and rotation. You can drag
     the red, green, and blue arrows to change the position of the glyph along the x-axis
     (horizontally), the y-axis (vertically), or the z-axis (toward or away from the viewer),
     respectively. You drag the hollow white circles to rotate the glyph around each of the
     x, y, and z axes.

7   Select the *G* in *Group* and experiment by dragging the various controls.

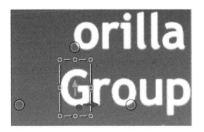

8   When you finish experimenting with the various manipulation tools on the glyph,
     press F4 to open the Text pane in the Inspector.

     Changes you make to the glyph in the Canvas are stored in the Scale, Offset, and
     Rotation parameters of the Advanced Formatting section in the Format pane (but
     not in the Scale, Position, or Rotation parameters of the Properties pane, which apply
     only to the text layer as a whole).

     You'll reset the Scale, Offset, and Rotation in the Advanced Formatting area to get the
     G back to our starting point.

9   Press Command-Z several times to return the *G* to its initial position.

10 Shift-drag a bounding box control handle to increase the G glyph's size to about 200%, or until the top of the G is at the same level as the top of the other letters in *Gorilla*.

Scaling the G positioned it far from the remaining letters in the word *Group* and too close to the remaining letters of *Gorilla*.

11 Select the *o* in *Gorilla*, and then Shift-click the *a* to select all the remaining letters in the word.

12 Drag the x-axis drag handle (red arrow) to reposition the *orilla* away from the G.

13 Select the *r* in *Group*, and then Shift-click the *p* to select all the remaining letters in the word.

14 Drag the y-axis drag handle (green arrow) with the x-axis drag handle (red arrow) to reposition the *roup* next to the G. Adjust the word fragment so that the *r* in *Group* and the *o* in *Gorillas* are directly under each other.

15 Select the *F* in *Fund*, and then Shift-click the *d*. With the entire word now selected, reposition it under the word *Group*, and line up the *F* of *Fund* under the *r* of *Group*.

You'll also make the word *Fund* slightly smaller than the *Gorilla Group*.

16 With the word *Fund* still selected, in the Inspector adjust the Scale slider in the Advanced Formatting section to 75%.

17 Do the same with the word *The*, bringing it in closer to the word *Gorilla* and positioning the *T* over the *o*. Then scale the entire word to 75% using the Scale slider in the Inspector.

NOTE ▶ When repositioning a character with the Transform Glyph tool, remember that you are changing its Offset parameter in the Format pane of the Text Inspector, not changing the Position parameter in the Properties pane.

18 Save your work, press Shift-Z to see the entire Canvas, and then press the ' (apostrophe) key to turn off the safe zones. Finally, press Tab to choose the Select/Transform tool.

You have one more text layer to create; this time you'll place the text along a path.

Placing Text on a Path

At times a project calls for just a bit more dynamic text placement than a straight horizontal line. Now, don't get all crazy with this effect. Use it judiciously and it can be a wonderful thing. Do it over and over, and it becomes gratuitous. It's a fine line, just not always horizontal.

1   In the Timeline, press Command-Option-Right Arrow to move the playhead to the fourth and final marker.

    This location has another piece of text created but disabled in the *Sidebar* group. You'll enable it and place it on a path around the Earth.

2   In the Layers list *Sidebar* group, select the activation checkbox to view the *Help save the mountain gorilla* text in the Canvas.

    The Layout pane in the Inspector contains typical page layout settings such as margins, but it also has more sophisticated layout options such as paths that allow you to convert a text baseline into a spline curve.

3   In the Layers list, select the *Help save the mountain gorilla* text.

4   In the Inspector, click the Layout pane, and from the Layout Method pop-up menu, choose Path.

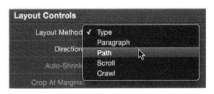

    When you set the Layout Method to Path, Path Options is enabled further down in the Inspector interface. By default, the path is an open spline you can modify by double-clicking the text in the Canvas. For this exercise, you will place the text on a circle around the Earth.

5 From the Path Shape pop-up menu, choose Circle.

6 In the Canvas, double-click the selected text to see the path.

You can drag the handles on the circular path to reshape the circle with movement constrained to a single direction. When you drag the handles extended from the right side of the path, you access freeform reshaping. In the next step, you'll drag the freeform handles in conjunction with the Shift key to scale the circle around the Earth.

7 Shift-drag one of the freeform handles to best fit the path around the Earth.

Take your time aligning the text. The tighter the fit, the nicer this layout will look. You may need to return to the Select/Transform tool and reposition the path to get the best fit.

8 When you complete the adjustments, save your work.

You've formatted and created a number of great layouts for all the text in your project. But this is a *motion* graphics project. It's time to animate the text using a mix of keyframes, basic behaviors, preset text behaviors, and even a text behavior of your own creation.

Applying Text Behaviors

Now that your text is nicely formatted, styled, and positioned, it's time to animate it on and off the screen. In addition to the keyframing methods and behaviors you already know, Motion includes a collection of text behaviors that are designed specifically to animate text.

1   In the Canvas, select *The Gorilla Group Fund*.

2   Press Command-2 to open the Library, and choose Behaviors > Basic Motion.

   Just about any behavior in the Library can be applied to text, and some—like the Fade In/Fade Out behavior—are very useful.

3   In the Layers list, drag the Fade In/Fade Out behavior onto the *Gorilla Group Fund* layer, and then click Play to see the results. Stop playback when you are done.

   The entire text block fades in smoothly and then fades out at the end. But instead of animating the entire text layer as a single object, you could attract more attention to the text by using a group of behaviors designed specifically to animate individual characters.

4   In the Layers list, close the *Sidebar* group and open the *Background* group. Make sure that the Select/Transform tool is still chosen.

5   Select the *A Species in Danger* layer. Press Shift-I to move the playhead to the layer's In point, press Command-Option-I to set a play range In point, and finally, press the Spacebar to start playback.

6   In the Library, choose the Behaviors category. You'll find two folders of text behaviors: Text Animation and Text Sequence.

7   Select the Text Sequence folder, and then click the disclosure triangle next to the Text-Basic folder (or, if you are in icon view, double-click the folder).

Each folder in the Text Sequence folder contains text sequence behaviors of various styles. A text sequence behavior creates animation that ripples or *sequences* through the characters in the layer, animating each one in the same manner but at different points in time, creating a falling domino effect.

8   Locate the Blur In behavior, and drag it to the *A Species in Danger* text layer in the Project pane's Layers list or the Timeline layer list. Click Play.

The behavior appears under the layer in the Layers list and the mini-Timeline. To see the animation, you'll need to temporarily hide the paint stroke.

9   In the Layers list, select the activation checkbox next to *Paint Stroke* to hide it in the Canvas.

The text in the Canvas animates onto the screen one letter at a time, with each letter starting very blurry and then coming into focus.

Notice that the behavior duration is shorter than the text layer duration. All other behaviors, filters, and masks last as long as the layer to which they are applied; but because the text behaviors are designed to animate text on and off the screen, they have a shorter default duration.

10 From the Library, drag the Blur Out behavior onto the same text layer, and in the mini-Timeline, drag the entire behavior to the right so that its Out point aligns with the end of the project. The text now animates on and off the screen.

If the text lasts too long, you can trim it and reposition the behavior.

11 Press the Spacebar to stop playback, and then position the playhead at 8:19. Drag the end of the Blur Out behavior to align it with the playhead. Then select the *A Species in Danger* layer, and press O to mark the current playhead position as its new Out point.

> **TIP** Shift-dragging layers in the Timeline snaps the layers to the playhead and/or markers and makes it easier to position tracks precisely.

12 In the transport controls, click "Play from Start" to view the play range. Now the text blurs on screen and blurs off with the correct duration.

13 In the Layers list, select the activation checkbox next to *Paint Stroke* to show the paint stroke.

14 Press Option-X to reset the play range to the start and end of the project, and then press the Spacebar to stop playback.

Motion includes well over 125 text behaviors. Some are designed to animate text onto the screen, some animate text off the screen, and others just ripple through text like a glint of light. When you have time to experiment, try combining various styles of text behaviors to produce very sophisticated title animations.

Animating Text Using the Sequence Text Behavior

All the behaviors in the Text Sequence folders are presets that were created using the Sequence Text behavior. When you understand how it works, you will be able customize any of the presets based on this behavior, and you will be able to create new animations from scratch.

1   In the Library, select the Text Animation folder. Tucked innocently among three other very useful behaviors is the Sequence Text behavior.

2   Drag the Sequence Text behavior to the *Mountain Gorillas* layer and play the project. Because the behavior has no default values it does nothing by default, and it lasts for the duration of the layer, which is much too long for this project.

3   In the mini-Timeline, drag the behavior's Out point to the left. Using the information box as a guide, trim it to a duration of 1:00. Next, set the play range to focus just on the area you are adjusting.

4   Stop playback and set the play range by positioning the playhead at 2:59, and pressing Command-Option-O. Press the Spacebar to start playback.

You'd like the letters to fall into place randomly. So they need to rotate forward at the start. As a reminder, as when you're using the Transform Glyph tool, you can drag the red, green, and blue arrows to change the position of the glyph along the x-axis (horizontal), the y-axis (vertical), or the z-axis (toward or away from the viewer). Drag the hollow white circles to rotate the glyph around each of those axes.

5   In the Canvas, locate the hollow white circle at the top of the letter *M* and drag it down until it is facing down 90 degrees.

This action sets the initial positions for *all* the characters. During the animation all the characters will start face down and animate back to their original positions by default.

6   Drag the y-axis drag handle (green arrow) to the right until the *M* starts to move offscreen.

NOTE ▶ The onscreen position arrows turn yellow when they are selected.

You don't have enough room around the Canvas to position the *M* and place all the letters offscreen. To make this a little easier, you can zoom out of the Canvas to provide more maneuvering space.

7   From the Zoom Level pop-up menu at the top of the Canvas, choose 25%.

8   Drag the y-axis drag handle (green arrow) and the z-axis drag handle (blue arrow) until all the letters start animating completely offscreen and fall into position. Then press Shift-Z to fill the Canvas with the project.

You can decide how many characters animate at any given time by adjusting the Spread parameter.

9   In the HUD, increase Spread to about 15. Up to 15 characters are now either finishing or starting to animate at once, which creates a smoother, overlapping animation. The total duration of the animation, however, remains unchanged.

10 In the HUD, from the Direction pop-up menu, choose Random. The letters now appear to animate into position in a random order.

While you can interactively change the starting position, rotation, and scale of a character, you can change additional parameters in the Inspector.

11 Press F2 to open the Behaviors pane of the Inspector. From the Parameter pop-up menu, choose Format.

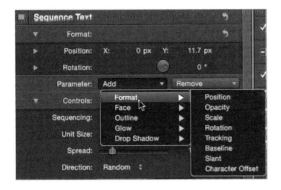

You can animate all the parameters in this pop-up menu, which includes most of the parameters from both the Format and Style panes of the Text Inspector. You can start to see why this behavior is so powerful.

Each parameter you choose is added to the Sequence Text behavior and appears in the Behaviors pane, where you can change its starting value.

12 Choose Format > Opacity, and then drag the Opacity slider to 0.

13 From the Speed pop-up menu, choose Ease Out to enable a smoother landing at the end of the behavior.

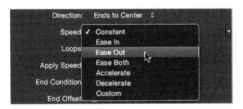

That animation is not bad, but you can still mix it up a bit for more visual variety. Each character animates on at a different time, but the animation is exactly the same for each. Adjust the Variance parameters to vary the animation for each character.

14 In the Behaviors pane, increase the Variance value to about 10%, and then experiment with changing the other parameters. The basic animation is the same, but Variance introduces a small amount of randomness to the attributes animated in the Text Sequence behavior.

15 Stop playback, save your work, and press Option-X to reset the play range.

Creating an animation like this with keyframes would take a very long time to set up, and the results would be impossible to modify! The Variance parameter makes it easy to vary the animation by dragging a single slider.

When you create a new text behavior or modify an existing one, you can save it as a Favorite so that you can reapply it at any time to any project.

16 At the bottom of the Library categories, select the Favorites category.

17 In the Layers list, triple-click the *Sequence* text layer to select its name, and type *Random Fly In* to rename it. Then press Return.

18 Drag the newly named Random Fly In behavior from the Layers list into the Stacks area in the lower half of the Library. This custom preset is now available for use with any Motion project on this computer.

Animating Text on a Path

To complete this project, you will animate the text you placed on the path around the Earth.

1   In the Timeline, press Command-Option-Right Arrow or Command-Option-Left Arrow to go to the last marker.

This marker is placed where the text comes onscreen. You'll choose a better rotation point for the text to appear and then use keyframes to rotate the text around the Earth.

2   Close the HUD, and in the Layers list, close the *Text* group.

3   Open the *Sidebar* group, and then select the *Help save the mountain gorilla* text layer.

4   In the transport controls, click the Record Keyframe button.

5   Press F4 to open the Text pane in the Inspector.

6   In the Path Options area, drag the Path Offset slider to 65.

The text now comes onscreen near the lower part of the Earth. Let's set a keyframe at the end of the project.

7   Press End, or drag the playhead to the end of the project.

8   Drag the Path Offset slider to –40.

9   In the transport controls, click the Record Keyframe button again to disable it.

10 Press Command-Option-Left Arrow to move the playhead to the last marker, and click Play to start the animation.

You are getting there. It would look smoother if the text typed onscreen instead of popping on. To achieve this, you can combine the keyframes you just created with a behavior to type the text onscreen.

11 Press Command-2 to open the Library, and choose Behaviors >Text Sequence Behaviors > Text Basic.

12 Drag the Rotate In text behavior to the *Help save the mountain gorilla* layer in the Layers list.

13 Press the Spacebar to play the entire project to see all your animations, if necessary, including the new type-on effect you just applied.

14 Press Stop, and then save your work.

This same animation could have been created solely with keyframes or behaviors. The choice is yours, but in most cases using behaviors will provide more flexibility when you need to modify the animation.

Adding Motion Blur

Sometimes, an animation can be made to look more natural by adding blur based on a layer's direction and speed. This type of blur is called motion blur. As a final step, let's try enabling and adjusting motion blur for this project. In Motion, motion blur is a universal property that you turn on or off for the entire project.

1 Position the playhead at 0:49.

2 From the Render Options pop-up menu at the top right of the Canvas, choose Motion Blur, or press Option-M.

> **TIP** ▶ You can also turn on motion blur by choosing View > Render Options > Motion Blur.

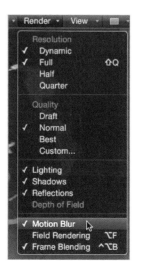

You can see how motion blur affects the *Mountain Gorilla* text and the Earth as it rotates, making it appear much more natural. Motion blur creates subframes between the current frame and adding them to the current frame with varying levels of opacity. Because each frame uses information from multiple subframes, the playback speed and render times are affected. You can adjust the number of samples and the shutter angle in the Project Properties window.

3   Choose Edit > Project Properties, or select the Project icon in the Layers list.

NOTE ► Motion blur does not affect motion within a QuickTime movie or image sequence.

The Properties pane now shows the Project Properties.

In the Motion Blur section, the default number of samples is eight, and the shutter angle is 360 degrees. Samples refer to the number of subframes rendered for every 360 degrees of shutter angle. The shutter angle acts like the shutter of a film camera. Increasing the angle increases the number of frames over which the shutter is open, thereby spreading out the samples.

4   Increase Samples to 16, decrease Shutter Angle to 180 degrees, and click OK. You now have more copies of each character, and they are spaced more closely together.

As with the Render Quality setting, it's a good idea to leave Motion Blur turned off while you are working and then turn it on before exporting, or turn it on as an Export option.

5   Press Option-M to turn off motion blur, and save your work.

Nice job. You've created, formatted, and styled text layers; changed the format and style of individual glyphs; saved and applied text styles; animated text layers with preset and customized behaviors; animated text on a path; and used motion blur. To expand your knowledge, feel free to dig deeper into the text animation presets and the text options available in Motion.

Lesson Review

1.   Name two of the three panes in the Text pane of the Inspector.

2.   How do you display the action-safe and title-safe overlays?

3.   When modifying an individual character in a text layer, which tool do you use to change its scale, position, and rotation; and how do you select that tool?

4.   How do you create a marker?

5.   From which two locations can you apply a preset text style?

6.   Which behavior was used to create all the text sequence presets in the Library?

7.   Which text layer parameters can you animate directly in the Canvas using a Sequence Text behavior?

8.   What parameter would you adjust to set the number of characters animating at once in a Sequence Text behavior?

9.   With the Transform Glyph tool, you can change the offset, scale, and rotation of a character directly in the Canvas. Where are those parameters located in the Inspector?

10.   After changing the Layout Method to Path, what must you do to see the path in the Canvas?

11.   Describe one method for turning on motion blur, and identify where you can adjust its settings.

Answers

1. Format, Style, and Layout

2. From the "View and Overlay" pop-up menu at the top right of the Canvas, choose Safe Zones, or press the ' (apostrophe) key.

3. You use the Transform Glyph tool, which you can select from the 2D Transform tools in the toolbar (the first of three View tools), or by Control-clicking a text layer in the Canvas and choosing Transform Glyph.

4. Select a layer and press M.

5. From the Style Preset pop-up menu in the Style pane of the Text Inspector, or from the Text Styles category in the Library

6. The Sequence Text behavior

7. Position, rotation, and scale

8. The Spread parameter

9. In the Format pane of the Text Inspector (as opposed to the Properties pane, which contains Position, Scale, and Rotation parameters for the entire text layer)

10. Double-click the text in the Canvas.

11. Turn on motion blur from the Render Options pop-up menu, by choosing View > Render Options > Motion Blur, or by pressing Option-M. To change its settings, open the Project Properties window by choosing Edit > Project Properties, or pressing Command-J.

Keyboard Shortcuts

T	Select the Text tool
Tab	Rotate through each available tool for the selected object
Esc (Escape)	Exit text-entry mode
Option-M	Toggle motion blur off and on
' (apostrophe)	Toggle safe zones display

7

Lesson Files
: Motion5_Book_Files > Lessons > Lesson_07

Media
: Motion5_Book_Files > Media > Rockumentary, Teaser

Time
: This lesson takes approximately 60 minutes to complete.

Goals
: Create and modify a particle emitter
Use an image sequence as a cell source
Browse, apply, and customize preset emitters and replicators
Create and modify a replicator

Working with Particle Emitters and Replicators

If you've ever wanted to add chimney smoke and falling leaves to an autumn scene, put blinking lights on a screen, or create an animated background pattern, you are going to love particle emitters and replicators.

Particle emitters shoot out a continuous stream of objects and can be used to create almost anything: natural phenomena like fog, smoke, fire, and rain; a flock of birds; pulsing light fields; or a cascade of video clips.

Replicators create a fixed pattern of objects you can animate to create an incredible variety of backgrounds, transitions, and moving elements such as video walls, splattering paint, or growing leaves.

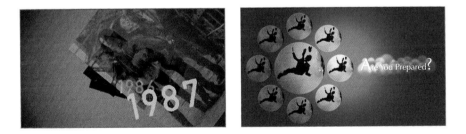

You can use just about any object as a source for both emitters and replicators, including your own graphics, image sequences, movies, or elements from the vast Motion Library. And both emitters and replicators have unique behaviors for creating compelling animations.

Motion contains a huge number of preset emitters and replicators to get you started; you can use them as is, modify them, or make your own from scratch.

In this lesson, you'll use a particle emitter to recreate the shower of cascading photos that starts your Rockumentary title project. Then you'll use a replicator to animate a pattern of video clips to form an animated background for a title animation.

Using Emitters to Make Particle Systems

You create particle systems in Motion with an object called an *emitter*. The emitter uses a source object to create a "spray" of copies, called *particles*, that appear, move, and disappear. The particles can be created from just about any object in Motion: a photo or graphic, a video clip, a text layer, or a shape—it's all fair game. In this exercise, you'll create particles using an image sequence, which is a sequentially numbered series of still images that Motion interprets as a movie. Then, you will animate the particles to look as if they are falling back in space. Let's start by inspecting the image sequence.

1   Open Motion5_Book_Files > Lessons > Lesson_07 > Particles Start. Save it to the Student_Saves folder, and examine the Layers list.

This project contains two groups: The *Background* group that contains the background elements you created in an earlier lesson, and the *Opening animation* group that contains an image sequence.

2 Select the *PD_[###]* layer, and Command-Spacebar-drag left in the Canvas to zoom out far enough to see the layer's bounding box. Press Shift-V to see the full view area, and then play the beginning of the project.

> **NOTE ▶** If Spotlight is invoked when pressing Command-Spacebar, turn off its default keyboard shortcut in System Preferences.

The photos play for one frame each. The first time you play the project, the photos preload into RAM, so playback may be slow. After the photos have been cached, play-back speed increases to real time. The large bounding box in the Canvas indicates that the photos' dimensions are much higher than the project dimensions. While looking at the full view area, you can see that some photos are tall and some are wide—something you couldn't determine by viewing only the bounding box, which represents the size of the largest photo in the sequence.

> **NOTE ▶** Although imported images are automatically scaled to fit the Canvas size, movies and image sequences are not. Before importing into Motion, it's a good idea to scale your media to the maximum pixel dimensions necessary for your project to improve playback performance and render times. In this exercise, the image sequence has already been scaled up to fill the Canvas.

Before making a particle system from this image sequence, let's determine how many images it contains.

3   Stop playback, and press Shift-O to move the playhead to the layer's Out point. If necessary, click the timing display pop-up menu to switch from timecode to frames.

Because the layer ends at frame 48, and an image sequence plays one image per frame, the layer must include 48 images. This information will be useful when you work with the particle emitter. Now let's make a particle system.

4   Resume playback, and in the toolbar, click the "Create a particle emitter" button, or press E.

A lot happens when you click that button. In the Layers list, the *PD_[###]* layer is deactivated, so it no longer appears in the Canvas. Two new objects appear in the Layers list: The *Emitter* layer is, surprisingly enough, the emitter—the object that emits particles. Tucked underneath the emitter is the particle cell, which represents and controls the emitted particles. It assumes the name of the source for the particle system, our image sequence layer.

The Canvas fills with dozens of overlapping images with new ones constantly appearing. Also, the HUD now displays several emitter parameters.

As you can see, creating a particle system is easy, but modifying it to look the way you'd like takes a bit more effort. You can start your modifications in the HUD.

5   In the HUD, reduce Birth Rate to 5 and Scale to 20.

> **TIP** ▶ To make small changes in the HUD, Option-click to the left or right of the dot on a slider.

6   Press Shift-V to turn off the full view area, and press Shift-Z to fit the Canvas to the window.

With only five new particles born every second—and each particle reduced to 20 percent of its original size—it's now easier for you to see what's going on in the animation. However, each particle changes over time, from one photo to the next. Before you go cross-eyed, let's change that, too.

7   Press F4 to open the fourth pane of the Inspector, which is now the Emitter pane.

You could adjust a lot of parameters here, but don't be overwhelmed. They are logically organized, and you can tackle them a few at a time.

8   Near the bottom of the pane, deselect the Play Frames checkbox, and leave the Random Start Frame checkbox selected.

Now each particle is born with a randomly assigned image from the image sequence, and displays only that image for its short lifespan of five seconds. Then it "dies," never to be seen again.

The particles are born in the center of the Canvas and move out in all directions. Often, you will want to change the direction, the range, and the speed of the particles. The emission control—the visual interface at the bottom of the HUD—lets you alter all three of those parameters.

9   In the HUD, drag the dot that rests at the left edge of the circle clockwise or counter-clockwise to create an emission range of less than 360 degrees. Drag inside the result-ing "pie slice" to change the emission angle, and drag in and out on the arrow(s) to adjust the particle speed.

The particles now appear to spray out of the center of the Canvas and in a specific direction, as if you were holding your thumb on the end of a hose to control the width of the spray, its direction, and its speed.

The controls in the HUD let you make basic changes to the particles' behavior, but precisely adjusting the emitter to look the way you want requires working in the Inspector. First, let's see how the emitter and the particle cell are related to each other.

NOTE ▶ Although you have full control of the emission range and angle in the HUD, speed adjustments are limited. You can make the particles go faster by using the Inspector.

10 In the Layers list, select the *PD_[###]* layer that is tucked under the *Emitter* layer (the layer with the round orange icon), and look at the fourth pane of the Inspector.

The layer you selected is the *cell* of the emitter, which is why the context-sensitive Object pane is now named Particle Cell. Once again, think of the cell as representing the objects created by the emitter, and the emitter as the device that spits out those objects. Or, in terms of the hose-and-water analogy, the hose is the emitter, and the cell represents the water droplets.

11 Now in the Layers list, select the *Emitter* layer, and examine the Inspector.

Below the parameters that control the emitter, you will see Cell Controls, which include the *same parameters* as those found in the Particle Cell pane. As a convenience, Motion places the parameters for both the cell and the emitter in the Emitter pane. Therefore, you can adjust both sets of parameters when the *Emitter* layer is selected.

12 Save your work.

Adjusting Emitter and Cell Controls in the Inspector

Now you'll alter the Emitter pane parameters to make the particles—the photographs—look as if they are falling back in space, and spinning as they become smaller. Right now, all the particles emanate from a single point in the center of the Canvas. It would look better if they started from different positions—even outside the visible Canvas area—and fell into view.

1 Continue to play the project.

2 You have many choices for the emitter's shape. In the Emitter pane, from the Shape pop-up menu, choose Rectangle.

When you choose a shape, parameters for that shape appear. By default, the rectangle is 300 x 300 pixels in size with five columns and rows, and all particles are born in this five-by-five grid. This pattern is easier to see if you stop the particles' movement.

3   Locate the Speed parameter near the middle of the Emitter pane and set its value to 0.

The bounding box in the Canvas is a square, and the center of each photo aligns to the five-by-five grid. However, you want a larger grid that matches the aspect ratio of the project, and has a more random layout.

4   In the Emitter pane, click the disclosure triangle to open the Size parameter. Set Width to 1280 and Height to 720, and then set Arrangement to Random Fill. Customizing a particle emitter is an iterative process, so you may later want to further adjust these settings. With the current settings, the photos are born in random positions all over the Canvas.

To make the photos look as if they are moving away, you can apply a behavior designed specifically for particles. The tricky thing to remember about this behavior is that you apply it to the cell, not the emitter.

5   Near the bottom of the Emitter pane, locate the Scale parameter and set it back to 100%. This way, the photos will start large and the behavior will make them grow smaller.

6   In the Layers list, select the *PD_[###]* cell below the *Emitter* layer. In the toolbar, click the Add Behavior button, and choose Particles > Scale Over Life.

By default, the particles now scale from 0% to 100% in size. The effect actually looks quite interesting, but it isn't what you want here.

7   In the HUD or the Behaviors Inspector, change Scale At Birth to 100 and Scale At Death to 0.

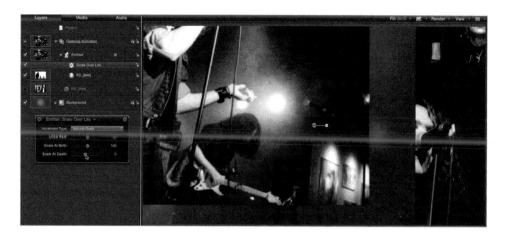

The photos now start at full size and scale down, but the new photos cover the old ones so quickly that you never see any of them become small. A few more adjustments will take care of that.

8   In the Layers list, select the *Emitter* layer, and in the Inspector's Emitter pane, change the Birth Rate to 1. You can now see the photos changing scale, which creates the illusion that they are moving back in space. Remember, Speed is still set to 0, so the movement is due only to the particles' change in scale.

This is still not quite the effect you want because each particle scales down around its anchor point and appears to move toward the edge of the screen. If the particles were truly falling back in space, they would appear to move toward the center of the screen.

Instead of changing the Scale Over Life parameter, you can make the particles actually move along the z-axis by turning the emitter into a 3D emitter.

9   In the Layers list, deselect the Scale Over Life checkbox.

While this behavior creates interesting animation, it won't let us achieve the look we are going for in this project.

10   In the Emitter pane's Emitter Controls, select the 3D checkbox. New emission parameters appear below the checkbox; but because the Speed parameter is set to 0, the particles aren't moving.

11   Set Emission Latitude to 0, Emission Longitude to 180, and Emission Range to 0. Then in the Cell Controls, set Speed to 1,000.

The photos now appear to fall quickly back in 3D space. It would be less jarring if they faded into view rather than popping onto the screen.

12 Near the bottom of the Emitter pane, click the Opacity Over Life disclosure triangle to reveal the gradient editor. Click the white bar to add three opacity tags near the ends of the bar, and set the Opacity value for the outer two tags to 0. The photos now fade into view when they are born and fade out when they die.

TIP ▶ You can also Control-click (or right-click) an opacity tag and change its value by sampling from the pop-up palette.

A key aspect of particle systems is the ability to introduce variations to create a more natural, organic look. If you inspect the parameters in the Cell Controls section of the Emitter pane, you will see several randomness parameters. For example, below Birth Rate is Birth Rate Randomness, below Life is Life Randomness, and so on. Randomness parameters are the keys to more natural-looking particle systems.

13 Change Speed Randomness to 500, Angle Randomness to 90, Spin Randomness to 60, and Scale Randomness to 50. These values are added to and subtracted from each parameter to create a range of values. For example, with Speed set to 1,000 and Speed Randomness set to 500, the speed of each particle will vary between 500 and 1,500 pixels per second.

Each photo now has a different speed, angle, spin rate, and scale, which makes your composition more interesting. If you don't like the type of randomness or you see too many repeating images, you can fine-tune the randomness by adjusting the Random Seed parameter. Because you have a total of 48 images to choose from and only about five appear onscreen at any one time, you should be able to avoid duplicates.

14 At the bottom of the Emitter pane, click the Random Seed's Generate button repeatedly to change the particle pattern until you find one you like.

TIP ▶ The number next to the Generate button lets you recreate the same random-ness in different copies of the project. If you or someone else creates the same project with the same settings and enters the same random number, both projects will have identical particle patterns.

Some of the photos are in black and white and some are in color. You can make them all black and white using a filter, and then tint them using the emitter's Color Mode parameter.

15 In the Layers list, select the original deactivated source layer, *PD_[###]*. In the toolbar, click the Add Filter button, and choose Color Correction > Hue/Saturation. In the HUD, drag the Saturation slider all the way to the left.

All the photos are now black and white. Effects applied to the source layer in the particle system are passed through to the particles—a powerful feature.

16 Reselect the *Emitter* layer, and in the Emitter pane from the Color Mode pop-up menu, choose Colorize to tint particles with the color specified in the Color param-eter. When this setting is selected, additional Color parameters appear. Click the downward-facing arrow next to the color swatch to sample a light reddish-orange color that matches the background. The particles are shaded with the selected color.

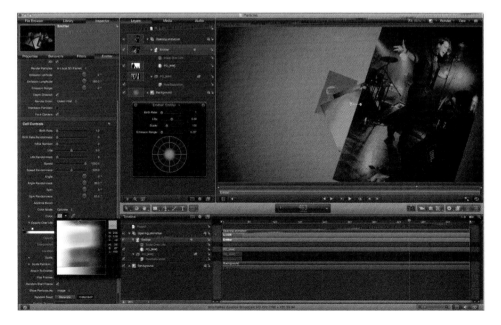

17 Feel free to experiment further, for instance by dramatically increasing the emitter shape's Width and Height settings and adjusting the other parameters. Then save your work.

Adding Cells

A particle emitter can have multiple cells, and each cell can be adjusted independently, allowing you to create complex particle systems. You can add a cell to this particle emitter so that it also creates particles for the years the band was together. The first step is to add the new particle source to the project.

1 In the File Browser, navigate to Motion5_Book_Files > Media > Rockumentary. Click the List View button. With the project still playing, select and drag the **[####].png:1984-1992** file into the *Opening animation* group.

NOTE ▶ Make sure the Show Image Sequences as Collapsed button at the bottom of the File Browser is selected in order to see these images as one file.

NOTE ▶ If you see only a white rectangle in the Canvas, it means that Motion is incorrectly interpreting the file's alpha (transparency) channel. In the Project pane, select the Media list and locate and select the **[####].png:1984-1992** file. In the Media Inspector, from the Alpha Type pop-up menu, choose Straight. Then reselect the Layers list.

This file is another image sequence in which the original filenames of each image are the years 1984 to 1992, so they've been interpreted by Motion as four-digit sequential file numbering and are therefore collapsed to #### in the image sequence filename. One way to create a new cell in the current emitter from this layer is to drag it to the emitter.

2   In the Layers list, rename the *[####]* layer to *Years*, deselect its activation checkbox, drag it to the *Emitter* layer, and when the + (plus sign) appears, release the mouse button.

A new cell named *Years* appears below the emitter, and the Canvas fills with animated dates. When you add a new cell in this manner, the cell uses the default settings. Rather than customize this new cell from scratch, let's start over by duplicating the current customized cell, and then replacing its source.

3   Press Command-Z to remove the cell you just created. Select the *PD_[###]* cell and press Command-D to duplicate it.

4   Drag the *Years* layer on top of the new *PD_[###] copy* cell layer. Wait for the hooked arrow before you release the mouse button. The hooked arrow indicates that you are exchanging the media. The year images now animate in exactly the same pattern as the photos, so a year image appears on top of every photo. It's not quite what you want, but it's close.

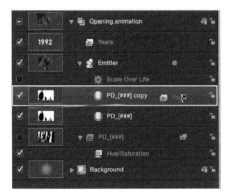 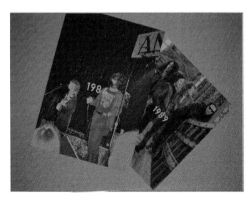

5   With the *PD_[###]* copy layer selected, at the bottom of the Particle Cell pane, click the Generate button. The year images now mix nicely with the photos. But they could use a little more tweaking.

6   In the Particle Cell pane, adjust the Cell Controls to increase the scale, modify the color, and change other particle cell settings to your liking.

NOTE ▶ If you select the Emitter pane, you will find that the Cell Controls are no longer available because you have more than one cell in the emitter. You need to select each cell individually to adjust its parameters in the Particle Cell pane.

7   Stop playback and save your work.

Using Emitters from the Library

The Motion Library includes a large, varied collection of particle emitter presets. Now that you know more about how particle emitters work, it will be easier for you to modify the presets to suit your own projects. Let's look through the presets, apply one, and modify it.

1   Close the current project, and then choose File > New, and click the Motion Project icon. Choose the Broadcast HD 720 preset with a frame rate of 29.97 and a duration of 300 frames, or 10 seconds, and click Open. You will experiment with particle emitters in this new project.

2   Press Shift-Z to fit the Canvas to the window. Press Command-2 to open the Library, and select Particle Emitters. Switch to icon view. Motion includes over 200 particle presets organized into eight categories.

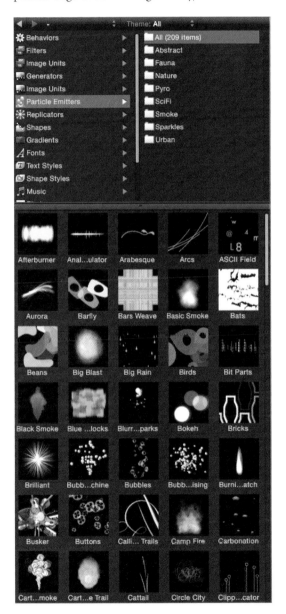

3   Select the Sparkles category. You'll see 16 types of sparkle emitters.

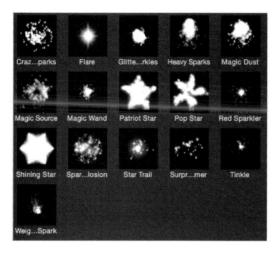

4   Select the Magic Wand preset, and drag your pointer around the preview area.

The emitter follows your pointer movements, providing a preview of how the emitter would look when animated. Let's animate it.

5   Click Apply to bring the emitter into the Canvas, and start playback.

6   In the toolbar, click the Add Behavior button, and choose Basic Motion > Motion Path.

7   In the Canvas, a red line appears with control points at each end. Drag the control points to reposition them. Option-click the red motion path line to add more control points. Drag the points and adjust the Bezier handles to create a curving, overlapping path.

> NOTE ► You may need to zoom or pan on the Canvas to view and select the control point on the right.

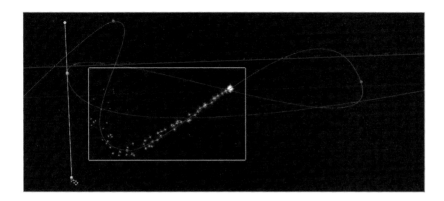

8   In the Layers list, you can see that this preset emitter contains two cells: one for the central flare and one for the stream of sparks. Because the emitter is moving so quickly, you won't see many sparks.

9   Select the *Spark06* cell layer, and press F4 to open the Particle Cell Inspector. Increase Birth Rate to around 250 to create many more particles, and then increase Life to around 5 seconds to create a longer trail.

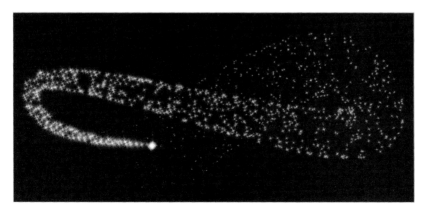

When you combine behaviors with particles, the creative possibilities are almost infinite.

10 Select and delete the *Group* that contains the emitter to start over. Browse, apply, and adjust some of the other particle presets. If you make something you like, drag it to the Favorites folder in the Library to make your customized preset available for future projects.

11 In the Library, select the Content folder, and then select the Particle Images folder. This folder contains hundreds of images and movies you can use to make particles. In fact, all the Emitter presets in Motion use particle sources from the Content folder.

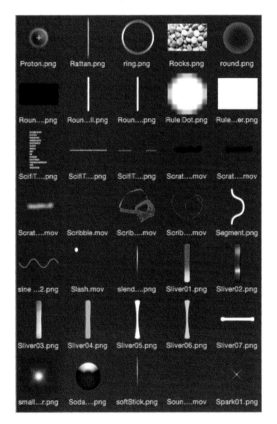

12 Select a particle image. Add it to your project, and make a particle system out of it by clicking the Make Particles button in the toolbar, or pressing E. Experiment with changing the parameters.

You should now understand the basics of particle systems. You can use this knowledge to modify a preset emitter to fit your project or to create your own particle emitter from scratch.

Replicating Elements

The replicator creates patterns from copies of a source object, and a replicator's structure is very similar to that of a particle emitter. Unlike a particle emitter, however, a replicator creates a fixed number of copies in a static pattern. You can animate a replicator using keyframes, behaviors, or a dedicated behavior called the Sequence Replicator behavior.

In this exercise, you'll start with a partially completed text animation and add a background design based on replicators.

1   Close any open projects. Open Motion5_Book_Files > Lessons > Lesson_07 > Replicators Start, and save it to the Student_Saves folder. Press Shift-Z to fit the Canvas to the window, open all the groups and layers in the Layers list, and play the project.

From the bottom of the Layers list, you can see that the project contains the following:

▶   A blue rectangle shape object for the background

▶   A video clip with three color correction filters to give it a highly stylized look

▶   An animated circle mask to reveal the video

▶   An empty *Replicators* group

▶   A text layer animated with a sequence text behavior

▶   Another rectangle placed on top for the vignette effect

You'll add a replicator to create additional copies of the video.

2   Stop playback, and close all the groups. Change the timing display to Timecode, if necessary, and move the playhead to 1:00. This is the frame where the circle mask on the video stops scaling down. It's a good place to bring on the replicated images. Instead of replicating the video clip directly, you'll replicate the group containing the clip and all the effects.

3   Select the *Video* group, and at the far right of the toolbar, click the Replicate button, or press L.

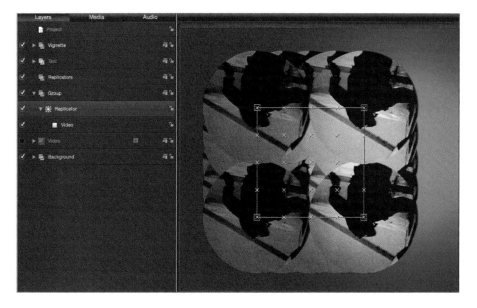

As with a particle emitter, several things happen at once when you create a replicator. In the Layers list, the *Video* group (the source for the replicator) is now deactivated. A new *Replicator* layer appears above the *Video* group in its own new group; and below the replicator, the replicator cell appears with the same name as the source object, *Video*.

In the toolbar, the Adjust Item tool is now selected, and a replicator bounding box appears in the Canvas. By default, the replicator creates 25 copies of the source object in the Canvas, in a five-by-five grid as indicated by each white X.

NOTE ▶ The Adjust Item tool changes its name depending on the type of object selected. Although the tooltip that appears when hovering over the tool in the toolbar reads *Adjust Item Tool*, if you Control-click in the Canvas, you'll see in the shortcut menu that the currently selected tool is called the Replicator.

4   In the HUD, decrease Columns to 3 and Rows to 2, and drag a corner of the replicator bounding box to see how you can adjust the layout of the copies.

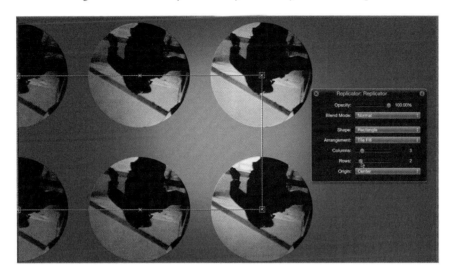

Let's build on the circle theme of this project by changing the replicator shape.

5   In the HUD, from the Shape pop-up menu, choose Circle. From the Arrangement pop-up menu, choose Outline, and set Points to 8.

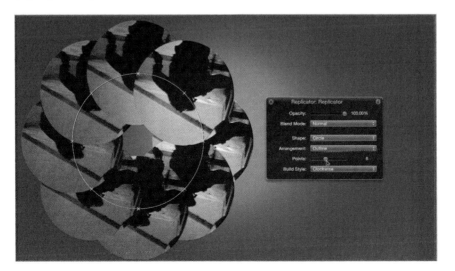

That's about all you can adjust in the HUD, so let's get busy in the Inspector.

6   Press F4 to reveal the Replicator Inspector. Many of these parameters are similar to those you used with particle emitters.

7   In the Replicator Controls, set Radius to 250. In the Cell Controls, set Scale to 52%, and then in the Layers list, select the *Video* group's activation checkbox to turn the group back on.

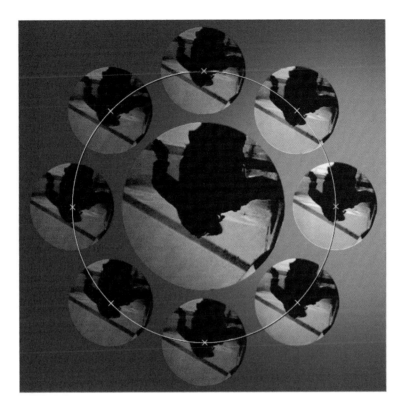

In this case, you want to see the original source object in the center of the replicated pattern. With the pattern in place, you can use a behavior designed just for replicators to animate the pattern onto the screen.

8   With the *Replicator* layer selected, in the toolbar, click the Add Behavior button, and choose Replicator > Sequence Replicator.

If you recall using the Sequence Text behavior in Lesson 6, you'll find that this behavior is very similar. It creates animation that *sequences* through each of the copies in the pattern. By default, it is applied to the full duration of the replicator. As a result, you need to trim it so that the animation ends before the text animation begins.

9   Choose Mark > Go To > Next Marker to move the playhead to the marker at 2:02. Press O to trim the behavior's Out point to the playhead. Press Command-Option-O to set a play range Out point at the same frame, and start playback.

The replicated pattern will animate onscreen from 1:00 to 2:02, ending at the point where the video freezes, right before the text animation starts. Just as with the Sequence Text behavior, you must choose the parameter (or parameters) you want to animate with the Sequence Replicator behavior.

10 In the Behaviors Inspector (which came forward automatically when you added the behavior), from the Parameter's Add pop-up menu, choose Scale.

11 In the Scale parameter that appears, change the value to 0, set Sequencing to From, and increase Spread to 3.

The copies now change their scales *from* 0% to their set Scale value, and the animation is spread so that at any point in time three copies are animating.

12 From the Add pop-up menu, choose Rotation, and set the Rotation value to –180.

The copies now scale up and spin into place in sequence. You can take the animation a little further by keyframing a couple of the replicator's parameters.

13 Stop playback, and press Shift-O to move the playhead to the behavior's Out point. In the Replicator pane, click the keyframe buttons for Radius and Offset to set keyframes.

14 Press Shift-I to move the playhead to the behavior's In point, and once again set keyframes for the Radius and Offset parameters. Then, change Radius to 0 and Offset to −30%, and resume playback.

The copies scale up from the center of the circle. It would look better if they were behind the original video.

15 In the Layers list, drag the *Replicator* layer into the *Replicators* group, and delete the empty *Group* group.

16 Select the Replicators group, and choose Object > Send Backward, or press Command-[(left bracket), to move the Replicators group below the Video group. The replicated pattern now emerges from behind the original video.

17 Save your work.

Modifying Replicator Presets

In addition to its particle emitters, Motion includes a large collection of preset replicators you can use "out of the box," or modify to your heart's content. You will modify a preset replicator to create a background to frame the text layer in this project.

1   Stop playback. Move the playhead to the marker at 2:02, and press Command-Option-I to set a play range In point. Move the playhead to the end of the project, press Command-Option-O to set a play range Out point, and resume playback.

In this section of the project, a short written question animates onscreen. A subtle animated background could give the question more focus and weight.

2   Press Command-2 to open the Library, and select Replicators. You will find over 200 presets organized into categories.

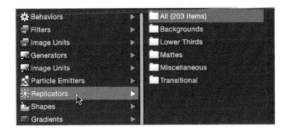

3   Select the Lower Thirds folder, and preview several of the presets.

Because most of these presets were created with a Replicator and animated using the Sequence Replicator behavior, it is easy to modify them.

4   With the project still playing, locate the Lower Lounge preset and drag it into the *Replicators* group.

5   If necessary, select the *Lower Lounge* replicator layer, and in the Canvas, drag the layer to position it under the text.

The rounded squares don't work well with the circle theme you've established. This replicator uses the deactivated *Shape* layer in the *Replicators* group as its source. You can change the source shape to change the cells.

6   Activate and select the *Shape* layer.

7   In the HUD, drag the slider to increase the Roundness parameter as far as it will go. The shape turns into a circle, as do the cells.

The replicator exists for the full project, but it should come onscreen just before the text animates on.

8   Stop playback and deactivate the *Shape* layer. Choose Mark > Go To > Play Range Start, and select the *Lower Lounge* replicator layer. Press I to trim the layer's In point to the playhead. Now move the playhead to a point where the text is visible.

The pattern is too wide and a little short. You can change it with the Replicator tool.

9   To choose the Replicator tool, Control-click the replicator in the Canvas, and from the shortcut menu, choose Replicator. Resize and reposition the layer to fit behind the text, and then press Shift-S to return to the Select/Transform tool.

10 In the HUD, decrease Opacity to about 60% so that it doesn't overwhelm the text.

11 In the Layers list, select the Sequence Replicator behavior below the Lower Lounge replicator, and move the playhead to 2:16. Press O to trim the behavior to a duration of 15 frames, and resume playback.

This behavior was used to animate the opacity of the copies, but you will repurpose it to animate the scale of the pattern onto the screen.

12 In the Behaviors Inspector, in the Sequence Replicator section, change Scale to 0, Spread to 4, and Loops to 1.

That looks good. However, the color of the replicator still makes the background stand out too much.

13 Stop playback and move the playhead to the point where all the text is visible. In the Layers list, select the *Shape* layer (the deactivated layer, not the cell under the replicator).

14 In the Shape Inspector, change the Fill Mode to Gradient.

15 If necessary, click the disclosure triangle to reveal the gradient editor, remove the center color tag by dragging it away, and then Control-click the remaining color tags to change them to shades of blue.

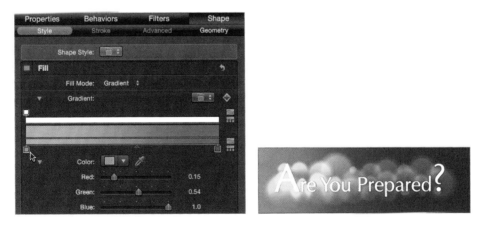

Great job! You have worked with both particle emitters and replicators in this lesson, building each from scratch as well as modifying presets from the Library. You now have the know-how to leverage the incredible arsenal of presets in the Motion Library, or to build your own custom particle emitters and replicators for your next project.

Lesson Review

1. Name the two particle system components that appear in the Layers list when you make a particle emitter.

2. You created particles from a leaf graphic you found in the Library, and made those particles spin by increasing the Spin value in the Emitter pane. But you now want to spin each of them at different rates. Which Emitter pane parameter do you adjust to do this?

3. What kind of particle-specific behavior do you use to change particles' sizes during their lifespan and what does it get applied to?

4. Your particles appear at random locations on the screen, but you want to change those random locations. Which button can you click to create a different random pattern?

5. What is a quick way to introduce variations that give your particle system a more natural, organic look?

6. What's the primary difference between a particle emitter and a replicator?

7. How can you animate a replicator's elements so that they fade onto the screen, one after the other?

8. You want to drag the bounding box to resize a replicator but the onscreen controls aren't appearing. How can you display them?

9. Name three shapes that can be chosen from the Shape parameter pop-up menu for a particle emitter or a replicator.

10. Can you use a QuickTime movie as the source for a particle emitter or a replicator?

Answers

1. The emitter and the cell

2. The Spin Randomness parameter

3. Apply the Scale Over Life behavior to the particle cell.

4. The Generate button for the Random Seed parameter

5. Use the randomness parameters that appear in the Cell Controls section of the Emitter pane. For example, below Birth Rate is Birth Rate Randomness, below Life is Life Randomness, and so on.

6. A particle emitter creates a continuous stream of particles that are born, stay onscreen for some time, and then die. A replicator creates a fixed number of elements in a fixed pattern that you can animate with keyframes or behaviors.

7. Use the Sequence Replicator behavior, add the Opacity parameter, set the parameter to 0, and set Sequencing to From.

8. The replicator bounding box becomes available when you select the Adjust Item tool is in the toolbar, or Control-click the replicator in the Canvas and choose Replicator from the pop-up menu.

9. Line, Rectangle, Circle, Burst, Spiral, Wave, Geometry, and Image. Particle emitters can also have a Point shape.

10. Yes, you can use images, image sequences, movies, or many of the Motion objects (text, generators, shapes) as sources for both emitters and replicators.

Keyboard Shortcuts

E	Create a particle emitter
L	Create a replicator
Shift-End	Move the playhead to the play range Out point (Shift-Fn-Right Arrow on a laptop)
Shift-Home	Move the playhead to the play range In point (Shift-Fn-Left Arrow on a laptop)
Shift-V	Show the full view area

8

Lesson Files   Motion5_Book_Files > Lessons > Lesson_08

Media   Motion5_Book_Files > Media > Rockumentary

Time   This lesson takes approximately 45 minutes to complete.

Goals   Work with audio in the Audio list and Audio Timeline

Automate audio levels using behaviors

Create and edit markers

Assemble a project from saved Motion groups

Edit to the beat of an audio track

Sync animation to audio with the Audio parameter behavior

Lesson **8**

Using Audio

Audio doesn't get the respect it deserves. Good-quality audio, used creatively, can turn a motion graphics spot from decent to spectacular. On the other hand, low-quality audio—or audio that's poorly selected, edited, or mixed—can kill a good animation.

With more and more media being watched on portable devices and heard through tiny speakers, making your audio memorable is more important than ever.

In Motion, you have a host of tools for importing, adjusting, and automating your audio—and for tightly integrating it with your motion graphics.

In this lesson, you will assemble the final Rockumentary title project and use a music track to time edits and create animation. You will explore the Motion audio interface, use markers to identify edit points, and apply behaviors that change audio levels over time. You'll finish by working with the powerful Audio parameter behavior.

Importing Audio

You can import audio into Motion just as you would import a video clip or image.

1   Navigate to Motion5_Book_Files > Lessons > Lesson_08, and open Rockumentary
     Audio Start. Choose File > Save As, and save the project to the Lesson_08 > Student_
     Saves folder.

2   In the Layers list, select the *Background* group, and then Option-click its disclosure
     triangle to open the group and all the elements inside it.

> **TIP** ▶ Holding down the Option key while opening or closing a group in the Layers
> list or the Timeline will open or close not just that group, but all the groups and/or
> layers it contains.

This group contains the Rockumentary project background image with the Colorize
filter and a Fade In/Fade Out behavior applied. Because you selected it, you can see in
the mini-Timeline that it lasts for the full project. If you play the project, you'll see the
now-familiar gradient.

3   Choose Edit > Project Properties, or press Command-J, and if necessary, set the
     Duration pop-up menu to Timecode.

The project preset, Broadcast HD 720, matches the other Rockumentary projects you created. The duration is 37;14, just long enough for the audio you'll add momentarily. The Background Color is set to the default black, but the Background setting was changed to Solid to ensure that any transparency in the final project appears with a black background.

4   In the Layers list, close the *Background* group and make sure that the playhead is at Home. Let's start building the project by importing the audio track.

5   Press Command-1 to open the File Browser. Then navigate to Motion5_Book_Files > Media > Rockumentary, and select **burn.00.aif**. The audio file plays, and in the preview area you can see that its duration is 37.5 seconds. You can also see that this is a stereo audio file.

6   In the preview area, click Import to add this audio file to the project. A green bar appears in the mini-Timeline to represent the file duration, and the HUD indicates that an audio track is selected. However, the Layers list is still empty because in the Project pane, audio tracks appear in an Audio list.

7   Click the Audio list to open it, or press Command-6.

In the Audio list, you can view and modify the file, including adjusting the level, pan, and output channels. If you had more than one audio track, you could also modify all the tracks at once using the Master controls at the bottom of the list.

NOTE ▶ Motion supports 5.1-channel audio with Left, Right, Center, LFE, Left Surround, and Right Surround channels. However, to hear all six channels, you need hardware (and speakers) that support multichannel surround sound.

8   In the transport controls at the bottom of the Canvas, make sure that the Play/Mute audio button is enabled, and play the project to hear the audio. This is the audio from the final Rockumentary QuickTime movie you watched in an earlier lesson.

You can also mute and solo individual tracks in the Audio list. But because you have only one track of audio in this project, you'll focus on level and panning adjustments.

9   In the Audio list, or the HUD, drag the Level slider as the project plays to change the audio volume. Watch the audio meters in the Master control strip at the bottom of the Audio list to make sure the audio doesn't trigger the peaking indicators—the red dots—at the top of the meters.

10   Adjust the Pan using either the control in the Audio list or the slider in the HUD. Listen to hear the audio move between the left and right speakers, and then return the Pan value to 0 and stop playback.

You'll leave the audio panned to the center position for now.

Working in the Audio Timeline

While you can adjust the level and panning of audio tracks in the Audio list, you must use the Audio Timeline and adjust the way the audio changes over time. The Audio Timeline displays a layer for each of a project's audio tracks and allows you to see waveforms, add markers, and apply audio behaviors to each track. In the Audio Timeline, you will fade up the volume with a behavior and set markers that help you edit to the beat of the music.

1   Choose Window > Audio Timeline, or press Command-9.

The Audio Timeline slides open in the Timing pane, underneath the Timeline, so that you can see both. Changing how audio plays back over time is called *automation*. You can use two audio behaviors to automate an audio track.

2 If necessary, select the *burn.00* layer. In the Toolbar, from the Add Behavior pop-up menu, choose Audio > Audio Fade In/Fade Out. In the HUD, set the Fade Out to 0 frames. Play the project.

The audio now fades in over the first 20 frames. You can also automate the track panning.

3 Click the Add Behavior pop-up menu, and choose Audio > Audio Auto Pan. While playing the audio, in the HUD change Loops to 12 and End Condition to Ping Pong. The audio now bounces back and forth between the left and right speakers, creating a spacey effect that matches the feel of the music.

NOTE ► You can also use keyframes to automate level and panning changes in the Keyframe Editor. (Choose Window > Keyframe Editor, or press Command-8.) Double-click the level or pan line to add a keyframe and then drag it to the value you want.

In the Audio Timeline, you can also display an image, called a *waveform,* that you can use to see how the volume of a track changes over time.

4   Move the pointer just below the name of the audio track and when it changes to the resize pointer, drag down to increase the height of the audio bar and reveal the waveform inside it.

5   Move the playhead to the frame where the waveform suddenly gets taller and stays that way for the rest of the project—at about 17:34.

This is the frame where the drums kick in—a great place to bring the final title slam onto the screen. Being able to identify this frame so you could find it more easily when you add graphics to the project would be great.

A marker is visible in the ruler area to the left of the playhead. Markers are a great way to flag and locate individual frames or a range of frames. They're particularly useful when you want to add a layer, record a keyframe, or synchronize an action across multiple layers at a specific point in time. You can create markers on layers, groups, and in the ruler of the Timeline. Markers in the ruler are called project markers; the others are called object markers.

6   With the playhead at 17:34, press Shift-M to add a project marker at the playhead. Then choose Mark > Markers > Edit Marker, or press Command-Option-M, to open the Edit Marker dialog.

NOTE ▶ Pressing M alone adds a marker to a selected layer or group. If nothing is selected, pressing M adds a project marker. Pressing Shift-M will always add a project marker—even when a layer or group is selected.

TIP ▶ You can also double-click a marker to open the Edit Marker dialog, but you'll first need to move the playhead away from the marker to be able to double-click it.

7   In the Edit Marker dialog, in the Name field, type *C_Title*. This is the frame where the main title will start.

8   Feel free to change the color of the marker, and click OK. The marker appears in the Timeline ruler.

9   Move the pointer over either of the markers in the ruler. A pop-up shows the name of the marker.

At this point, you can use object markers to identify other key edit points for the project.

Editing to the Beat

One way to more tightly integrate audio into your project is to time your edits to match audio cues, such as the beats of a music track. Because Motion lets you set markers as the project plays, or "on the fly," you can quickly identify key audio cues for your edit points.

In the following steps, you will set a play range and add markers to the audio track, tapping out the beats as the music plays. In the next exercise, you'll add photos and trim each photo layer to a marker.

1   With the playhead placed anywhere to the right of the *C_Title* marker, Control-click in the ruler. From the shortcut menu, choose Previous Marker, and press Command-Option-I to set a play range In point. You will set markers on the audio track in this play range.

2   Now move the playhead to the *B_Graphics* project marker, and if necessary, select the *burn.00* audio layer.

    TIP ▶ You can press Command-Option-Left Arrow to move the playhead to the previous marker or press Command-Option-Right Arrow to move the playhead to the next marker.

    You are going to add markers to the audio layer as the project is playing, so it's helpful to start a few frames early to get ready to start placing markers right after the *C_Title* marker.

3   Start playback. As the playhead hits the *C_Title* marker, start tapping the M key on every other beat to lay down markers on the audio layer.

    To help you do this most effectively, here are a few tips:

    ▶   The music is in 4/4 time, or four beats to a measure. Try to place markers when you hear the drum hit on beats 1 and 3—not on beats 2 and 4.

    ▶   If you want to start over, choose Mark > Markers > Delete All Markers.

    ▶   Add markers for the last beats 3 and 4 (the beats with the drum hits).

    ▶   Drag the zoom slider to zoom in on the play range.

▶   You should end up with about 19 markers.

▶   Play the project. If some of your markers are a bit late, simply drag them to the left to more precisely match the beat.

▶   To remove a marker, drag it up off the bar, where it will disappear in a puff of smoke.

4   Save your work.

Next, you will assemble all the visual elements of the project using the markers as guides.

Working with Audio and Video

Previously, you created three sections for the Rockumentary title. In Lesson 2, you built the ending composite and added a sequence of images. In Lesson 3, you used behaviors to animate the opening dates and pictures to fall through space. And in Lesson 4, you used keyframes to create the middle section, in which the title graphics animate into position.

Now you will assemble the full project by importing each of those completed projects as groups, and use markers to line them up. Then you'll edit the photos to sync with the markers on the audio track.

1   Close the *burn.00* layer to hide the behaviors applied to it. Drag up on the top of the Timing pane to make the window much larger, and drag down on the top of the Audio Timeline to make more room for video layers.

2   Press Shift-Z to fit the Timeline to the window, press Option-X to reset the play range, and then click in the Canvas and press Shift-Z to fit the Canvas to the smaller window.

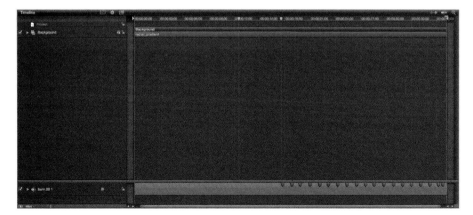

3   In the File Browser, navigate to the Lesson_08 folder, and select the A_Opening
file. With the playhead placed at the start of the project, drag the file above the
Background group in the Timeline and release the mouse button.

This file consists of groups and layers that contain the animated photos and dates you
created earlier.

4   Move the playhead to the *B_Graphics* marker, and then drag the B_Graphics & Stills
project file from the File Browser to the Timeline, above the *A_Opening* group. Wait
for a pop-up menu to appear, and choose Composite.

This group contains all the title graphics. It overlaps the *A_Behaviors* group as the elements animate into place. Notice the red object marker that indicates where all the
elements "land" in place—it should line up with the *C_Title* project marker.

NOTE ▶ If the *B_Graphics & Stills* group imports inside the *A_Behaviors* group, undo
your work and try again.

5   Move the playhead to the *C_Title* marker, and then drag the C_Title file from the File
Browser to the *C_Title* marker in the Timeline, above the *B_Graphics & Stills* group.
Once again, perform a composite edit.

This group contains the actual title and graphic that appear on top of everything else
at the first drum hit.

6   Play the project.

The music plays, the photos and dates fall back in space, and the title elements ani-mate into position. However, the photos in the upper-right corner of the screen don't change at all.

NOTE ▶ Depending on your hardware, playback may appear jumpy. When audio is enabled in the transport controls, by default Motion skips video frames as neces-sary to sync the audio with the video and play in real time. If you turn off the audio, Motion will revert to what you are probably used to seeing. It will play every frame, taking as long as necessary to do so, with the result that the frame rate may vary. You can change this default behavior in the Time pane of Motion preferences. Choose Motion > Preferences, click the Time pane and in the Playback Control section, select Pause Audio Playback.

Another option is to create a RAM preview by choosing Mark > RAM Preview > Play Range, or pressing Command-R. Doing so will load as many frames as possible into your available memory. You can then play those frames in real time.

You can now trim each photo layer to a marker.

7   In the Timeline, open the *B_Graphics & Stills* group.

8   Open the *Stills* group and scroll down so that you can see the bottom layer in the group *vid_pix_001*.

NOTE ▶ Because some layers reference the same media, you may see an additional number in a layer name, such as *vid_pix_001 1*. You can delete or ignore the extra digit.

9   Drag the zoom slider to fit the *vid_pix* layers to the window.

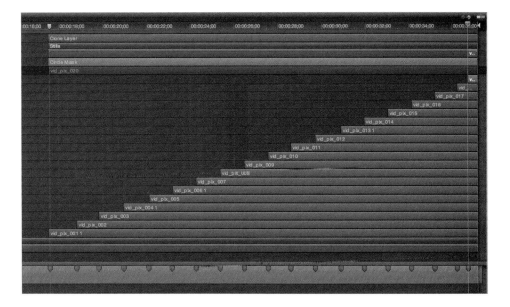

The In point for the *vid_pix_001* layer is already at the first marker on the audio layer.

10 Starting with the *vid_pix_002* layer, move the playhead over the next marker in the audio track, select the *vid_pix_002* layer, and press I to trim its In point to the playhead.

11 Continue moving to the next marker and up to the next layer, trimming the In point of each layer in the group to create a stair-step pattern.

> **NOTE ▸** Because you have more images than markers, the *vid_pix_20* layer is extra, and you can turn it off. It is good practice to include extra graphics in case they are needed.

12 Close the *Stills* and the *B_Graphics & Stills* groups. Drag down on the top of the Timeline to make the Canvas larger. Press Shift-Z while the Timeline is active to fit it back to the window, and play the project. The pictures now change to the beat of the music.

13 Save your work.

Great job! For the final task in this lesson, you'll use the powerful Audio parameter behavior to automatically animate layers to the music.

Animating with Audio

In addition to editing to audio cues, animating to audio is a powerful way to combine audio and video. Although you can turn on recording and set keyframes to animate a layer to an audio track, Motion automates this process via the Audio parameter behavior.

This powerful behavior lets you animate any keyframeable parameter of any layer, group, or effect based on an audio track. (A keyframeable parameter is one that contains an Animation menu—the small downward facing arrow that appears when you move the pointer over the far right of a parameter.)

To apply the Audio parameter behavior, you select a layer and choose the parameter you want to animate. For this project, you will animate the scale of the *One* layers so that they pulsate to the music.

1 In the Layers list, open the *B_Graphics & Stills* and *Graphics Over* groups, and select the top layer, *One_title_b copy*. Press Shift-I to move the playhead to the In point of the layer, and then press Command-Option-I to set a play range In point.

2   Press F1 to open the Properties Inspector. From the Animation menu for the Scale
     parameter, choose Add Parameter Behavior > Audio.

The Audio parameter behavior appears under the selected layer. The Behaviors pane
comes forward, displaying the parameters for the Audio parameter behavior. Now you
need to indicate which audio track to use to generate the animation.

3   In the Behaviors pane, from the To pop-up menu, choose burn.00.

Motion analyzes the audio, and in the Audio Graph window a bar graph appears, representing the levels of different frequencies in the audio track. The low frequencies are on the left, and the high frequencies are on the right.

You can drag the sliders underneath and to the right of the Audio Graph to limit the animation to a specific frequency and level range—the very loud notes of a low-frequency bass drum, for example.

4   Drag the sliders to set a range that uses the middle-to-lower frequencies at all but the lowest volumes.

> **TIP** You can also perform these actions in the HUD.

5   Press the Spacebar to play the project and see the animation.

The *One_title_b copy* layer animates, but it gets much too large. To make the animation subtler, you can change the Scale parameter—not the Scale parameter of the layer, but the Scale parameter for the behavior, which controls how dramatically the selected parameter changes as it animates.

6   In the Behaviors pane, Option-drag in the Scale value field to set a value of about 0.05. The layer now pulses nicely to the music, but it appears to animate just a tiny bit late, which is most noticeable on the last two beats.

7   In the Behaviors pane, set the Delay value to –1. The animation now plays one frame sooner and more closely matches the music.

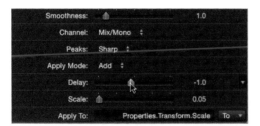

8   Experiment using different volume and frequency ranges in the Audio Graph to see how the animation changes. Play around with other parameters as well, such as Smoothness, Peaks, and Apply Mode.

> **TIP** ▶ For better playback performance, turn off the groups that don't contain the layer you are working on.

9   When you are satisfied with the results, in the Layers list, Option-drag the Audio behavior from the *One_title_b copy* layer to the *One_title_b* layer beneath it so that both layers animate together.

The Audio parameter behavior is very powerful because it can be applied to any key-frameable parameter of a layer, filter, or behavior.

10   At the bottom of the Behaviors pane or the HUD, click the To pop-up menu to view a list of all available parameters, and try applying the behavior to a few different parameters.

11   When you finish experimenting, save your work.

Congratulations—you've learned many different approaches to manipulating and editing audio in this lesson. Audio is a crucial component for enhancing motion graphics, and you now have some powerful tools at your disposal for molding it to your needs.

Lesson Review

1. Can Motion be used with 5.1-channel surround sound audio files?

2. Name two locations in the Motion interface where you can work with audio.

3. In what two ways can you adjust audio with behaviors?

4. What is the difference between project markers and object markers?

5. You are adding audio markers on the fly and realize that your timing was off. How can you remove all markers to start over?

6. If you can't remember the keyboard shortcuts to create, edit, jump to, and delete markers, what is the menu containing all these commands?

7. You enabled audio in the transport controls and now Motion is skipping video frames as necessary to sync the audio with the video and play in real time. How would you turn off the audio to play every frame?

8. True or false: The Audio parameter behavior lets you animate any keyframeable parameter of any group, layer, or effect to an audio track's specific frequency range and volume range.

Answers

1. Yes, but you can hear all six channels only when your hardware supports 5.1-channel surround sound.

2. The Audio list in the Project pane and the Audio Timeline in the Timing pane

3. You can automate the audio level with the Audio Fade In/Fade Out behavior, and you can automate panning with the Audio Auto Pan behavior.

4. Project markers appear over the ruler area of the Timeline, whereas object markers are applied directly to a selected layer, group, or effect.

5. Choose Mark > Markers > Delete All Markers.

6. The Mark menu

7. Disable audio in the transport controls, or choose Motion > Preferences. Click the Time pane, and in the Playback Control section, select Pause Audio Playback.

8. True

Keyboard Shortcuts

M or ` (grave)	Add a marker
Shift-M	Add a project marker
Command-Option-M	Edit a marker
Command-6	Reveal the Audio list in the Project pane
Command-9	Reveal the Audio Timeline in the Timing pane
Command-Option-Left Arrow	Move the playhead to the previous marker
Command-Option-Right Arrow	Move the playhead to the next marker

Visual Effects Design

9

Lesson Files Motion5_Book_Files > Lessons > Lesson_9

Media Motion5_Book_Files > Media > Retiming

Time This lesson takes approximately 30 minutes to complete.

Goals Speed up and slow down a video clip

Apply optical flow frame blending

Use keyframes to create a variable speed ramp

Apply, trim, and combine Retiming behaviors

Use and modify Time filters

Speed Changes and Optical Flow

It's rare to see a title sequence or an advertisement where the video hasn't been sped up, slowed down, or both: A car races toward the camera and suddenly slows to a freeze before it passes by; a skateboarder flies off the edge of a ramp and freezes at his apex; a new laptop spins around in a blur, slows down suddenly so that it's barely moving, and speeds up again just as suddenly.

In Motion, you can change and animate the playback speed of a video clip using keyframes and behaviors.

In this lesson, you'll apply a constant speed change to a video clip to create smooth slow motion using different frame blending options, including optical flow.

Then you'll vary the speed of the clip over time, creating *ramping* effects—first by using keyframes and then by using Retiming behaviors. Finally, using the Motion Time filters, you'll create time-based special effects.

Creating Constant Speed Changes

The simplest way to change the speed of a clip is to apply a constant speed change—for example, slowing a clip down to 50 percent of its original speed or speeding it up to 200 percent. Constant speed changes are great for adjusting a clip's length to fit within a sequence, creating a time-lapse effect, or playing a clip in slow motion.

1   Navigate to Motion5_Book_Files > Lessons > Lesson_09. Open the Lesson_09_Start project, save it to the Lesson_09 > Student_Saves Folder, and play it.

The project contains a clip from an Audi promotional video shot at 24 frames per second. Notice that the project duration is longer than the duration of the clip. This extra time will come in handy when you slow down the clip.

2   With the project still playing, select the clip, press F1 to open the Properties Inspector, and in the Timing section, click Show.

TIP ▶ The Show text is displayed only when you hover over the Timing section of the Inspector.

In the Timing section, you can control a clip's playback speed. The Speed parameter is currently set to the default value of 100%. Notice that the clip Duration is 192 frames, or eight seconds if you are displaying timecode.

3   Drag in the Speed value field to change the Speed value to 50%. The clip now plays in slow motion. Notice that the bar in the Timeline has become longer, and the duration field now reads about 16 seconds, or 384 frames.

Because the clip plays half as fast, it now lasts twice as long. The clip plays more slowly, but the motion is not very smooth.

When you slow down a clip, you extend the existing frames over a longer time period, so frames are repeated. So when a clip is slowed by 50 percent, every frame is played twice so that half the original frames can play in the same amount of time. This repetition of frames can create a distracting, step-like effect. Motion has other options for altering clips that produce smoother changes at less than 100 percent speed.

Using Frame Blending and Optical Flow

When you slow down a clip, you can control the slow motion appearance by choosing one of several frame blending options from the Frame Blending pop-up menu. The Blending option blends adjacent frames, quickly creating the most predictable results. Optical flow can produce more fluid and realistic slow motion results. This option estimates the motion between two frames of video and renders an intermediate frame that interpolates the motion. However, optical flow requires processing and affects playback performance most significantly.

1   In the Properties Inspector's Timing pane, from the Frame Blending pop-up menu, choose Blending. Rather than repeating each frame, blending creates new frames by combining the original adjacent frames with varying levels of opacity to smooth out the transition from one frame to the next.

2   Stop playback, and press the Left and Right Arrow keys to step through the clip. Between every original frame you can see a frame that blends the preceding and following frames.

3   Locate the playhead on a frame in which you can see two blended images. Then, from the Frame Blending pop-up menu, choose Motion-Blur Blending.

Motion-Blur Blending creates blur between frames when a clip's frame rate is higher than the project's frame rate. Because this clip has been slowed down, blending has no impact.

NOTE ▶ Motion-Blur Blending is unrelated to Motion Blur, which is located in the Render pop-up menu and is adjusted in the Render Settings pane of Project Properties. Motion-Blur Blending creates blur within a video frame, whereas Motion Blur affects only animated objects.

The remaining Frame Blending option, Optical Flow, needs some time to do its magic because it first analyzes movement from frame to frame to generate entirely new frames in real time.

4   From the Frame Blending pop-up menu, choose Optical Flow. Then play the clip. Nothing seems to change, but an animated icon appears under the mini-Timeline on the right. This icon is the *analysis indicator*. It tells you that Motion is analyzing the optical flow or the directional movement of pixels.

NOTE ▶ The more movement in a clip, the longer the analysis will take.

5   Click the analysis indicator. The Background Task List window opens and displays the analysis progress. In this dialog, you also can pause and restart the analysis. The process runs as a *background task*, so you can continue to work in Motion while the analysis is performed.

> **TIP ▶** You can batch-process multiple clips in a project. Each clip is analyzed in the order in which it was added to the queue. You can reorder clips by dragging them up and down in the Background Task List window.

6   After the analysis is completed, play the project. The clip now plays much more smoothly.

> **NOTE ▶** Depending on the source material, you may see artifacts in individual frames where optical flow has attempted to interpret the motion. Optical flow works best on clips that have little or no camera movement and a primary subject moving in the scene. A panning camera can create a tearing effect in the background.

When you perform the optical flow analysis, Motion creates a *cache* file that contains information about the clip. After this cache is created, you can change the speed of the clip as much as you want—including adding keyframes and behaviors—without analyzing the clip again. The cache file is large because it contains information to enable all possible speed changes.

You can choose how the cache file is handled in Motion Preferences.

7   Choose Motion > Preferences, or press Command-, (comma).

8   Click the Cache icon. In the Optical Flow Retiming section, you can choose a different location in which to store the cache file, and delete the cache file.

TIP When your project is complete, consider deleting the cache files to free up disk space.

9   To see how large the cache file is, click the "Reveal in Finder" button, and then select the cache file to view its properties. This cache file is roughly 350 MB.

The cache file includes the optical flow analysis of only the portion of the clip used in the project. The longer the clip's duration and the greater its resolution, the larger the cache file will be. If you are analyzing long HD-resolution clips, make sure you have adequate disk space to store the cache files.

10   Return to Motion and close the Preferences window.

NOTE ▶ If you extend a clip's In or Out points, Motion will analyze the added media as a background task.

11 Change the Speed value from 50% to 40%. The clip immediately plays at the new speed with optical flow frame blending applied.

12 Return the Speed value to 100%.

> **TIP** ▶ At the top left of the Canvas, keep an eye on the project's frame rate (displayed only when the project is playing). Optical flow processing during playback is GPU intensive, and you may need to export the clip to play at a full frame rate.

Next, you'll work with ways to change speed over time. Because the optical flow analysis was performed, the results of your changes with optical flow frame blending will be visible immediately. You can return the Frame Blending type to one of the other options at any time. If you later return to optical flow, it will use the existing cache file.

Creating Speed Ramps with Keyframes

The real fun of retiming clips starts when you change the speed over time. For example, a clip can start in slow motion, suddenly speed up, stop in a freeze frame, and speed up again.

1 Stop playback. Set the play range Out point at the end of the video layer by dragging the white arrow in the mini-Timeline, or press Command-Option-O.

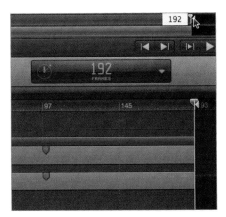

2 Press Home to move the playhead to the start of the project.

NOTE ► If you are using a keyboard that does not have a Home key, such as a MacBook or MacBook Pro, press Fn-Left Arrow to move the playhead to the start of the project.

3   In the Properties Inspector's Timing pane, from the Time Remap pop-up menu, choose Variable Speed. A Retime Value field appears with a value of 1. A solid diamond in the Animation menu indicates that a keyframe is located at the playhead.

4   Next to the current time field, click the clock icon to toggle from timecode to frames. The Retime Value of 1 refers to frame 1, which is the current playhead location. Working in frames will clarify the relationship between the current time field and the Retime Value field.

5   Drag the playhead to frame 30, and look at the Retime Value field. No matter where you move the playhead, the frame under the playhead is the same as the frame in the Retime Value field. This indicates that the clip will play at its native speed: At any given frame in the project, the same frame of the video is seen.

6   Press Command-8 to open the Keyframe Editor. If necessary, drag the zoom slider to view the full curve in the window.

The project plays at 100 percent speed. The curve in the Keyframe Editor contains keyframes at the beginning and end of the clip. The first keyframe tells Motion to play the first frame of the clip at the beginning of the project, and the second keyframe tells Motion to play the last frame of the clip when the playhead reaches the corresponding frame in the Timeline. Between those keyframes, Motion interpolates a straight line, and therefore the project plays at normal speed.

Now that you have a curve, you can manipulate which frames of the video play and at what times. You'll now create a freeze frame by adding two keyframes to the curve that have the same value.

7   Hold down Command-Option and press Right Arrow twice to move the playhead to the second marker on frame 99. Double-click the keyframe curve directly under the playhead to add a keyframe. In this frame, you can clearly see the Audi branding on the side of the car, which makes it a good frame to freeze.

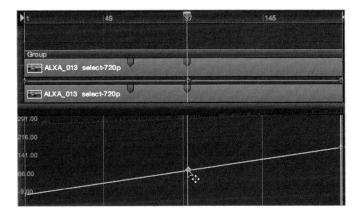

8   Hold down Command-Option and press the Left Arrow to move the playhead to the first marker, and double-click to add a keyframe on the curve. Then double-click the keyframe, and in the Value field, enter 99. Press Return, and play the project. Because both the new keyframes are playing the same frame of the video clip, the curve between them is flat, and the video appears to freeze between them.

The car stops and starts again rather suddenly. You can slow it to a stop and speed it up again by changing the interpolation of the keyframes.

9   Control-click (or right-click) the first new keyframe and choose Ease In from the shortcut menu.

10 Control-click the second keyframe and choose Ease Out from the shortcut menu. The combination of the eased keyframes and optical flow frame blending creates a very smooth freeze-frame effect.

> **TIP** If you just want to change the location of a keyframe without changing its value, drag it in the Timeline instead of dragging it in the Keyframe Editor, where you could accidentally drag it up or down, thereby changing its value. (You may need to click the Show/Hide Keyframes button at the upper left of the Timeline.)

11 Stop playback, press Command-8 to close the Keyframe Editor, and save your work.

Using keyframes to change clip speed lets you precisely control which frame of video plays at any point in time.

Creating Speed Effects with Retiming Behaviors

If you can animate an element in Motion using keyframes, it's likely that you can also animate it using behaviors. Time remapping is no exception. While keyframes allow great animation precision, Retiming behaviors have their own strengths. They can be added and adjusted quickly; they can be combined with keyframes; and they can create effects that would be difficult or time-consuming using keyframes.

Also, Retiming behaviors will not change those parts of a clip they are not applied to. If you slow down the first half of a clip with a behavior, the rest of the clip will still play at 100 percent, and the clip will become longer. If you use keyframes to slow down the first half of a clip, the second half will speed up so that the total clip length remains the same.

You will start this exercise by building the same freeze-frame effect using a Retiming behavior. Then you'll modify the behavior, duplicate it, and try a few variations.

1   Return the Time Remap parameter to Constant Speed.

The clip returns to its default settings. However, if you were to return the Time Remap value to Variable Speed, the keyframes you created would still be intact. And the optical flow frame blending also would be intact.

Let's create a speed ramp effect using the Set Speed behavior.

2   Press Command-2 to open the Library, choose Behaviors, and then choose the Retiming folder.

You have 11 available Retiming behaviors. Selecting a behavior displays a sample movie and written description in the preview area.

3   Move the playhead to the first marker at frame 65. Let's start the speed ramp at the same point as the freeze frame in the previous exercise.

4   Drag the Set Speed behavior from the Library onto the video clip in the Canvas, and then press I to trim the behavior's In point to the playhead.

5   Drag the playhead to the second marker at frame 99, and press O to trim the Out point. We'll end the speed ramp at the same point the freeze frame ended in the previous exercise.

   TIP ▶ If you press Command-Option-Right Arrow to move to the markers after you add the behavior, you must reselect the video layer. If you do not, Motion will look for a marker on the selected behavior.

6   Start playback, and in the HUD, drag the Speed slider to 0 to create a freeze-frame effect.

   The Ease In Time and Ease Out Time parameters determine how many frames it takes to get from full speed to the Speed value. The Curve parameters set acceleration and deceleration over the Time values and work much like the Bezier handles on keyframes.

7   Adjust the Time and Curve values in the HUD as you like.

   One of the advantages to Retiming behaviors is that you can change their locations and durations right in the mini-Timeline.

8   Try dragging the Set Speed behavior earlier and later in time, and drag the In and/or Out points to change their durations. Adjust the play range as needed.

   You can also quickly duplicate, add, and stack Retiming behaviors.

9   Press Command-D to duplicate the Set Speed behavior, and then reposition and trim each behavior to create two separate speed ramp effects.

Finally, you can combine Retiming behaviors and keyframes.

10 Press F1 to open the Properties Inspector, and in the Timing section, change the Time Remap parameter to Variable Speed. The keyframe curve you previously created is added to the Retiming behaviors (look at the Keyframe Editor to see the curve), and as the clip plays, both keyframes and behaviors manipulate its playback speed.

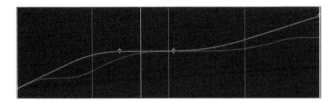

The other Retiming behaviors in the Library create a variety of time-related effects and can be freely mixed and matched in the Timeline.

11 Return the Time Remap parameter to Constant so that the keyframes no longer affect the animation.

12 At the top of the toolbar, click the Add Behavior pop-up menu and try several of the behaviors in the Retiming group. Trim them, move them, and adjust them in the HUD or the Behaviors Inspector to understand how they work. You may need to remove the existing behaviors to make more space available for the new behaviors you want to try.

Using Time Filters

Time filters are designed to create time-based effects you can use alone or in combination with time remapping and optical flow frame blending.

1 Delete all the Retiming behaviors you applied to your clip. It will be easier to see the effects of the Time filters if you use the speed of the original footage.

2 Press Command-2 to go to the Library. Choose Filters, and then choose the Time folder, which contains five Time filters.

3 Select each filter and watch its preview. Most of the filters work by holding and/or combining frames on top of each other.

4 Drag the WideTime filter to the clip.

5   In the HUD, increase Duration to 0.2 and increase Decay to 1.

The filter holds frames before and after the current frame to create a blurry series of images surrounding the cars. You can combine this effect with Retiming behaviors or keyframes.

TIP ▸ You can also keyframe the filter parameters. For example, you could set a Duration of 0 until immediately after a freeze frame, and then increase the value to create a "spray" of copies that shoot out of the freeze frame.

With constant and variable time remapping, frame blending options such as optical flow, retiming behaviors, and time-based filters, Motion provides you with a vast arsenal of time-manipulation tools.

Lesson Review

1. In which pane and section do you change the speed of a clip?

2. Name the two kinds of Time Remap speed changes.

3. Identify three of the four frame blending options.

4. You created a slow motion effect using the Optical Flow option. How can you determine the size of the resulting cache file?

5. Can you continue working on a Motion project while the optical flow analysis is performed?

6. Describe four reasons to create a speed effect with a Retiming behavior instead of using keyframes.

7. Which Retiming behavior lets you create a speed ramp effect?

8. Can you combine Retiming behaviors with keyframes?

9. Name two of the Time filters.

Answers

1. The Properties Inspector in the Timing pane

2. Constant Speed and Variable Speed

3. None, Blending, Motion-Blur Blending, and Optical Flow

4. Choose Motion > Preferences. In the Cache pane, click the "Reveal in Finder" button, and then select the cache file to view its properties.

5. Yes, it's a background task.

6. Behaviors can be added and adjusted quickly; they can create effects that would be difficult or time-consuming using keyframes; Retiming behaviors only change the parts of a clip to which they are applied; you can change the locations and durations of Retiming behaviors in the mini-Timeline.

7. The Set Speed behavior

8. Yes, if you apply a keyframe curve to a Retiming behavior, both keyframes and behaviors manipulate the clip's playback speed.

9. Echo, Scrub, Strobe, Trails, Wide Time

10

Lesson Files   Motion5_Book_Files > Lessons > Lesson_10

Media   Motion5_Book_Files > Media > Green Screen

Time   This lesson takes approximately 90 minutes to complete.

Goals   Stabilize a shot

Match move one shot to another

Use the Keyer to remove a green screen

Create and animate a B-Spline mask

Match foreground and background color

Add and customize a particle effect

Lesson **10**

Keying and Compositing

When producers want an actor to hang off the edge of a cliff, blast aliens on a distant planet, or read a book at a Parisian outdoor café, they'll frequently save time, money, and work-safety violations by shooting the actor in a studio against a green screen and then replace the green background with a new background. But replacing the green screen is just one aspect of visual effects compositing, as you'll find out in this lesson.

In this lesson, you will prepare a background for the composite and then remove a green screen background using a keying filter. After finessing the key, you will animate a mask to cut out problem areas of the image, and finish by matching the tone and color of the foreground clip to the background.

Stabilizing a Clip

When you combine any two shots to look as if they are one shot, the framing and camera movement of each shot must match exactly. To accomplish this, you first remove unnecessary camera movement from one of the clips. In Motion, you can do this with the Stabilize behavior. But before you begin stabilizing, let's look at the simple structure of this project.

1   Close any open projects, and choose File > Open. Open Motion5_Book_Files > Lessons > Lesson_10 > Lesson_10_Start. Choose File > Save As and save a copy to the Student_Saves folder. This project has a resolution of 1280 x 720 pixels and includes two groups, each containing a single clip.

2   In the Layers list, click the disclosure triangle for the *Foreground* group, and then press the Spacebar to play the clip. After you play the clip a few times, stop playback.

This clip has two actors on a green screen. The evenly lit green screen makes it easier to place subjects onto a new background because you can remove the green using a process called keying.

In this clip, the camera moves behind the actors, and at the end of the clip, they duck down. We can assume that this action is the important part of the shot and signals that something spectacular happens here. In this exercise, you'll key the clip in preparation for adding the "spectacular" bit.

3 In the Layers list, deselect the activation checkbox next to the *Foreground* group to hide it, and then click the disclosure triangle for the *Background* group. Press the Spacebar to play the clip. After you play the clip a few times, stop playback.

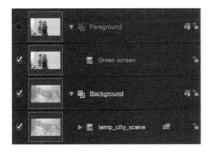

This background already includes a Levels filter to provide more contrast. This 1920 x 1080 pixel clip is much larger than the project. It's convenient to have a larger background for your composite in case you need to stabilize it or pan the background to fit the action in the scene

NOTE ► In this exercise, the background is really just a temporary placeholder. For an actual composite, you would need a live action background filmed with the same camera move as the foreground, or a 3D background matching the foreground camera move.

TIP ► You can mix and match codecs and frame sizes in a composition; but if possible, match frame rates to avoid any skipped or repeating frames.

If you examine the background clip as it plays, you'll see a slight shake in the camera probably caused because the camera is zoomed in quite far and the tripod might have been a bit unstable. In any case that movement is enough to ruin the illusion that the foreground and background are a single shot. So the first thing to do is remove the unwanted background movement using the Stabilize behavior.

4   Press Command-2 to go to the Library. Select Behaviors, and then select Motion Tracking. You use the four behaviors in this category to perform a variety of tracking-related operations.

Tracking operations analyze and record the movement of objects or regions within a clip. Once you acquire the motion data, you can invert it and apply that inverted motion data to stabilize the clip. When the camera moves right, the inverted motion data creates a move left that negates the camera movement.

5   Drag the Stabilize behavior onto the *temp_city_scene* layer in the Layers list, and then press F2 to open the Behaviors pane in the Inspector.

The Stabilize behavior can function automatically if you click Analyze and let it do its thing, but that method works best for smoothing a clip and not as well when locking a clip down or stabilizing it.

When stabilizing, you can adjust several parameters to ensure you get the results you want.

6   To completely remove the camera movement from this clip, leave Method set to Stabilize in the Inspector. The camera moves only horizontally and vertically in this shot, so you'll also leave the Adjust options enabled for Position. The Stabilize behavior can also stabilize camera tilting and zooming transforms by enabling the Scale and Rotation options. You won't need those two options for this shot so you will also leave those at their default setting.

> **TIP** Setting Method to Smooth is a great way to reduce shaky moving camera footage, such as when a camera is on a dolly or attached to a car.

The next step is to add a tracker to the Canvas. When stabilizing, a tracker is used to identify an area in the image that should remain stable. Motion locks onto the defined area as it moves across the screen to determine its movement over time. Ideally you want to position the tracker over a high contrast clear pattern that is not obscured and does not change shape for the duration of the clip.

7   In the Inspector, click the Tracker Add button.

The small circular tracker is added to the center of the Canvas. Although it is sometimes called a tracking point, the tracker actually identifies a small region. Because tracking begins at the start of the behavior, it's critical that you place the tracker while looking at the first frame of the behavior, which in this case is the start of the project.

8   Position the playhead at the start of the project, and then drag the tracker around the Canvas.

TIP ▶ As you drag the tracker, Motion displays a magnified inset view under your pointer to help you precisely select the tracking reference pattern. You can control the level of magnification in the Inset view from the Auto-Zoom menu in the Inspector.

9   In the Canvas, Option-drag the tracker.

After a brief pause, Motion displays suggested tracker points for that frame. Because these reference points are chosen for this frame and not for the entire clip, they may not all be ideal tracking reference patterns. Still, they are a huge help in the somewhat hit-and-miss process of selecting a tracking point.

10 Drag the tracker to the upper-right corner of the building in the center of the screen. The tracker will snap to the reference point.

11 In the Inspector, click Analyze.

TIP ▶ If you were stabilizing a clip of the same size as the project, you would choose Zoom from the Borders pop-up menu. Motion would then automatically scale the clip as necessary to ensure that black borders wouldn't appear in the Canvas as the clip is repositioned to eliminate camera movement.

Motion analyzes the clip frame by frame. When the analysis is completed, you can play the clip and Motion will attempt to remove all movement by changing the layer's position at every frame (and the rotation or scale, if those are selected in the Inspector) to lock down the buildings.

12 Play the project, and stop playback after you confirm that the clip no longer has any unwanted movement.

In the Canvas, the bounding box of the layer moves and a small dotted line appears under the tracker to indicate the motion path of the layer that causes the buildings to appear motionless. With the background stabilized, your next step is to have it inherit the movement of the foreground shot.

Creating a Match Move

Since the camera moves in the green screen clip, the background must track that movement to make the composite look realistic. Tracking works almost exactly like stabilization. You set up trackers to calculate the movement of objects as with stabilization, but the acquired motion data is applied to a different layer, in this case, the background.

Motion's main tracking behavior is the aptly named Match Move behavior. It matches the movement of one layer to another. You apply the Match Move behavior to the layer that you want to inherit the new movement.

In this exercise, you want the layer stabilized prior to applying any match-moving data. To achieve this, you'll apply the Match Move to the *Background* group. The hierarchy of layers within groups dictates that the Stabilize behavior on the layer is applied first and the group's Match Move behavior is applied second.

1 Press Command-2 to open the Library. Drag the Match Move behavior onto the *Background* group in the Layers list, and then press F2 to open the Behaviors pane of the Inspector.

2 Drag the *Green screen* layer from the Layers list to the Source well in the Inspector. Select the activation checkbox for the *Green screen* layer to view it in the Canvas.

The tracker appears in the center of the Canvas. By default, the behavior will match only the position of the layer, so only one tracker is required.

TIP ▶ When you want to track the layer's scale and/or rotation, a second tracker is needed. When you enable Scale and Rotation in the Inspector, Motion automatically displays a second tracker.

Trackers are positioned on the Canvas to identify which object in the frame should be followed to match the movement. And again, the location of the playhead is critical for the Match Move behavior because it assumes the playhead is on the first frame of the behavior.

3   Press Shift-I to move the playhead to the In point of the layer.

NOTE ▶ If the source layer is obscured under another layer in the Canvas, clicking the tracker will still correctly show a zoomed-in view of it.

When selecting a pattern to track, choose an area of high contrast that stays in the frame. Luckily the people who shot this clip knew you would need to track it so they conveniently placed tracking references on the green screen wall. The light green rectangles are perfect for tracking because they are clearly defined for the duration of the clip.

4   Drag the tracker over the green rectangle in the upper-right corner of the frame, and center the rectangle in the magnified inset view

5   In the Inspector, click Analyze.

> **NOTE** ▶ If you are trying to track a fast moving object, you may have to increase the Search Size value in the Anchor or Rotation-Scale sections of the Inspector. A larger search size helps ensure that the tracker won't be lost when a lot of movement occurs from one frame to the next.

As the tracking begins, white dots in the Canvas indicate the path of the tracker over the duration of the clip. As you watch the Canvas, you'll notice the woman's head obscures the tracking reference pattern (the green rectangle) before the analysis is complete. The tracker stops prematurely because it can no longer find the tracking reference pattern you selected. When a tracking reference pattern is obscured or goes offscreen during a track, you can use the Track Offset to select a new pattern to pick up where the original pattern is lost. Motion calculates the offset between the new and old tracks to create a single continuous track.

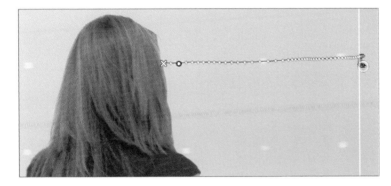

6   Drag the playhead to the frame just before the tracking point is obscured. Use the Tracker Preview in the Inspector to make sure you clearly see the green rectangle. You'll want to position the playhead at 4:10 (or frame 131).

7   In the Inspector, select the Offset Track checkbox.

8   In the Canvas, drag the yellow tracker to a green rectangle in the upper-right of the frame, and then in the Inspector, click Analyze.

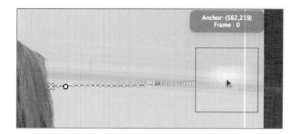

The tracker picks up where the previous one left off; but once again, the woman's head obscures the green rectangle before the analysis is completed. You'll have to repeat the offset process by selecting yet another track reference pattern in the upper-right of the Canvas.

9   With Track Offset still enabled, position the playhead at 5:00 (or frame 151) just before the second tracker is obscured. Drag the tracker to a third green rectangle in the upper-right corner of the Canvas, and then click Analyze in the Inspector.

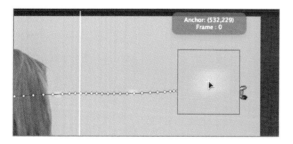

Now the Canvas has a perfect tracking line that will act as a motion path for your background clip. Let's review the applied motion.

10   In the Layers list, deselect the activation checkbox next to the *Foreground* group to hide the group. Press the Spacebar to play the background clip. Stop playback after you view the clip a few times.

The clip clearly has the right motion applied to it, but the movement is much greater than the clip size so the background pans offscreen. The only solution is to scale the background clip to fill the Canvas.

11   In the Layers list, select the *temp_city_scene* layer, and then select the Properties pane in the Inspector. Set the Scale to 125, and then drag the playhead to the start of the project.

The camera moves only to the right so you know that at the start of the project, the right edge of the frame can be placed against the right edge of the Canvas.

12 In the Canvas, drag the *temp_city_scene* layer until its left edge is against the left edge of the Canvas. Also drag down until you can see the rooftops and some sky. Then move the playhead to the end of the project.

You can see the edge of the frame no longer moves into the Canvas so that resize works. The background clip now matches the camera move from the green screen clip, and it no longer pans off the Canvas thanks to the resize and repositioning.

13 Save your project.

You are now ready to key the green screen.

Keying in Automatic Mode

Motion includes an excellent keying filter for replacing a green screen or blue screen background with a new background from a different layer.

The Keyer in Motion starts in an automatic mode by analyzing the image to determine what color range to select. The color range is then keyed to make it transparent and reveal the background layer. In this exercise, you'll apply the keying filter to see how well this automatic mode works for your shot.

1 Position the playhead at 4:00 (or frame 121).

2   In the Layers list, select the activation checkbox for the *Foreground* group, and select the *Green screen* layer inside the *Foreground* group.

Instead of using the Library to add the Keying filter, you'll use the alternative toolbar method.

3   From the toolbar, click the Add Filter pop-up menu, and choose Keying > Keyer.

As soon as it is applied, the Keyer samples the dominant green color and makes it transparent to reveal the background clip.

NOTE ▶ Although typically used for blue and green screens, the Keyer filter works on any color range.

4   Play the project a few times and then stop playback and return the playhead to 4:00 (or frame 121).

At first look this key seems to be very good; but when you are keying, always view the matte created by the key because it can reveal more subtle problems.

5   Press F3 to open the Filters pane in the Inspector, and then click the center View button to view the matte in the Canvas.

The matte is a grayscale representation of the key displayed in the Canvas. Areas of white are opaque in the actual composite, areas of black are completely transparent, and areas of gray are partially transparent. Ideally, the background is completely black and the subject is completely white to the edges, which should have smooth edges, without any stair-stepping.

NOTE ▸ How easy or difficult it is to create a clean matte is dependent upon the way the subject was shot; how brightly and evenly the background screen was lit; how far the subject was from that background; what colors the subject was wearing; how much movement and detail were in the shot; and the type of camera, recording media, and compression in use.

Perfect mattes are never created without some adjustments, and this shot is no exception. As you can see, the key that looked great when viewed as a composite has lots of semi-transparent gray areas on the actors. You can make adjustments to remove some of these gray semi-transparent areas while maintaining others (especially around hair).

Start your adjustments with the Strength slider, which adjusts the core transparency. When you reduce the slider value, you reduce the areas of transparency by narrowing the range of green used to create the matte.

6   Drag the Strength slider to 50%.

In the Canvas, the white areas of the matte now have no gray or semi-transparent areas within them. Unfortunately, by narrowing the green color range, you also revealed the green rectangles you used for tracking. Those rectangles are a slightly different shade of green and show up as gray rectangles in the black area of your matte. When you have several shades of green or blue in the background that you want to include in the key, you can use the Sample Color tool.

7   From the Zoom Level pop-up at the top of the Canvas, choose 200% to see the
     rectangles more clearly. Then press H to choose the Pan tool, and drag the Canvas
     until the male actor's head is centered on the screen.

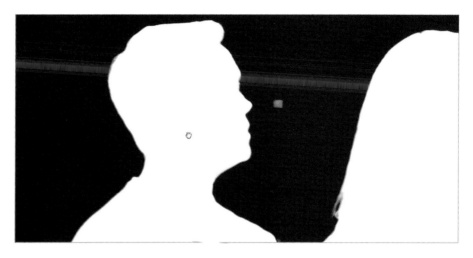

8   In the Inspector, click the Sample Color button. In the Canvas, drag a selection
     rectangle around the gray rectangle that appears between the two actors' heads.

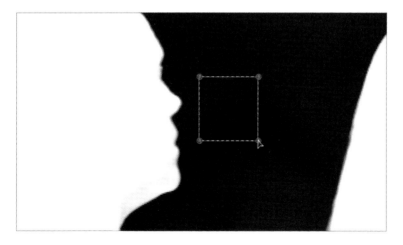

TIP ▶ Instead of clicking the Sample Color button in the Inspector, if the Keyer
is selected in the Layers list, you can Shift-drag in the Canvas to create a Sample Color
selection rectangle.

The black areas of the matte are now totally black, just as you want them.

TIP ▶ You can add sample regions in different areas and on different frames. When you add sample regions on different frames, keyframes are created to interpolate the difference from one frame to the next. These keyframes are not shown in the Motion user interface, but you can move to each keyframe by clicking the "Jump to Sample" buttons in the Inspector.

9   Press Shift-Z to see the entire frame in the Canvas.

Although the Sample Color tool corrects the color range problem, it can remove some nice soft edges, especially around hair. Let's view a different frame to see if any new problems have arisen.

10 Drag the playhead to 5:25 (or frame 176) to better see the matte around the woman's hair.

The Edges tool is used to refine semi-transparent areas such as hair, smoke, and motion blurred objects by drawing a control line over the edge of the matte you want to work on. Let's use the Edges tool to improve the transparency on the actor's hair as she ducks down.

11 In the Inspector, choose the Edges tool.

12 In the Canvas, drag from the white area at the top of her head to just above the black area of the background to create a control line.

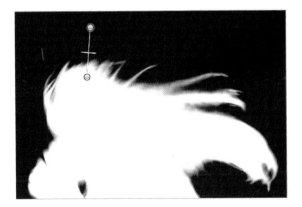

> **TIP** ▶ Instead of selecting the Edges tool in the Inspector, if the Keyer is selected in the Layers list, you can Command-drag in the Canvas to create a control line.

Once the control line is in place, the matte can be made softer or harder by dragging the control line slider handle in the Canvas.

13 Drag the slider handle toward the white portion of the matte to soften the edges of her hair, and then drag toward the black side of the matte to harden the edges. Leave the slider handle set about two-thirds of the way to the top of the control line.

As you drag the slider handle toward the white side of the matte, more gray semi-transparent areas are revealed, which is not the way you want to go. Dragging toward the black side of the matte improves the matte slightly, and gives it a good mix of pure white with gray strands. But this is beginning to feel like a seesaw because those pesky rectangles reappear. One more sample color addition should remove them for good.

> **TIP** ▶ You can change the size of the Edges control line and the sample region anytime by dragging their control handles in the Canvas.

14 In the Inspector, click the Sample Color button. Then in the Canvas, drag a selection rectangle around the gray rectangle above the male actor's head.

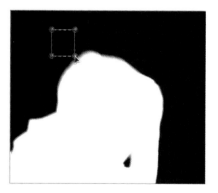

> **TIP** ▶ You can delete a sample color range rectangle or an Edges control line by Option-clicking it in the Canvas.

The rectangles are now gone, and the hair still looks great! The only remaining problem with the matte is some gray areas under the male actor's chin. One way to fill in unwanted holes or subtle gray areas in the white part of your matte is to drag the Fill Holes slider. But that technique can also ruin the softness you just achieved on her hair. You could cut her hair and reshoot, but that might be too expensive. Instead you'll correct this problem later using the Matte tools. For now, review the project and see if you have other basic adjustments to make here.

> **TIP** ▶ If you are filling holes near semi-transparent edges you want to keep, use the Edge Distance slider to determine how close the Fill Holes parameter gets to the edges of your matte.

15 Click the left View button to view the composite in the Canvas, and continue to play the project. Stop playback after you watch the entire project a few times.

The basic key adjustments are almost complete. The final slider you'll use in this exercise is Spill Level, and by default it is already applied. When a subject is shot in front of a green screen, the light from the screen can often bounce back and add a green tint to the subject. This green fringing is called *spill*, and one way to get rid of it is by using a spill suppressor. Let's lower the Spill Level slider to see what the shot looks like without it.

16 In the Inspector, move the Spill Level slider to 0.

Without spill suppression the actors look a little radioactive with green fringe around them. The spill suppression pushes the color in the opposite direction of the key color (green, in this case). Adjusting the Spill Level slider is a balancing act between reducing the green and adding magenta.

17 Slowly drag the Spill Level slider to about 30. Then stop playing after you are satisfied with the amount of spill suppression.

You are done creating your matte. In some cases that might be enough to complete your key. In other cases, such as this one, you will want to refine the matte a bit more before making color adjustments.

Refining the Matte

The additional tools found in the Keyer filter are a bit more advanced; in fact, one set of parameters is labeled Advanced. Because the Keyer begins in an automatic mode, the Advanced parameters are primarily used as an alternative mode.

1   In the Inspector, click the Advanced disclosure triangle to open the controls.

The Advanced section reveals a circular graph for adjusting the core key color selection and softness or edge transparency. When using the Keyer filter in Motion, you can use the Automatic mode, or manually select the core color and softness using the Advanced Chroma and Luma graphs. To use the Advanced mode, click the Manual button and define the core color, softness, and luminance regions in the graphs. The graphs are most useful when you know what you want but can't quite find it on your image.

TIP   When selected, the Fix Video checkbox in the Advanced section corrects the horizontal chroma blending found in video captured at 4:2:0/4:1:1/4:2:2. You can deselect it when you use clips captured at full bandwidth 4:4:4.

2   In the Inspector, click the Advanced disclosure triangle to hide the controls.

Your key is nearly complete, so you won't need the Advanced tools, but the sections below the Advanced tools can significantly add to the realism of your composite by refining your existing matte. The Matte tools don't recreate the matte, they process it. Think of them as filters that are applied to the matte.

3   Position the playhead to 4:00 (or 121 frames) to view the frame where the actor's chin was still semi-transparent. In the Inspector, click the center View button to view the matte.

4   From the Zoom pop-up menu, choose 200%. Press H to choose the Pan tool, and then drag in the Canvas to pan the frame until you can see the actor's chin.

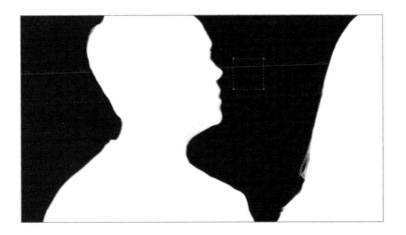

Using the Matte tools on subtle matte problems like this chin—instead of applying Fill Holes adjustments—can make a fix easier because the controls are more precise.

5   In the Inspector, click the Matte Tools disclosure triangle to open the controls.

The first of the Matte tools is the Levels control. This is similar to a Levels control in color correction because you can adjust the contrast by moving the black point, white point, and midtones. The chin area probably falls within the white point and midtone areas so you can adjust those first and check the results.

6   In the Levels controls, drag the White point handle to 0.8 and the center Bias point to the left to around 1.5.

TIP ▶ The disclosure triangle on the Levels control reveals parameters for the gradient handles. Keyframing these parameters can make it easier to create a key for blue screen and green screen backgrounds that change over the duration of a clip due to lighting or shadows.

In the Canvas, the semi-transparent gray area is almost completely gone, and the matte is definitely improved. To be sure, let's check the Matte view.

7   Press Shift-Z to fit the frame in the Canvas. Click Play to play the project once and then stop.

The matte for his chin and her hair look pretty good, but all these adjustments have weakened the black matte at the start of the project. While watching playback, notice that the lower-left area of the black matte has a lot of gray in it. To address this, you can adjust the black point to clip or crush more of the black areas.

8   In the Inspector, drag the Black point handle to .15 to darken the black matte a bit, and then click the Composite view button to view the composite in the Canvas.

The key looks nearly perfect, except for the nagging white outline around the actors. The Shrink/Expand tool can alter the matte size, which is exactly what you need to remove the white outline.

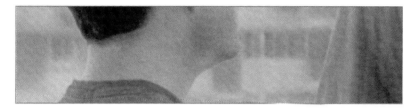

9   Drag the Shrink/Expand parameter to –1, slightly shrinking the matte.

The white outline is gone, but the Shrink parameter change has made the matte a bit hard, especially around the female actor's head and arms. A small amount of softness will help.

10   Drag the Soften parameter to 2.5, and then play the project a few times to review your key. Stop playback.

The softness adds a slight blur to the edges of the matte so they don't appear so hard. It also blended in a tiny bit of the white ring. The easiest way to remove the ring without eating away at your matte by shrinking it again is to use the Spill Suppression tools.

11   In the Inspector, click the Spill Suppression disclosure triangle to open the controls.

The Spill Level you previously adjusted controls the amount of applied suppression. The Spill Suppression controls allow you to customize the color and luminance of the suppression. The tint and saturation parameters modify the magenta color (orange, when you are using a blue screen) that replaces the green spill when the Spill Level is increased. Spill Contrast helps remove the white outline that can appear around keyed subjects, just like the one here.

12 Position the playhead to 1:00 (or 30 frames). From the Zoom Level pop-up menu, choose 200% to get a better look at the problem.

13 Press H to choose the Pan tool. Drag in the Canvas until you see the male actor's head and back, which will make it easier for you to see the white outline problem.

The white fringe that remains after the softness adjustment is most clearly seen around the head and back of the male actor. To remove this, you'll move the White point handle on the Spill Contrast parameter.

14 Slowly drag the White point handle to about 0.70 to remove the white outline. The white outline darkens until it is no longer noticeable.

15 Press Shift-Z to fit the frame in the Canvas. Click Play to view your composite. Stop playback after you watch the project a few times.

The key looks complete. The last parameter in the Keyer, the Light Wrap parameter, is a bit of secret sauce that can really sell this shot by blending it with the background. You could apply it here in the Keyer as the last step, but if you are going to perform color corrections, it's better to leave it alone in the Keyer and set it later. But before you get to all of that, you'll quickly add and animate a shape mask that can remove unwanted areas in the foreground not covered by the green screen.

Creating a Garbage Mask

Your next step is to mask off the extraneous parts of the foreground that are not covered by the green screen. This so-called *garbage mask* creates a hole in the foreground layer to reveal the background layer underneath. It is meant to hide mike booms, C-stands, clamps, gaffer's tape, or anything in the foreground not covered by the green screen. You'll create the garbage mask using the B-Spline mask tool. Then you'll animate it to follow the camera move.

1   Move the playhead to the start of the project, and from the Zoom Level pop-up menu, choose 50% so you have enough room in the Canvas to draw outside the frame.

2   In the Layers list, select the *Green Screen* layer, and from the toolbar, choose the B-Spline Mask tool, or press Option-BB.

   B-splines, as you recall, are infinitely easier to deal with than Beziers when creating smooth curved shapes like your mask.

   The green screen does not cover the entire set to the left of the frame so it is visible in your composite. You'll draw the mask around this entire unwanted area to remove it.

3   Draw a rough mask around the left side of the shot that the green screen does not cover.

TIP ▶ As you adjust shapes, it is sometimes easier to toggle the Canvas overlays off and on from the View menu, or by pressing Command-/ (slash). Doing so will hide the red mask lines and control points so that you can better see the final result.

4   After you complete the mask shape, Command-click the upper-right control point, and drag out to create a sharp corner. Do the same for the lower-left control point and the upper-left point, if necessary.

TIP ▶ To create a sharp corner on a B-spline shape, you can also Control-click the control point and choose Linear from the shortcut menu.

By default, the mask protects what is inside it and makes transparent whatever falls outside it. But you need the reverse of this behavior.

5   Open the HUD and set the Mask Blend mode to Subtract so the mask now hides the offending area instead of isolating it.

TIP ▶ Alternatively, you can choose Subtract or select the Invert checkbox in the Inspector.

You've already done the work to animate the mask, even though you may not realize it. The Match Move you applied to the background is the same animation needed for your mask. You just need to duplicate the Match Move behavior onto the B-Spline Mask layer.

6   Option-drag the Match Move behavior from the *Background* layer in the Layers list to the *B-Spline Mask* layer.

TIP ▶ You can also animate a mask by tracking each control point on the shape by using the Track Points behavior.

7   Press Shift-Z to fit the Canvas in the window, and in the transport controls, click "Play from start" to view the composite. Save your work when you finish viewing the project.

You had it pretty easy with this animation. When you have to animate a mask using keyframes, keep a couple of things in mind: First, you want to create as few control points as possible. It's better to create several shapes than to create one large shape with many points. Remember, however, that the more control points you have, the more time it will take to animate them.

Second, you may not need to animate every control point on every frame. You can save time if you animate just the first and last frames, animate the frame in the middle of those keyframes, and keep "splitting the difference" by animating the frame in the middle of two other existing keyframes until you are satisfied with the result.

Color Correcting a Shot

A critical step when completing your composite is to blend the color and tone of the foreground subjects and background so they look like a single seamless shot.

You can match the contrast and color levels of the foreground shot to the background using a flexible Levels filter, then match the vibrancy in the clips (or lack thereof) with a slight saturation change, and finally improve the edge blending using a new blend mode developed just for keying.

1   Select the *Green screen* layer, and in the toolbar, click the Add Filter pop-up menu and choose Color Correction > Levels.

TIP ▶ If you don't select the layer first, the filter is applied to the B-Spline mask and will have no effect.

The Levels filter is added to the Filters pane in the Inspector. The Levels filter is a great all-around filter because in one filter it gives you instant access to multiple fundamental color correction parameters.

2   Press F3 to open the Filters pane of the Inspector, and position the playhead around 4:00 (or frame 121) so the two actors fill a large part of the Canvas.

The background has a very low-contrast, low-saturation look. You need to match that by reducing the contrast areas in your foreground shot. You can do so by adjusting the midtones in the Levels control.

3   In the Filters pane of the Inspector, drag the middle gray handle under the Level's histogram to flatten the midtones of the foreground until they closely match the contrast of the background (about 1.2).

Flattening the midtones, or gamma, evens out the overall foreground without affecting its brightest or darkest areas, and more closely matches the clip's tones to the background. But the actors still appear quite a bit redder than the background. To more precisely examine the differences, you can compare the red, green, and blue values of the background pixels to the foreground pixels.

4   Choose Motion > Preferences to open the Motion Preferences window.

5   In the Appearance pane, select the Color checkbox, and then close the Preferences window.

The status bar above the Canvas now displays red, green, and blue (RGB) pixel values. As you move the pointer over the Canvas, these values update to reflect the RGB values of the pixel under the pointer.

6   Move the pointer over the tan building to the left of the actor's head.

In the status bar, the values are close for red and green at about 0.500, and slightly lower for blue.

NOTE ▶ The RGBA values are calculated based on 32-bit floating-point bit depth. A value of 0 means no color in that channel, and a value of 1 means full color for that channel.

7   Move the pointer over the male actor's neck.

Here, the status bar shows consistently higher red values—in the mid 0.600s or so—while green and blue values are lower.

You can use the Levels filter to reduce the red value and more closely match the green and blue levels to the background.

8   In the Filters pane, from the RGB pop-up menu, choose Red. Any changes you make to the histogram will now affect only the red channel.

9   Drag the red midtone handle very slightly to the right to about 0.90. Then position the pointer in the Canvas to check the RGB values on the man's neck to verify that the red value is lower and green has risen. Be sure to also visually check that the actors match well with the background.

The Levels filter has handled most of the work, but the color still looks a bit too vibrant on the actors compared to the background. You'll add a Saturation filter to reduce the color vibrancy of your actors.

10 In the Layers list, select the *Green Screen* layer. In the toolbar, click the Add Filter pop-up menu, and choose Color Correction > Hue/Saturation.

11 In the Filters pane of the Inspector, drag the Saturation slider to –0.2 to slightly reduce the color on the actors.

The last color-related task for this project is to revisit the Light Wrap parameter you skipped when adjusting the Keyer. Light wrap blends the background tones with edges of the foreground, creating a subtle but realistic edge-blending effect. If you were not going to color correct the actors, you could have applied light wrap in the Keyer. But when you do color correct the foreground, you want to do that before you add light wrap. Thoughtfully, Motion includes light wrap in the Properties pane so you can add it after all the color correction filters are applied.

12 With the *Green Screen* layer selected in the Layers list, press F1 to open the Properties pane in the Inspector. From the Blend Mode pop-up menu, choose Light Wrap.

The default settings are pretty good. However, you can click the Light Wrap disclosure triangle to view the parameters and manually try to improve the default. But be careful not to create a halo effect around the actors by increasing the Amount parameter too much.

13 When you are done adjusting the Light Wrap values to suit yourself, play the project, and save your work.

You have just about completed the entire composite. Feel free to adjust the levels further to refine your composite and even go back and adjust the Keyer. You should now have a solid understanding of compositing fundamentals. But remember, you have to do one last thing to complete this project. You have actors ducking in a shot for no apparent reason. Because you have some experience using Motion particles, let's add a particle effect to complete your shot.

Using Particles in a Composite

You can use Motion particles as design elements, as you have done in previous lessons, or as realistic visual effects, as in this exercise. You'll add and customize a Motion explosion particle effect to finish your composite.

1   Drag the playhead to 5:15 (or frame 166).

This is a good location to place your particles because it is just a frame or two before the actors begin to duck.

2   Press Command-Shift-A to make sure nothing is selected in the Layers list.

3   Press Command-2 to open the Library. Click Particle Emitters and select the Pyro category.

4   Drag the Shrapnel Explosion particle into the Layers list. Release the mouse button when the insertion line appears just below the project icon.

The particle is added to the Canvas as a group called *Group*. It's a bit unwieldy in the Timeline and Layers list because all the groups are open showing all of their inner layers. Let's close all the groups to make the list more manageable, and then correctly position *Group* between the *Foreground* group and the *Background* group.

5   Click the disclosure triangles to close *Group*, the *Foreground* group, and the *Background* group in both the Timeline layers list and the Layers list.

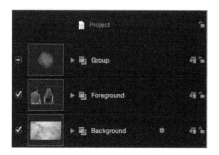

6   In the Layers list, select *Group*, and then choose Object > Send Backward.

The group is now correctly layered beneath the actors and above the background.

7   Click Play to see the explosion and then stop playback. Position the playhead at the end of the project.

It's not that impressive an explosion. You'll need to position and scale the explosion so that it appears more like something the actors would duck from and not just a spark from your BBQ igniter.

8   With *Group* selected, drag it to the lower-center of the Canvas, and watch the dynamic alignment guides to ensure that it is centered.

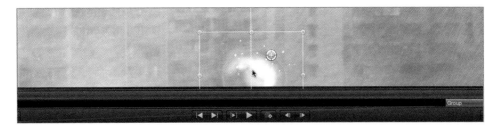

9   In the Canvas, Shift-drag the top-center scale handle for the *Group* group until it reaches just above the roofs of the buildings in the background. You will need to reposition *Group* to recenter it in the Canvas after scaling.

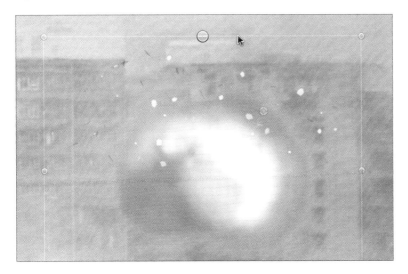

10 Play the project to view the explosion, and then stop playback and position the play-head at the end of the project.

You may need to finesse the explosion's position, but overall it's looking good. Scaling the entire particle explosion worked for the most part, but the pieces of shrapnel look a little too comical for this shot because they are so large. You can easily customize any portion or cell of a particle system in the Inspector.

11 In the Layers list, click the disclosure triangle for the group to reveal the *Shrapnel Explosion* layer. Then click the disclosure triangle for the *Shrapnel Explosion* layer.

The three particle cell layers that make up this particle effect are revealed in the Layers list. One of the cell layers is named *shrapnel*, which makes it easy to decide which cell you need to scale down.

12 Select the *shrapnel* cell layer.

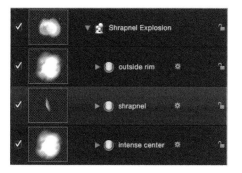

13 Press Command-3 to open the Inspector for the cell layer.

The Scale parameter is located at the bottom of the Inspector. You'll use the Scale slider to scale down the shrapnel to a size that is more appropriate for your composite.

14 Drag the Scale slider to 2%, and then play the project to review the new shrapnel size. Stop playback when you are done viewing the explosion.

Two more things will really make this explosion fit within your composite: correcting its color and its blending. First, to better fit the color of the explosions within the scene, duplicate the color correction filters you applied to the *Green screen* layer and copy them onto your particles.

15 In the Layers list, open the *Foreground* group, and then open the *Green screen* layer to view the filters applied to it.

16 In the Layers list, click the Hue/Saturation filter, and then Command-click the Levels filter.

17 With both filters selected, Option-drag the filters onto the *Group* group in the Layers list.

The color adjustment is done. In the last step, you will apply a Screen blend mode to the particles to integrate them with the background.

18 In the Layers list, select the *Group* group, and in the Inspector, click the Properties pane. Set Blend Mode to Screen, and play the project.

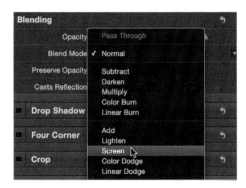

The Screen blend mode blends most of the explosion with the background but maintains its dark smoky shadows and bright white core explosion.

19 Stop playback and save your project.

You've done it. You started with two simple clips and created a realistic composite using stabilization, tracking, keying, color correction, masking, and particles. Although Motion excels at creating motion graphics and animating design elements, it also makes realistic visual effects fairly simple to achieve.

Lesson Review

1. You want to create a hole in a layer to reveal the layers underneath. You add a mask with the B-Spline tool, but instead of creating a hole in the layer, it restricts the layer's visibility to the area inside the circle. How can you make it do the opposite?

2. What types of camera movements can you stabilize using the Stabilize behavior?

3. When using the Match Move behavior to track the position of one layer to another, do you apply the behavior to the layer that will inherit the new movement or to the layer that has the movement you want?

4. How can you create a sharp corner in a B-Spline mask?

5. If shades of the green or blue screen are not totally removed when you first apply the Keyer filter, how can you add additional shades?

6. You are looking at a keyed shot and the foreground subject has some areas of green fringe around it. Which parameter of the Keyer filter do you adjust?

7. You've perfected the matte on your subject, but a white ring appears around the foreground subjects. Describe one of two approaches to remove the white ring.

8. In what two areas can you find the Light Wrap parameters, and when would you adjust them in each location?

9. How can you check the actual RGB values of an area in your clip?

10. What does the Strength slider do in the Keyer filter?

Answers

1. In the HUD or the Mask pane of the Inspector, choose Subtract from the Mask Blend Mode pop-up menu, or click Invert in the Inspector.

2. Position, Rotation, and Scale

3. The Match Move behavior is applied to the layer you want to inherit the new movement.

4. Command-drag the control point (or Control-click the control point), and from the shortcut menu, choose Linear.

5. In the Inspector, click the Sample Color button and drag a selection rectangle around the additional color shades you want to remove.

6. The Spill Level parameter

7. Adjust the Shrink/Expand parameter to shrink the matte, or adjust the White point handle in the Spill Contrast graph.

8. The Light Wrap parameters can be found in the Keyer filter or in the Blend Mode menu on the Properties pane. You would use the Light Wrap in the Blend Mode menu when you plan to color correct the foreground of the key. Otherwise you can use the Light Wrap setting in the Keyer.

9. Select the Color checkbox in Motion Preferences, and move the pointer over pixels in the image.

10. The Strength slider adjusts the core transparency. When you reduce the slider value, you reduce the transparency by narrowing the range of green or blue used to create the matte.

Keyboard Shortcuts

Option-BB   Choose the B-Spline Mask tool

An Introduction to Publishing and Rigging

11

Lesson Files	Motion5_Book_Files > Lessons > Lesson_11
Media	Motion5_Book_Files > Media > Audi_FCP_X, Audi_Motion
Time	This lesson takes approximately 45 minutes to complete.
Goals	Preview, apply, and adjust Final Cut Pro title effects
	Modify Final Cut Pro effects in Motion
	Create a Smart Motion Template from scratch
	Publish template parameters

Publishing Smart Templates for Final Cut Pro X

Motion is a powerful motion graphics and effects tool on its own. But when you add Final Cut Pro X to the mix, a new world of possibilities opens up. All the preset effects that are available in Final Cut Pro—titles, transitions, generators, and other effects—are actually Motion project files, called Smart Motion Templates. They were created in Motion and can be modified in Motion.

Furthermore, you can create your own Smart Motion Templates from scratch and then *publish* them to Final Cut Pro. And not only can you publish the project, you can choose to publish *specific parameters* of the project, which makes those parameters available to the Final Cut Pro editor.

In this lesson, you'll open and review an edited Final Cut Pro project. You'll then apply, adjust, and modify a preset title. From there, you'll create your own smart template title and choose several parameters to publish to Final Cut Pro.

> **NOTE ▶** In order to follow all the steps in this chapter and the next, Final Cut Pro X must be installed on your computer.

Setting Up the Final Cut Pro Project

In this lesson, you will create effects for an edited project in Final Cut Pro. To enable Final Cut Pro to see the project, however, you must move the Final Cut Pro project folder and event folder to the proper locations.

1   In the Finder, open a new window, navigate to Motion5_Book_Files > Media > Audi_FCP_X and open the Final Cut Events and Final Cut Projects folders.

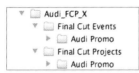

In each of these folders you'll find a folder named Audi Promo. You must place these two Audi Promo folders in the enclosing folders that already exist in your Movies folder with the same names (Final Cut Events and Final Cut Projects). When you've done this, Final Cut Pro will be able to find them.

2   Open a new Finder window, and from the sidebar, select the Movies folder.

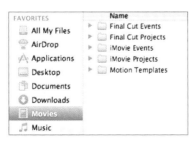

> **NOTE ▶** If you have already been working with Final Cut Pro, you may find other folders inside the Final Cut Events and Final Cut Projects folders. If you don't have Final Cut Events and Final Cut Projects folders in your Movies folder, you should create them for this lesson.

3   Drag the Audi Promo folder from Media > Final Cut Events to Movies > Final Cut Events.

4   Drag the Audi Promo folder from Media > Final Cut Projects to Movies > Final Cut Projects.

5   Confirm that the Audi Promo folders are now contained in Movies > Final Cut Events and in Movies > Final Cut Projects.

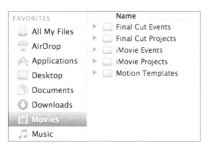

6   Open Final Cut Pro. If necessary, press Command-0 to open the Project Library.

The Audi Promo project now appears in the Project Library, along with any other projects you may have created.

7   Double-click the Audi Promo project to open it, and play the project.

The project is a short promotional spot for the Audi R8, shot on location at the Infineon Raceway in Sonoma, California. The edit is completed, or "locked," but the speaker needs to be identified.

Working with Effects Presets

Final Cut Pro contains a huge number of preset effects, transitions, titles, and generators collectively called "effects"—and you can modify all of them in a variety of ways. In this exercise, you'll work with a title effect from the Titles Browser.

1   Click in the middle of the **Paul_006** clip to select it, and then press the Up Arrow to move the playhead to the first visible frame of the clip, which will appear in the Viewer.

To identify the speaker, Paul Gerrard, you can add a title on top of the video clip.

2   In the Toolbar under the Viewer, hover the pointer over the Titles Browser (T) button to view the tooltip, and then click it.

As the tooltip indicates, clicking this button shows or hides the Titles Browser, which contains over 150 titling effects organized into five categories.

NOTE ▸ In addition to the Titles Browser, Final Cut Pro X includes browsers for Effects, Transitions, Generators, Themes, Photos, and Music and Sounds.

3 Select the Lower Thirds category, and then move the pointer across the first title, *Clouds*.

By moving the pointer, or *skimming*, across the preview thumbnail, the title animation plays in both the thumbnail and in the Viewer so you can preview the title before
applying it to your project.

4   Scroll down to the Boxes section and skim the Left title to preview the animation.
    With a few adjustments, this title may work with your video clip.

5   With the playhead still located on the first visible frame of the Paul_006 clip, double-
    click the Boxes > Left title to add it to the project at the playhead position. The title
    appears as a purple bar over the video clip.

6   Press Command-= (equals) twice to zoom in on the playhead position and then select
    the title.

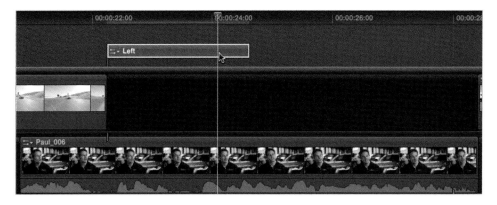

When the title is selected and the Timeline active, the title is outlined in yellow. In the
Viewer, the two lines of text each have a box around them, indicating that they are
editable.

NOTE ▶ You may need to move the playhead to a frame of the title where you can see
all the text on the screen.

7   In the Viewer, double-click the *Up Next* text to select a single word, and then press
    Command-A to select all the text in that text box. Type *PAUL GERRARD*, and press
    the Esc key to exit the text editing mode.

8   Now replace the *Name* text with Paul's title: *Director of Training, Audi Sportscar Experience*. That's a long title. It doesn't even fit on the screen! You can fix that in the Inspector.

9   At the far right of the toolbar, click the Inspector (I) button to open the Inspector.

The Inspector has buttons across the top for adjusting different aspects of the title.

10 Select the Text button. In the Canvas, reselect all the title text in the Viewer, and then in the Inspector, adjust the Size parameter to about 52 so that Paul's full title fits on the screen.

11 In the Inspector, move the pointer over the Face bar, and click Show when it appears. Click the Color swatch, and choose a red color for Paul's title.

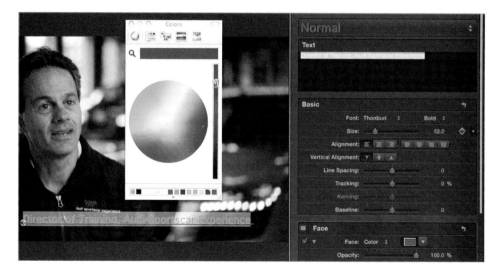

12 Close the Colors window, click the red title text, and press the Esc key to exit the text editing mode.

The Text Inspector contains many of the parameters for modifying text you have already seen in Motion. Feel free to change the font; add an outline, glow, or drop shadow; or change other properties to your liking.

NOTE ▶ The first text box (containing Paul's name) has a blend mode applied to "cut out" the text from the blue background and reveal the video underneath. Therefore, you can't alter its color as you can for the second text box.

NOTE ▶ Unlike Motion, where you should save your work often, Final Cut Pro X has no File > Save command! A Final Cut Pro project is saved for you automatically after every change you make.

13 In the Inspector, click the Title button, and from the pop-up menus, try out the different values available for Color Theme and Shape.

The parameters available in the Title Inspector have been "published" by the title designer—that's why they are called Published Parameters. Although the arrow shape works for this promo, none of the color theme choices work that well. But you can create more options by modifying the title in the application that created it: Motion.

Modifying Effects Presets

The beautiful thing about all these titles in the Titles Browser (and just about all the transitions, effects, and generators in their respective browsers) is that they were created using Motion. This means that you can modify them in Motion! Although these presets are very flexible, if you can't get them to look precisely the way you want, you can open a copy in Motion, and change the preset to suit your purpose exactly. In this exercise, you'll make a few changes to the Left title to make it a better match for the Audi project.

1   In the Titles Browser, Control-click (or right-click) the Boxes > Left thumbnail, and
    from the shortcut menu, choose "Open a copy in Motion."

The title opens in Motion with the name Left Copy.moti. The *.moti* indicates that this
project is a Motion *Title* project. In the Layers list, you'll find a new layer called a *rig*
with two layers beneath it: *Color* and *Shape*. These layers are "widgets." You'll create
your own Rig and widgets in Lesson 12.

2   Select the *Color* widget, and press F4 to open the Widget Inspector.

The Color pop-up menu contains the same color options you saw in Final Cut Pro. Let's add a new item to the list.

3   From the Color pop-up menu, choose Purple (the last option). Click the Add (+) button next to the Color pop-up menu, and in the highlighted Color field, type *Red*.

By selecting the last menu item before adding a new one, your new menu option appears at the bottom of the list.

4   Use the color picker to change the color of the middle color swatch to a light red, and then change the color of the bottom color swatch to a darker red.

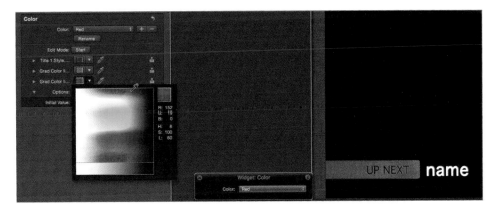

NOTE ▶ The top swatch for the text color has no visible effect because the text within the colored shape is transparent.

Let's also change the default shape and font so that you won't need to make these changes in Final Cut Pro.

5   In the Layers list, select the Shape widget; and in the Widget Inspector, from the Shape pop-up menu, choose Arrow.

6   Open the *Scene 2* group, the *Lower 3rd* group, and the *text* group. Select the *Title 1* text layer, and use the HUD to change the font to Arial Bold and Size to 46. Then change the *Title 2* text layer to Arial Regular and its Size value to 52.

7   Select the *Gradient* layer. In the Canvas, Control-click the gradient to choose the Edit Position tool, and drag the rightmost color tag to the left to brighten more of the arrow tip.

8   Press Shift-S to return to the Select/Transform tool, and then press Command-S to save your work.

Because this project is a ".moti" title project, it is automatically published to the Titles Browser in Final Cut Pro. Let's see for ourselves.

9   Press Command-Tab to switch to Final Cut Pro X. The title in the Timeline hasn't changed. When you change a Final Cut Pro effect project in Motion, only the Browser copy is changed.

10   In the Titles Browser, reselect the Lower Thirds category, and scroll down to the Boxes section.

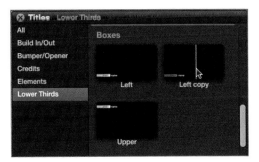

There's your new "Left Copy" title, and its preview reflects the new default color and arrow shape.

TIP ▶ "Left Copy" may not be the best name for this title. While you could choose Save As in Motion to change the name, the "Left Copy" project would remain in the Titles Browser. To change the name, in the Finder, navigate to User/Movies/Motion Templates/Titles/Lower Thirds/Boxes. Rename the Left Copy folder and the Left Copy. moti Motion project as you want. Then quit and reopen Final Cut Pro.

11 With the title still selected in the Timeline (as indicated by the gray outline), in the Titles Browser, double-click the Left Copy title to update the Timeline version.

The Timeline title name updates to Left Copy, and the design updates in the Viewer. Notice, however, that the custom text you previously entered remains intact, so you don't need to retype it.

12 Move the playhead to the start of the title, and play the project to watch the animation. Clearly, a viewer won't have enough time to comfortably read the full title.

13 Drag the right edge of the title to extend its duration by 2 seconds, and then play the title. It now lasts long enough to read.

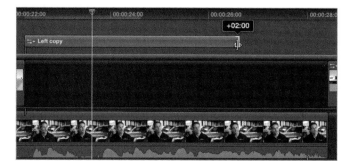

Terrific. You can see how easy it is to apply Final Cut Pro preset effects and modify them in Motion. But for the most creative control, you'll want to create your own Smart Motion Templates from scratch.

Creating Smart Motion Templates

As you've learned, the effects in Final Cut Pro X (effects, transitions, titles, and generators) were created in Motion using special project types called Smart Motion Templates. In this next exercise, you'll make your own Smart Template and a custom title for the Audi Promo. You'll also publish some parameters so that you can modify it in Final Cut Pro.

1   Press Command-Tab to return to Motion from Final Cut Pro, choose File > Close or press Command-W to close the current project, and then press Command-N to open a new Motion project.

When you create a new project in Motion, you have to choose the project type. The Project Browser displays five project types. So far, you have worked only with standard Motion projects. The other projects types are Smart Motion Templates for Final Cut Pro.

2   In the Blank category, click the Final Cut Title icon. Change the Preset pop-up menu to Broadcast HD 1080, the Frame Rate to 29.97, and the Duration to 5 seconds.

NOTE ▸ To see the Final Cut Pro Title icon text, you may need to resize the Project Browser by dragging its lower-right corner.

Because you chose the largest HD preset, this title will automatically scale down when used in Final Cut Pro Timelines with the same aspect ratio but lower resolution project settings. In this case, five seconds should be enough time for the title animation. If not, you can always adjust it in Final Cut Pro.

3   Click Open to open the new project, and press Shift-Z to fit the Canvas to the window.

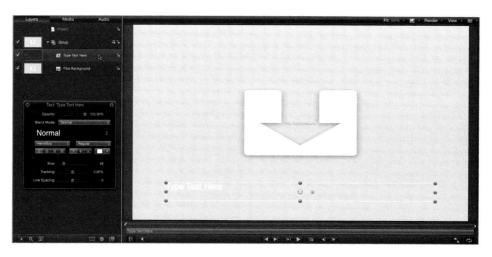

Unlike standard Motion projects that are empty when first opened, each new Smart Motion Template has content specific to each effect type. Final Cut Title projects contain a *Text* layer, and a "placeholder" layer named *Title Background*.

This placeholder represents the video under your title in Final Cut Pro and serves two purposes. First, it allows you to add a video clip or an image to the background of the project so that you can design "in context." Second, any effects you may choose to apply to it (such as filters, behaviors, and masks) will be applied to the video underneath the title in Final Cut Pro.

For this title, you won't apply any effects to the underlying video, but because you are designing this title to work for a specific shot, it can be helpful to add that shot here.

NOTE ▸ Although the placeholder layer looks like a Drop Zone (available under the Object menu), it is not the same. Do not delete the *Title Background* placeholder layer. If you do, it cannot be added back into the project.

4   In the File Browser, select the Movies folder. Locate Final Cut Events > Audi Promo > Original Media > **Paul_006.mov**, and drag it to the Canvas. When you see the yellow outline, release the mouse button.

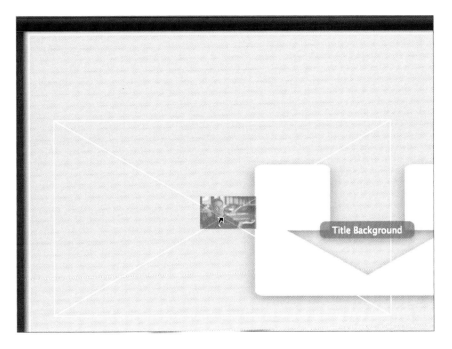

The video clip now appears in the Canvas. However, it can be distracting to see it during the design process, so let's turn it off for the time being.

5   In the Layers list, deselect the activation checkbox to turn off the *Title Background* layer.

Now you can design on a blank, empty Canvas, but at any time you can turn on the video clip layer to make sure that graphics aren't blocking the speaker. Speaking of graphics, let's add some after we save this project.

6   Press Command-S to save the project.

A new dialog appears. Because this project is a Smart Motion Template (specifically, a Final Cut Pro Title), you need to provide some information to establish how it will appear in Final Cut Pro.

7 For the Template Name, type *Audi Lower Third*.

8 For the Category, choose New Category, and name it *Audi*.

9 Leave the Theme as None, deselect "Include unused media," and make sure Save Preview Movie is also deselected because you haven't designed anything yet.

> Enter a name for the Final Cut Pro Title, and choose which folder to keep it. You may also assign a theme to your template.
>
> Template Name: | Audi Lower Third
> Category: | Audi
> Theme: | None
>
> ☐ Include unused media
> ☐ Save Preview Movie
>
> (Cancel) (Publish)

10 Click Publish.

The project is published to Final Cut Pro's Titles Browser and is immediately available. However, it's not very interesting yet, so let's add some graphics and animation.

NOTE ▶ The project is saved to ~/Movies/Motion Templates, in the appropriate folder for the type of effect—in this case, Titles. The project, media, and thumbnails are contained in a folder with the Category name (Audi), and within that, a folder with the Template name (Audi Lower Third).

11 In the File Browser, navigate to Motion5_Book_Files > Media > Audi_Motion.

This folder contains graphics you can use for designing the title.

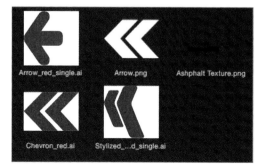

12 With the playhead still at the start of the project, add the Asphalt Texture.png and Arrow.png files to *Group*, and move the *Asphalt Texture* layer beneath the *Type Text Here* layer.

13 Select the *Arrow* layer, and in the Canvas, rotate it 180 degrees. Move it to the right of the text, using the dynamic guides to align it vertically with the text.

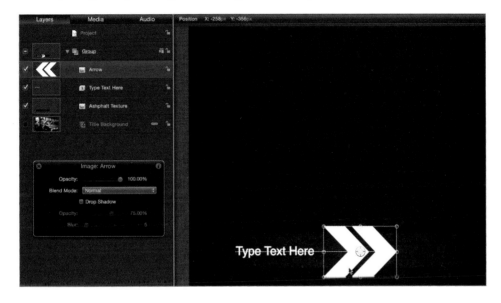

> **TIP** ▶ If you don't see the yellow dynamic guides, press N.

You can animate the arrow graphic across the screen, and use it to reveal the asphalt background.

14 With the *Arrow* layer selected, in the toolbar, click the Add Behavior pop-up menu, and choose Basic Motion > Motion Path.

15 Hold down Command-Spacebar, and drag left in the Canvas to create some room. Then move the starting control point for the motion path off the left side of the screen.

NOTE ▶ If pressing Command-Spacebar activates the Spotlight search field at the upper-right of your screen, deactivate this keyboard shortcut in the Spotlight section of System Preferences. Or, you can press Z to choose the Zoom tool and drag left in the Canvas, then press Shift-S to return to the Select/Transform tool.

16 Move the playhead to 1:00 and press O to trim the Out point of the Motion Path behavior. Play the project.

NOTE ▶ If the timing display is currently displaying frames instead of timecode, click the arrow to switch to timecode.

The arrows move across the screen in one second.

17 Save your work.

Completing the Animation

Now, with the basic elements in place, you'll reveal the asphalt background as the arrows move across the screen by using a new shape and an image mask. Then you'll animate the text onscreen, and fade everything out to complete the animation.

1   With the Motion Path behavior selected, press Shift-O to move the playhead to the Out point of the behavior. Choose View > Show Full View Area so you can see the arrows when they are offscreen.

2   In the toolbar, choose the Bezier tool, and in the Canvas, draw a shape that fits inside the first arrow on the right and extends all the way back to cover the asphalt image

on the left. It doesn't need to be perfect. It just needs to completely cover the asphalt image.

3   Press Shift-S to return to the Select/Transform tool. Return the playhead to Home, and press I to trim the In point of the new shape to the playhead. Rename this shape layer *Mask*.

4   In the Canvas, drag the *Mask* shape back so that it lines up with the arrow to the left of the screen.

5   Now Option-drag a copy of the Motion Path behavior from the *Arrow* layer to the *Mask* layer so that the shape will move along with the arrow.

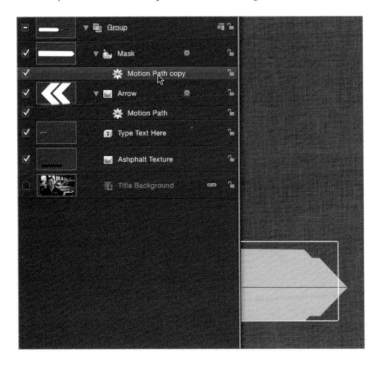

The *Mask* shape now follows the same motion path as the arrow.

6   Select the *Asphalt Texture* layer, choose Object > Add Image Mask, and drag the *Mask* layer to the well in the HUD. This action automatically turns off the visibility of the *Mask* layer.

7   Play the project. The *Asphalt Texture* layer is now revealed as the arrows pass over it.

> **TIP**   If you find the audio from the video clip annoying, click the small speaker button at the bottom left of the Canvas to mute the audio. Or, in the Project pane, select the Audio list, click the Link button for the audio track to unlink it from the video, and delete it.

Let's trim the text layer to have it appear after the arrows pass by, and then apply a behavior to animate the text onscreen.

8   Select the *Type Text Here* layer, move the playhead to 0:07, and press I to trim the layer to start at this frame. In the toolbar, click the Add Behavior pop-up menu, and choose Text Basic > Blur In.

9   In the mini-Timeline, trim the right edge of the behavior to a duration of 20 frames.

10 Scale down the *Arrow* layer to align with the top and bottom of the *Asphalt Texture* layer, and play the project.

The opening animation is complete. Now you can put all the elements into a group to fade them out at the end.

11 Close the *Arrow*, *Type Text Here*, and *Asphalt Texture* layers, and then Shift-click them. Choose Object > Group (not New Group), or press Shift-Command-G, to group them. Name the new group *Elements*.

12 Click the Add Behavior pop-up menu to add the Basic Motion > Fade In/Fade Out behavior to the group, and in the HUD set Fade In to 0.

13 Move the playhead to the end of the project, and press O to trim the Out point of the behavior.

14 Turn on the *Title Background* layer and play the project to see how it looks in context.

15 Turn off the *Title Background* layer and save your work.

Using Build In and Build Out Markers

Your title now animates on, remains still so you can read it, and animates off. And you've spent some time getting the animation to work just as you want. However, in Final Cut

Pro, if the title is trimmed, your animation will speed up or slow down to match the new length. That's not what you want here.

Fortunately, Motion has anticipated this situation and provides a solution in the form of two specialized markers you can use to force the opening and closing animations to play at their designed speeds, no matter how much your title is "stretched" or "squashed" in Final Cut Pro.

1　Move the playhead to a point a few frames past the opening animation, about 1:05.

2　Choose Edit > Deselect All. Choose Mark > Markers > Add Marker, and then choose Mark > Markers > Edit Marker. A project marker appears in the ruler area of the Timeline.

> **TIP** Remember, pressing Shift-M will also add a project marker even if a layer, group, or effect is selected. When the playhead is parked on a marker, you can press Command-Option-M to open the Edit Marker dialog. You can also double-click a marker to edit it (but you may first need to move the playhead out of the way).

3　From the Type pop-up menu, choose Build In – Optional.

The Build In and Build Out markers "lock in" the opening or closing animation to the number of frames established in the Motion project. "Optional" markers differ from the "mandatory" markers in that they offer the Final Cut Pro user the option to completely bypass the build-in or build-out animation.

4　Click OK.

5   Move the playhead to a point a few frames before the ending fade-out animation, about 4:05.

6   Press Shift-M to add a project marker, and press Command-Option-M to edit the marker. Choose Build Out – Optional, and click OK to change the marker type.

7   Move the playhead out of the way so you can see both markers, and move the pointer over each one.

The marker shapes have changed to small green flags, each pointing toward the animated part of the project. Moving the pointer over a marker displays the marker type. The ruler area between the markers is shaded gold to indicate that this region of the project will be extended or shortened when the title is trimmed in Final Cut Pro. Because this region has no animation, the animated portions are "protected." That is, they will play at the same speed no matter how long or short the full title plays in Final Cut Pro. Let's test it.

8   Press Command-S to save your work, and then press Command-Tab to switch to Final Cut Pro.

9   In the Timeline, select the Left Copy title.

10 In the Titles Browser, select the new Audi category, and skim over the Audi Lower Third preview thumbnail.

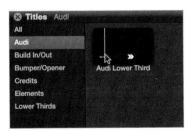

Your title animates in both the thumbnail and the Viewer, even though you haven't created a preview movie! This is because when no preview movie is available, Final Cut Pro plays the Motion project itself.

NOTE ► If you do not see the new Audi category in the Titles Browser, quit and reopen Final Cut Pro.

TIP Although Final Cut Pro will play the preview directly from the Motion project, it is good practice to create a preview movie in Motion when your project is completed. The preview movie will load faster and play more smoothly than a preview of the Motion project.

11 Double-click the Audi Lower Third title to replace the selected title in the Timeline, and play the title.

The new title design animates, and it is automatically updated with Paul's name and title.

12 Trim the title to make it shorter or longer, and play the title animation.

The title still animates on and off at the same speed. What if you didn't want it to animate at all?

NOTE ► To ensure that the title is playing in real time, select it and press Control-R to render it.

13 Select the title, and then go to the Title Inspector and click the Title button.

Because you chose optional Build In and Build Out markers, checkboxes appear in the list of published parameters. If you don't want the title to animate on or off, simply deselect the appropriate checkbox.

14 Deselect the Build In checkbox, and play the title.

As you can see, Build In and Build Out markers are automatically published to the Title Inspector in Final Cut Pro. But you can manually select other parameters to publish as well.

Publishing Parameters

By publishing specific parameters of a Smart Motion Template, you can give a Final Cut Pro editor more control over the look of an effect. For this Audi title, let's publish parameters that will allow a Final Cut Pro editor to change the color of the arrows, the opacity of the background graphic, and the overall position of the entire title animation.

1 Press Command-Tab to switch back to Motion.

2 Move the playhead to a frame where you can see the *Arrow* layer. Select it in the Layers list, and from the Add Filter pop-up menu, choose Color Correction > Colorize.

3 In the HUD, click the downward-facing arrow next to the Remap White To color swatch, and choose a red color.

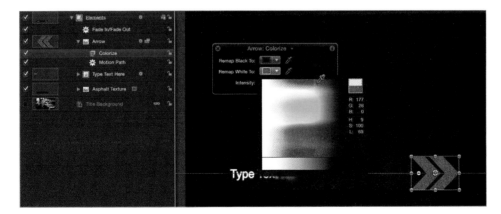

This red will be the default color of the arrows, but you want to be able to change the color in Final Cut Pro.

4   Press F3 to open the Filters Inspector.

5   Click the Animation menu for the Remap White To parameter (the small downward-facing arrow at the far right of the parameter name) and choose Publish.

That's all you need to do to make a parameter available in Final Cut Pro! But you may want to change its name. To do so, use the Project Inspector.

6   In the Layers list, select the *Project* layer, and then go to the Project Inspector and click the Publishing button.

There is your color swatch. However, "Remap White To" isn't going to make much sense in Final Cut Pro. Luckily, you can change published parameter names to anything you like.

7   Double-click the Remap White To parameter name, and change it to *Arrow Color*.

Next, the dark asphalt texture might look better if it were partially transparent over certain shots. Or maybe the Final Cut Pro editor will want to remove it completely. You can enable both scenarios by publishing the opacity of the layer.

8   In the Layers list, select the *Asphalt Texture* layer.

9   In the HUD, Control-click the parameter name Opacity, and from the shortcut menu, choose Publish.

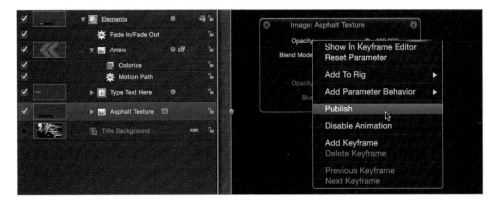

As you can see, you can publish certain parameters directly from the HUD. Now, let's allow the Final Cut Pro user to shift the vertical position of the entire animation, just in case it's blocking something important in the underlying video.

10   In the Layers list, drag the *Mask* layer into the *Elements* group.

You'll change the position of the *Elements* group, and you want the mask to move with everything else.

11 Select the *Elements* group, and press F1 to open the Properties Inspector. Click the disclosure triangle for Position, Control-click the Y, and choose Publish. This action publishes the vertical (Y) position of the group containing the entire title animation.

12 Select the project in the Layers list, and return to the Publishing pane of the Project Inspector.

13 Rename Opacity to *Asphalt Opacity*, and rename Y.Position to *Vertical Position*.

You can even change the order of published parameters.

14 Drag the Asphalt Opacity parameter above the Arrow Color parameter. Then drag it back down again.

TIP The last selected parameter in the Inspector remains selected, as indicated by a highlight. Command-click the parameter to turn off the highlight.

Let's see how your newly published parameters work in Final Cut Pro.

15 Save your work and switch to Final Cut Pro.

16 With the Timeline title selected, double-click the Browser version of the title to update the Timeline version.

17 In the Timeline, select the title, and in the Title Inspector, experiment with changing the values for Arrow Color, Asphalt Opacity, and Vertical Position. In the Viewer, you can see the arrows change color, the asphalt background fade or completely disappear, and the entire animation move up or down.

Great work! You've learned how to work with preset title effects in Final Cut Pro, how to modify a preset title in Motion, how to create your own Smart Motion Template from scratch, and how to publish parameters to give a Final Cut Pro editor more control. In the next lesson, you'll take this process a step further through the power of parameter rigs.

Lesson Review

1. Name the four kinds of effects in Final Cut Pro.

2. In Final Cut Pro, if you can't get the look you want for an effect by using the Published Parameters in the Inspector, how could you modify the effect?

3. How do you exit text editing mode in Final Cut Pro?

4. In Final Cut Pro, how can you preview a title animation in both the thumbnail and in the Viewer before applying it to your project?

5. In Motion, what content does a Final Cut Title project already contain?

6. How can you force Final Cut Pro to play your opening title animation at the same speed as your Motion project, no matter how the duration of the title is trimmed in Final Cut Pro?

7. Describe two ways you can publish a parameter of a Motion Smart Template so that it's available in Final Cut Pro.

8. How can you change the name of a published parameter?

Answers

1. Effects, Transitions, Titles, and Generators

2. Control-click the effect in the Browser, and choose "Open a copy in Motion" from the shortcut menu. Then change anything you like.

3. Press the Esc key.

4. Move the pointer or *skim* across the preview thumbnail.

5. A text layer and a placeholder layer named *Title Background*

6. In Motion, add a Build In marker to the Timeline on a frame after the opening animation has completed.

7. In Motion's Inspector, use the Animation menu, or Control-click the parameter name. Also, for some parameters, you can Control-click the parameter name in the HUD.

8. Select the project in the Layers list. Open the Project Inspector, and click the Publishing button. Double-click any parameter name to change it.

Keyboard Shortcuts

Command-Tab	Rotate through open applications
Command-0	In Final Cut Pro, opens the Project Library
Command-4	In Final Cut Pro, opens the Inspector
Q	In Final Cut Pro, connects the selected clip or effect to the primary storyline

12

Lesson Files	Motion5_Book_Files > Lessons > Lesson_12
Media	Motion5_Book_Files > Media > Audi_FCP_X, Audi_Motion
Time	This lesson takes approximately 90 minutes to complete.
Goals	Rig and publish a checkbox widget for a Final Cut Pro title
	Analyze the structure of a Final Cut Transition project
	Connect parameters with the Link behavior
	Rig and publish a pop-up widget
	Create a Final Cut effect project
	Rig and publish a slider widget

Lesson 12
Rigging and Publishing Widgets

In the previous lesson, you published both a project and specific project parameters from Motion to make them available for use in Final Cut Pro.

Parameter rigs take the publishing concept to a whole new level. A *rig* allows you to connect many parameters into a single control, called a *widget*. Instead of publishing several individual parameters, you publish a single widget that controls the parameters in ways that you specify, making it faster and easier to adjust an effect in Final Cut Pro.

Motion provides three types of widgets, and in this lesson, you'll work with all of them—checkboxes, pop-up menus, and sliders—to publish simple, powerful controls for Final Cut Pro X. You'll do this for three types of projects: a title, a transition, and an effect.

Rigging a Checkbox Widget

You finished the previous lesson by publishing an animated title and several parameters. Now, you'll give Final Cut Pro editors even more flexibility by publishing a rig to control the direction of that title animation.

1   Navigate to Motion5_Book_Files > Lessons > Lesson_12 > Audi Lower Third Start, and open the Audi Lower Third.moti project.

This file is a completed version of the project you made in the previous lesson. Before you work with it, however, you need to publish it to Final Cut Pro X.

2   Choose File > Save As. Name the template *Audi Lower Third*, and save it to the Audi category. (Create the category, if necessary.) Do not include unused media, click Publish, and if necessary, click Replace.

NOTE ▸ This project will replace the one you created in the previous lesson unless you give it a different name.

3   Play the project to reacquaint yourself with the animation.

The arrows fly onto the screen from the left to the right, revealing the asphalt texture. The text then animates on in the same direction. But what if you wanted to reverse this animation?

In this exercise you'll enable your Final Cut Pro editor to change the direction of the animation so the arrows and the text move from right to left.

While you could publish all the individual parameters required to make these changes, a rig enables you to connect these parameters to a single control, called a widget, that you can publish to Final Cut Pro. But before you can add a widget to your project, you need to create a rig to contain it.

4   Stop playback. Choose Object > New Rig.

A new layer named *Rig* appears in the Layers list. A rig is a container for widgets much like a group is a container for layers.

5 Press F4 to open the Rig Inspector.

The Rig Inspector contains three buttons representing the three types of widgets that you can add to a rig: Slider, Pop-up, and Checkbox.

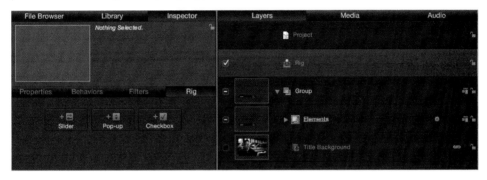

6 Click the Checkbox button.

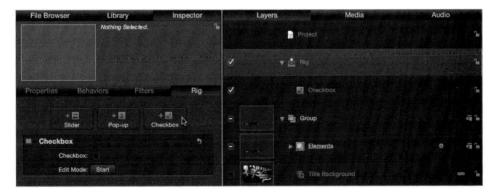

The checkbox widget appears under the *Rig* layer in the Layers list. Let's change its name to something that describes its function: reversing the animation's direction when the checkbox is selected.

7 In the Layers list, double-click the *Checkbox* layer name to select the text, type *Reverse*, and press Return.

With the widget selected in the Layers list, the fourth pane of the Inspector becomes the Widget Inspector. In addition to containing your renamed Reverse checkbox, it also contains an Edit Mode option that has a Start button.

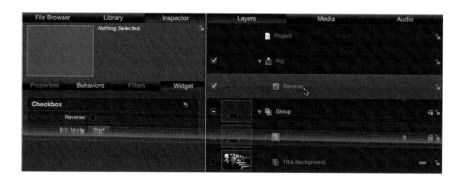

8 Click the Reverse checkbox to select it.

A checkbox is the simplest type of widget, because it has only two states: selected or deselected. Each of these states is called a *snapshot*, and each snapshot contains parameter values you select. When you change the snapshot by selecting and deselecting the checkbox, those parameter values change. That may seem confusing now, but it will be more understandable after you "rig" the widget.

In order for the checkbox widget to affect a parameter value, the parameter must be added to the widget. This process is called *rigging* the parameter to the widget. You can rig parameters to a widget manually or automatically. Let's rig parameters automatically using a special mode called Rig Edit Mode.

9 With the Reverse checkbox selected, in the Widget Inspector, click the Edit Mode Start button.

A window appears to remind you that you are in Rig Edit Mode. Any parameter changes you make will now be stored as part of the checkbox widget's "checked" state. So you'll now make all the changes necessary to reverse the animation.

10 In the Layers list, open the group named *Group*, the *Elements* group, and the *Arrow* layer. Select the *Motion Path* behavior, and in the HUD or the Behaviors Inspector, change the Direction parameter from Forward to Reverse. Play the project.

The arrow now moves to the left, but it's still pointing to the right.

11 Press F1 to go to the Properties Inspector, and change the Rotation parameter from 180 degrees to 0.

That's better, but the mask revealing the asphalt graphic also needs to point and animate in the opposite direction.

12 In the Layers list, open the *Mask* layer. Select the *Motion Path copy* behavior, and in the HUD or the Behaviors Inspector, set its Direction parameter to Reverse.

The mask now animates in the correct direction, but it isn't properly revealing the graphic.

13 Stop playback and click the *Mask* layer's activation checkbox so that you can see the layer in the Canvas. In the Properties Inspector, change its Rotation Z value to 180 degrees, and then in the Canvas, with the playhead at or near frame 23, drag the mask to the right to line it up with the first red chevron shape. Deselect the activation checkbox to hide the *Mask* layer and scrub through the project.

The mask reveals the asphalt texture as the arrows pass over. Now let's tackle the text.

14 Open the *Type Text Here* layer, select the Blur In behavior, and in the HUD or the Behaviors Inspector, change the Direction parameter to Backwards.

15 Move the playhead to a frame where the red chevrons have passed over the last letter of the text, at about frame 23. Select the *Type Text Here* layer, and press Shift-[(left bracket) to move the In point of the layer and behavior to the playhead. Play the project.

Now the text animates from right to left, matching the arrow animation; and it doesn't start to appear until after the chevrons have moved past it.

You've changed everything needed to reverse the entire animation.

16 In the floating window, click the Stop Rig Edit Mode button, and save your work.

Modifying, Testing, and Publishing a Widget

After you stop Rig Edit Mode, it's time to inspect the widget, test it, and publish it to Final Cut Pro.

1 In the Layers list, close *Group*, select the *Reverse* widget, and go to the Widget Inspector.

Every parameter you adjusted while in Rig Edit Mode now appears under the Reverse checkbox widget. Next to the Animation menu of each parameter, a joystick icon indicates that the parameter is rigged. What this joystick means is that the parameter's value is tied to a specific snapshot of the widget. Because the checkbox was selected while in Rig Edit Mode, the values you set are tied to the "checked" snapshot for the widget. You can see the values change when you change the snapshot.

2 Deselect the Reverse checkbox.

Notice that the values of most of the parameters change back to the original values that existed before you changed them in Rig Edit Mode.

NOTE ▶ The reason all the values don't necessarily change is that when parameters are added to a snapshot in Rig Edit Mode, all the channels of the parameter are added. For example, even if you just change the Z-rotation of a layer, Motion adds the X, Y, and Z rotation values to the widget.

3   Start playback and click the checkbox a few times.

When the checkbox is deselected, the animation plays left to right as it did when you first opened it. When it is selected, the animation plays right to left. This one simple checkbox widget controls the values of all the parameters rigged to it.

Now that you've rigged and tested the widget, the next step is to publish it.

NOTE ▶ When in Rig Edit Mode, you also moved the start of the *Type Text Here* layer to a new frame. But when you toggle the checkbox, the text layer does not return to its original position. This is because some project changes don't have an associated parameter you can rig to a widget. These changes include trimming and moving layers, and selecting or deselecting layer activation checkboxes. In this case, the animation still looks good in both directions with the text starting a little later, so you can leave it as it is.

4   Make sure the checkbox is deselected. This snapshot will be the default. Click the Animation menu for the Reverse widget, and choose Publish.

The widget now appears as a published parameter.

5   In the Layers list, select the *Project* layer.

6   Press F4 to open the Project Inspector, and if necessary, click the Publishing pane.

The Reverse checkbox appears below the other parameters you published in the last lesson. Let's see how this widget works in Final Cut Pro.

NOTE ▶ You can also test any published parameters here in the Project Inspector by changing their values. When you are satisfied, leave each parameter with the default value you want to publish to Final Cut Pro.

7   Save your work, close the project, and switch to Final Cut Pro, or open it, if necessary.

NOTE ▶ If you did not complete Lesson 11, you'll need to return to that lesson and complete the seven steps in the "Setting Up the Final Cut Pro Project" section. You'll then need to click in the middle of the **Paul_006** clip to select it, and press the Up Arrow to move the playhead to the first visible frame of the clip, which appears in the Viewer. You can then proceed to step 9.

8   Select the title in the Timeline.

9   In the Titles Browser, select the Audi category, and double-click the Audi Lower Third thumbnail to replace the Timeline version.

10   Select the title in the Timeline once more, and go to the Title Inspector. (If necessary, press Command-4 to open the Inspector, and then click the Title button.) Select the Reverse checkbox and play the title.

 Pressing the / (slash) key will play the selected item in the Timeline.

The animation plays in the opposite direction with the checkbox selected.

Congratulations, you've built and published your very first parameter rig! Next, you'll explore the pop-up widget using a completed transition project.

Deconstructing a Transition Project

The checkbox widget toggles between two snapshots, but sometimes you need more than just two options. The pop-up widget lets you set up as many snapshots as you like and display them in a list. In this exercise, you'll use a pop-up widget to rig three shape options for a transition that you will then apply to the Audi project in Final Cut Pro. You'll start with a completed Final Cut transition so that you can focus on the rigging process. Let's see how the transition is constructed.

1   Navigate to Motion5_Book_Files > Lessons > Lesson_12 > Audi Chevron Wipe Start, and double-click the Audi Chevron Wipe.motr project to open it in Motion.

   NOTE ▸ The file extension .motr indicates that the project is a Motion transition.

2   Choose File > Save As, and in the window that appears, name the template *Audi Chevron Wipe*. Create the Audi category, deselect "Include unused media," select Save Preview Movie, and click Publish.

Enter a name for the Final Cut Pro Transition, and choose which
folder to keep it. You may also assign a theme to your template.

Template Name: Audi Chevron Wipe

Category: Audi

Theme: None

☐ Include unused media

☑ Save Preview Movie

Cancel   Publish

Motion saves the project, and after a few seconds, generates a preview movie. Because
the design of this project is complete, you can immediately publish it to Final Cut Pro
along with a preview movie. Now, while you rig the project, you can save as you go by
pressing Command-S without the need to specify the publish settings.

3   In the Layers list, open the *Transition Placeholder* group. Press Shift-Z to fit the Canvas
to the window, and play the project.

A Final Cut title project contains one placeholder layer, whereas a Final Cut transition
contains two placeholder layers: one for each side of the edit point. The green layer,
Transition A, represents the outgoing video clip; the red layer, Transition B, represents
the incoming video clip.

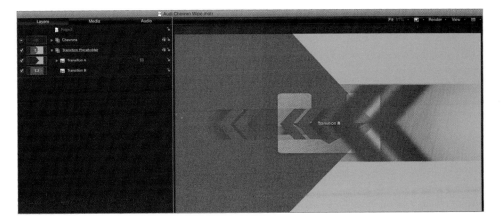

4   Stop playback. In the transport controls at the bottom of the Canvas, click the Go To
Start and Go To End buttons to move the playhead to the first and last frames of the
project.

A clean view of Transition A fills the first frame, and a clean view of Transition B fills the last frame. Transitions always start and end with an unaltered view of the outgoing and incoming video. Between these points, graphics fly across in both directions as Transition B wipes onto the screen.

In the Layers list, the small arrow on the icon on each of the transition placeholders indicates that you can replace the default graphic with video or graphics, much like a drop zone, to see how the transition will look in Final Cut Pro.

5   In the File Browser, navigate to Movies > Final Cut Events > Audi Promo > Original Media. With the playhead at the start of the project, drag the first clip, **ALXA_004.mov**, over the Canvas, wait for the yellow outline around the Transition A placeholder to appear, and release the mouse button. The video clip replaces the green graphic.

6   Move the playhead to the end of the project, and from the File Browser, drag the **ALXA_074.mov** clip to the Canvas to replace the Transition B placeholder. Play the project. Now you can see what the transition might look like in the context of the Audi Promo project.

Your goal with this project is to rig it so that an editor working with Final Cut Pro can choose different graphics to wipe across the screen. But before you can build the rig, you need to understand how the project is constructed.

7   Stop playback. Switch the Timing Display to frames, if necessary, and move the play-
    head to about frame 28 so you can see both clips. Close the *Transition Placeholder*
    group, and open the *Chevrons* group.

The *Chevrons* group contains four groups of its own. The top *Master Chevron* group's
activation checkbox is deselected, so that group isn't visible in the Canvas. Even
though its content is not visible, the *Master Chevron* group is being used to control
the content in all the other groups. Let's see how.

8   Open each of the four groups inside the *Chevrons* group.

NOTE ▸ To see all the layers, you may need to resize their heights by dragging up
between any two layers.

The *Master Chevron* group contains three graphics layers. You can tell from the preview icon that only the top layer, *Double Arrows*, is visible. The other layers are activated, but their Opacity parameters are set to 0.

You may wonder why you can see the *Double Arrows* layer in the Canvas, when the group that contains it, *Master Chevron*, is deactivated. It's because you are actually seeing a *clone* of that group.

The three groups below the *Master Chevron* group contain clone layers of the *Master Chevron* group. The silhouette badge on each layer icon indicates that the layers are clones.

9   In the *Chevrons huge wipe* group, select the bottom layer, *Chevron huge 1*, and if necessary, press F4 to open the Layer Inspector.

This layer is a clone of the *Master Chevron* group, and therefore displays the content of that group (even though the source group is deactivated). If you change which layer is visible in the source group, the content in the Canvas updates.

10 In the *Master Chevron* group, select the *Double Arrows* layer. In the HUD, change its Opacity to 0 percent. Then select the *Single Arrow* layer below it, and in the HUD, increase its Opacity to 100 percent.

In the Canvas, all the double arrows are replaced with single arrows. Because all the animated graphics in this project are cloned from a single group, you can change all the graphics in the project simply by "turning on" the appropriate layer in the clone source, the *Master Chevron* group. Thanks to this efficient project design, it will be easy to build a parameter rig to control all the graphics that animate across the screen during the transition.

NOTE ▶ Similarly, all shape layers in the project (indicated in the Layers list by orange shape icons) are clones of the *Arrow Background* shape in the *Master Chevron* group. These shape layers create the blurred red background behind the graphics, and they don't need to change when the graphics change.

11 Close all the groups inside the *Chevrons* group except for the *Master Chevrons* group. By doing so, you can focus your attention on the group that controls the look of the project.

Rigging a Pop-Up Widget

This project contains three different graphics options, so for this widget you need a way to choose three different "states," or snapshots. The pop-up widget contains a menu to which you can add as many snapshots as you like. You create the snapshots, name them, rig parameters to them, and set the appropriate parameter values for each snapshot. First, however, you must create a rig to contain the widget.

1 Choose Object > New Rig, or press Command-Control-R.

2   From the Rig Inspector (press F4, if necessary), click the Pop-up widget button.

3   In the Layers list, rename the *Pop-up* widget layer to *Shape* to make it clear that this widget will let you choose the shape of the graphics for the project.

4   In the Widget Inspector, click what is now the Shape pop-up menu.

By default, this menu has three choices: Snapshot 1, 2, and 3. You can change the name and number of snapshots in the menu.

5   With Snapshot 1 selected, click the Rename button, and type *Double Arrows*. Press Return. The rigging process will be easier if you name the snapshots in the same order as the layers in the Layers list.

6   Select and rename Snapshot 2 to *Single Arrow*, and rename Snapshot 3 to *Stylized Arrows*. Refer to the Layers list to match the order and naming of the snapshots to the layers.

You need only three snapshots here, but let's see how you would add another.

7   Next to the Shape pop-up menu, click the + (plus sign) button.

A new snapshot appears, named appropriately enough, *New Snapshot*.

TIP   New snapshots are created beneath the currently selected snapshot.

8   Press Return to accept the snapshot name, and then click the – (minus sign) button to delete the snapshot. The three snapshots are all you need in this exercise.

Now that you've created your snapshots, you can turn your attention to rigging parameters to the widget. In the previous exercise, you used Rig Edit Mode to automatically add parameters to the widget for multiple layers and effects as you changed their values. In this exercise, you want to rig only a few parameters (the Opacity parameters for the graphics layers in the *Master Chevron* group). Because you're rigging only three layers, you can easily rig the parameters and set their states manually.

9   In the Layers list, select the *Double Arrows* layer. Press F1 to open the Properties Inspector. Locate the Opacity parameter, and from its Animation menu, choose Add To Rig > Rig > Add To Shape.

The submenu lists available rigs and widgets. Since you didn't rename the rig, it appears as *Rig;* but your widget appears in the menu with its new name, *Shape.*

TIP ▶ You can use the Add To Rig command even if you haven't yet created any widgets—or even if you don't yet have a rig in your project! Choose Add To Rig > Create New Rig > Add To New Checkbox, Pop-up, or Slider. This is an efficient way to create a rig, add a widget, and rig a parameter to the widget in one step.

A small joystick icon next to the Animation menu for the Opacity parameter indicates that the parameter is now rigged.

10 Repeat the same process to rig the Opacity parameter for the *Single Arrow* and *Stylized Arrows* layers. Then, select the Shape widget in the Layers list.

In the Widget Inspector, the Opacity parameters for each of the three layers now appear, along with their current values. Notice, however, that the stacking order is reversed compared to the order in the Layers list. This is because each time you rig a parameter, it is added to the top of the list.

TIP ▶ When rigging more than a few parameters, it can be helpful to first add the lowest one in the Layers list and work your way up to match the order of the Layers list.

NOTE ▶ You cannot drag rigged parameters in a widget to change their order the way you can drag published parameters to reorder them in the Project Inspector. Instead, you need to use the Animation menu to remove parameters from the widget, and then add them again in the order you desire.

With all the necessary parameters rigged, you now can set the values of these parameters for each snapshot.

11 From the Shape pop-up menu, choose Double Arrows.

12 Set the Double Arrows Opacity value to 100, and the value of the other two parameters to 0.

13 Choose Stylized Arrows from the pop-up menu. Set the Stylized Arrows Opacity value to 100 and the others to 0.

NOTE ▶ You can skip the middle snapshot, Single Arrow, because the opacity values are already set correctly for that snapshot.

14 In the HUD, select each of the snapshot states and watch as the graphics update in the Canvas.

The final step is to publish the widget to make it available in Final Cut Pro.

15 From the Animation menu for the Shape pop-up menu widget, choose Publish. In the Layers list, select the Project, and in the Publishing pane of the Project Inspector confirm that the widget is published.

You can now choose the shape of the graphic for this transition in Final Cut Pro. Before testing it, however, let's also give the Final Cut Pro editor the ability to change the color of the graphics.

Using the Link Parameter Behavior

The color of the graphics in this project comes from filters applied to the three layers in the Master Chevron group. While you could directly publish the color swatch for each of the three filters, every time the Final Cut Pro editor changed the Shape snapshot, she would also need to change the corresponding color for that graphic.

You can be more efficient by connecting the color of all the shape graphics to a single "master" layer using the powerful Link parameter behavior. With this method, the Final Cut Editor can quickly customize the colors of the transition elements using a single color swatch in order to apply that new color to all three Shape options.

1   In the Layers list, in the *Master Chevron* group, open each of the three arrow layers to reveal the Tint filters.

You'll link the tint color of the lower two layers to the top layer. To make it clear that the top Tint filter will control the other two filters, you can rename it.

NOTE ▶ In this simple project, you could apply a single Tint filter to the *Master Chevron* group to tint all the shape options. However, in many projects it is necessary to use filters on multiple layers, and the Link behavior is a great way have them work in unison.

2   In the *Double Arrows* layer, double-click the Tint filter, and rename it to *Tint Master*.

3   In the *Single Arrow* layer, select the Tint filter, and press F3 to open the Filters Inspector.

4   Click the Animation menu for the Color parameter (or right-click the word *Color*), and from the pop-up menu, choose Add Parameter Behavior > Link.

The Link behavior appears underneath the layer in the Layers list. It is disabled because it has no source. In the Behaviors Inspector (which appeared automatically after you selected the Link behavior), you'll find a well for adding a source object. You can't add filters directly to the well, so you'll add the layer to which the filter is applied.

5   Drag the *Double Arrows* layer from the Layers list to the Source Object well in the Behaviors Inspector.

Next, you'll choose the source object parameter to which you want to link the color of the Tint filter.

6   In the Behaviors Inspector, from the Compatible Parameters pop-up menu, choose
    Filters > Tint Master > Color > All.

The color of the *Single Arrow* layer is now linked to the color of the *Double Arrows*
layer. Let's link the *Stylized Arrows* layer color in the same manner, this time using
both the Filters Inspector and the HUD.

7   Under the *Stylized Arrows* layer, select the Tint filter. Press F3 to open the Filters
    Inspector. Control-click the Color parameter, and choose Add Parameter Behavior >
    Link.

8   Drag the *Double Arrows* layer from the Layers list to the well in the HUD. Then from
    the Compatible Parameters menu, choose Filters > Tint Master > Color > All.

Finally, you must link the color of the blurred *Arrow Background* shape layer.

9   In the Layers list, select the *Arrow Background* layer. In the Shape Inspector, add the
    Link Parameter behavior to the Fill Color parameter.

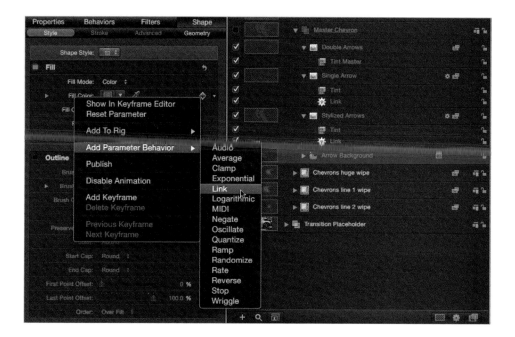

10 Drag the *Double Arrows* layer to the well in the Behaviors Inspector or the HUD, and from the Compatible Parameters pop-up menu, set the Source Parameter to the Tint Master filter color.

Let's test all the linked layers.

11 In the Layers list, select the *Tint Master* filter. In the HUD, change the color of the color swatch. The colors of all the graphics in the Canvas change because they are cloned from the *Master Chevron* group.

12 In the Layers list, select the Shape widget, and in the HUD, choose each of the snapshots. Every snapshot is the same new color because they are all linked to the Double Arrows snapshot.

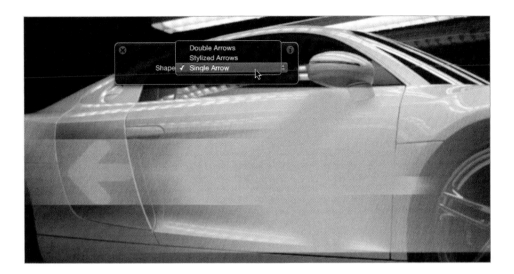

13 Press Command-Z a few times to undo the color change. Let's keep red as the default color. To finish, you just need to publish the Tint Master color swatch.

14 Select the *Tint Master* filter, and in the Filters Inspector, from the Animation menu for the Color parameter, choose Publish.

15 In the Layers list, select the Project, and in the Publishing pane of the Project Inspector, confirm that the color swatch is published. Test the published parameters, and then undo any changes to restore the default values.

You need to do one more thing to make this transition play correctly in Final Cut Pro.

16 With the project still selected in the Layers list, open the Properties Inspector.

This project's duration is two seconds. Final Cut Pro's default transition duration is one second, which is too fast for this project.

17 Select the Override FCP Duration checkbox. Now the transition will play for the full Motion project duration, two seconds, when it is applied in Final Cut Pro.

18 Close all the groups in the Layers list, and press Command-S to save the project. Deselect the Include Unused Media checkbox, and click Don't Copy.

NOTE ▶ Because you replaced the placeholder images with video clips after the previous save, you are now presented with some options. If you choose Copy, the video clips and the project file are copied to Home > Movies > Motion Templates > Transitions > Audi. The content you added will also appear in the static thumbnail in Final Cut Pro. For templates designed to be used in many types of projects, it's often a good idea to clear the placeholder content before closing the project by selecting each placeholder and clicking the Clear button in the Image Inspector. You don't need to clear the placeholder content for this exercise.

19 Switch to Final Cut Pro, select the Transitions Browser, select the Audi category, and skim the Audi Chevron Wipe thumbnail.

NOTE ▶ If you do not see the Audi category in the Transitions Browser, quit and relaunch Final Cut Pro X.

The thumbnail displays the video clips, but as you skim, the clips are replaced with the default lake and trees images. This is because you did not copy the placeholder media.

20 Drag the transition onto an edit point between any two clips in the Timeline, select the transition, and adjust the published parameters in the Inspector.

Excellent work! You explored a Final Cut transition project, rigged it with the pop-up widget to publish multiple shape options, and applied the Link Parameter behavior to enable changing the color of all the shape options in Final Cut Pro with a single control. For the final exercise in this lesson, you'll create a Final Cut effect project and rig it with the third and final kind of widget.

Creating a Final Cut Effect

To work with the third type of widget, the slider, you'll build a simple Final Cut effect project using clones and filters, and then rig the effect so a single slider can control its overall intensity in Final Cut Pro X. Finally, you'll publish a few additional parameters to provide even more design flexibility.

1   Switch back to Motion, close any open projects, and press Command-N to open a new project. Click the Final Cut Effect icon, set the Preset to Broadcast HD 1080, the Frame Rate to 29.97, and the Duration to 5;00. Click Open.

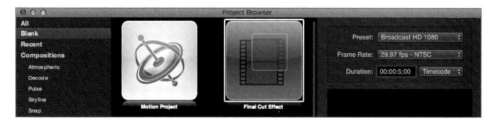

2   Press Shift-Z to fit the Canvas to the window.

Much like a Final Cut title or transition, a Final Cut effect project contains a place-holder. In this case, it's called the Effect Source, and it represents the video clip to which you will apply the effect in Final Cut Pro. When designing an effect, it's very helpful to replace the placeholder default graphic with an image or video clip.

Your goal is to make a stylized look for the slow-motion car clips, so you'll add one of those clips to the placeholder.

3   In the File Browser, navigate to Movies > Final Cut Events > Audi Promo > Original Media. Drag the **PHNTM_001.mov** clip to the Canvas, wait for the yellow outline to appear around the Effect Source placeholder, and release the mouse button. The video clip replaces the graphic.

The video looks very dull and flat compared to the same clip in the Final Cut Pro X Timeline. That's because the clip in Final Cut Pro has been color corrected, and here we are looking at the original, unaltered clip. Let's create an effect that can be used as an alternative to that color correction.

One way to punch up a flat image with little contrast is to copy it on top of itself and combine the two layers with a blend mode. Although an Effect Source placeholder cannot be duplicated like ordinary layers, it can be cloned.

4   With the *Effect Source* layer selected, choose Object > Make Clone Layer, or press K. Then, move the *Clone Layer* below the *Effect Source* layer.

5   Reselect the *Effect Source* layer, and in the HUD, change its Blend Mode to Overlay.

The image immediately looks better because the blend mode gives it darker blacks and brighter highlights. You'll take this look further by color correcting the image using a few filters.

You may wonder why we moved the clone layer below the original effect source. When a filter is applied to a source layer that has been cloned, the filter will also be applied, or "pass through," to the clone. However, filters (and other effects) applied to clones directly do not affect the source. With the clone layer placed beneath the original, you can change its look independently of the original layer. Let's try that now

6   Select the *Clone Layer*, and in the toolbar, click the Filters pop-up menu and choose Color Correction > Gradient Colorize.

The Gradient Colorize filter maps an editable gradient to the tones of the image. The default gradient creates more contrast, but also makes the image a little too dark.

7   Click the Filters button again, and choose Color Correction > Gamma. In the HUD, set the Gamma parameter to about 1.52.

The gamma filter lets you adjust the midpoint of the brightness values without affecting the darkest and lightest areas.

Because the Effect Source layer isn't affected by the filters, you can compare your results so far to the original clip by simply turning off the clone.

8   In the Layers list, toggle the activation checkbox for *Clone Layer* to switch between the original clip and the current design.

You can see how a blend mode and a few filters have given the clip a much punchier look. Let's take the technique a step further by adding one more filter to the group containing the layers so that the filter affects them both.

9   In the Layers list, select *Group*. In the toolbar, click the Filters pop-up menu, and
    choose Stylize > Bad Film. Play the project.

The Bad Film filter adds dirt, hair, and scratches to the clip; makes it shake and
flicker; and even shifts the focus. You can adjust several parameters to change the look
of the filter. Feel free to play with their settings.

With the basic design of the effect completed, you can now decide how to make the
effect adjustable in Final Cut Pro. First, however, save your work.

10 Press Command-S to save the project.

11 Name the template *Gradient Contrast-Bad Film*, and create a new Audi category.
    Deselect Include Unused Media, leave Save Preview Movie deselected, and click
    Publish.

Enter a name for the Final Cut Pro Effect, and choose which
folder to keep it. You may also assign a theme to your template.

Template Name: Gradient Contrast–Bad Film

Category: Audi

Theme: None

☐ Include unused media

☐ Save Preview Movie

Cancel   Publish

NOTE ▶ Because the placeholder contains a video clip, it is included when you create a preview movie. You can choose to create the preview movie later, after clearing the placeholder, to get a generic preview.

Also because the placeholder does contain a video clip, a copy of the clip is saved with the effect, which can waste disk space. You can remove the clip by navigating to Movies > Motion Templates > Effects > Audi > Gradient Contrast-Bad Film > Media and moving it to the Trash.

Rigging the Slider Widget

At this point, your new effect can be applied in Final Cut Pro, but it can't be adjusted without returning to Motion. The great thing about rigging and publishing is that you can choose what elements of a Motion project to "expose" to a Final Cut Pro editor so he can change the look of the effect directly in Final Cut. There are a lot of options! Often you'll want to find the balance between giving the editor enough control to modify an effect to his liking, while not overwhelming him with dozens of published parameters. The slider widget is a great tool for controlling multiple parameters at once, over a range of values you specify.

For this project you've just created, you'll add and publish a slider to control the overall impact of combined effects—from no impact at all, to the fully stylized look you have now. You'll also give the Final Cut Pro editor the ability to change the gradient used by the Gradient Colorize filter by publishing the Gradient editor. Finally, because the Bad Film filter is such a dramatic effect, you'll publish a separate control so the Final Cut Pro editor can add it independently of the color and contrast adjustments.

1   In the Layers list, turn off the Bad Film filter by deselecting its activation checkbox.

    Now you can focus on the impact of the other filters and the blend mode. Let's add the slider widget.

2   Choose Object > New Rig, or press Command-Control-R.

3   Press F4 to view the Rig Inspector, and click the Slider button.

    The slider widget appears below *Rig* in the Layers list. You want it to control the over-all intensity of the project, so let's rename it right away.

4   In the Layers list, rename the slider widget to *Intensity*.

In the Widget Inspector, the slider appears with the new name, *Intensity*. Underneath each end of the slider you'll see dots that represent snapshots. The left dot is blue because it is the active snapshot. Before working with the slider and the snapshots, you'll rig the parameters to the widget.

Your goal is to choose parameters to add to the rig that change the intensity of the effect. Often, multiple parameters will have a similar impact. By using Rig Edit Mode, any parameter changes you make are automatically added to the widget. Let's start with the Gamma filter.

5   In the Widget Inspector, click the Start button to enter Rig Edit mode.

6   Select the Gamma filter, and press F3 to reveal the Filters Inspector.

In addition to filter-specific parameters, most filters have a Mix parameter that modulates the impact of the filter.

7   Drag the Mix slider all the way to the left.

8   Drag the Gamma slider left and right, and then leave it at a different setting from the starting value.

The Gamma parameter makes the image brighter or darker. When you change each parameter in Rig Edit Mode, you add both parameters to the widget.

NOTE ▶ If you change a parameter and then restore its original value, the parameter is not added to the widget.

Below the Gamma filter controls in the Filters Inspector, you'll find the controls for the Gradient Colorize filter. This filter has several parameters, but only the Mix parameter will eliminate its impact.

9   In the Filters Inspector, set the Mix slider for the Gradient Colorize filter to 0.

10   Select the *Effect Source* layer, and in the HUD, drag the Opacity slider to 0.

The clip now looks as it did originally.

11   In the floating window, click the Stop Rig Edit Mode button.

12   In the Layers list, select the Intensity widget, and return to the Widget Inspector.

The four parameters you adjusted in Rig Edit Mode appear below the slider.

Since the active snapshot is the blue dot at the left of the scale, you need to set the values for all the parameters to make the clip look like the unaffected original.

13   Set the values for all the parameters that you added to the widget to 0 except the Clone Layer.Gamma.Gamma parameter. Set that parameter to a value of 1 so that it has no impact.

With the Intensity slider positioned all the way left, the clip isn't affected at all. Now, you'll set values for all these parameters when the slider widget is at its maximum value.

14 Click the dot below the right side of the slider widget to select that snapshot.

The parameter values automatically return to their values before you started Rig Edit Mode.

15 If necessary, set all the parameter values to 100% except the Clone Layer.Gamma. Gamma parameter. Set its value back to 1.52. The filters and blend mode now all affect the image.

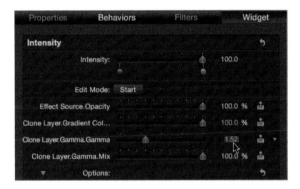

16 Drag the Intensity slider between the two snapshots. As you drag, all the rigged parameters values change simultaneously to reduce the overall effect.

17 Leave the Intensity slider at about the middle position and save your work.

The single Intensity slider now controls four separate parameters from two filters and an image layer. Nice work. The final step is to publish the widget and test it—but let's publish a few other parameters as well to give the Final Cut Editor more flexibility.

TIP You can add intermediate snapshots to the slider widget by clicking anywhere underneath the slider. You can move the snapshots left or right, and set new parameters values for each snapshot. In this way, you can control how quickly parameter values change as you drag the slider from one end to the other.

Publishing Widgets and Parameters

Let's publish our new Intensity widget, the Gradient editor for the Gradient Colorize filter, and the Bad Film filter; then you'll modify the published parameters and test them in Final Cut Pro.

1   In the Widget Inspector, from the Animation menu for the Intensity widget, choose Publish.

2   In the Layers list, select the *Gradient Colorize* filter, and if necessary, press F3 to open the Filters Inspector.

The default gradient is white on the left and changes to black on the right. But the gradient colors can be edited to create a completely different look. Let's publish the entire gradient to Final Cut Pro. Although the Gradient parameter doesn't have an Animation menu, you can still publish it.

3   Control-click the word *Gradient*, and from the shortcut menu, choose Publish.

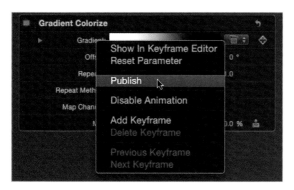

Finally, let's return to the Bad Film filter. Rather than publish individual parameters, you can publish the filter's activation checkbox.

4   Select the Bad Film filter, and in the Filters Inspector, Control-click the words *Bad Film*, and from the shortcut menu, choose Publish.

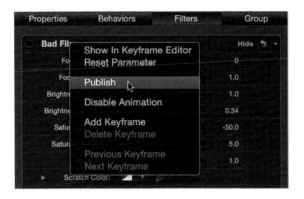

Now, let's look at what we have.

5   In the Layers list, select the Project, and go to the Publishing pane of the Project Inspector.

The Intensity slider widget, the Gradient editor, and the Bad Film activation checkbox are all here.

6   Test each of the published parameters by changing their values, and then return them to their default values.

NOTE ▸ Although the Gradient editor includes a pop-up menu of gradient presets in the list of Published Parameters, that menu will not appear in Final Cut Pro. Instead, you'll edit the gradient directly.

In terms of workflow in Final Cut Pro, it may make the most sense to first edit the gradient, and then adjust the overall intensity of the effect. Then, you can add the Bad Film effect if you desire. Therefore, let's change the order of the published parameters.

7 Drag the Gradient editor above the Intensity slider.

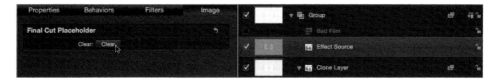

As a final step, let's clear the Effect Source.

8 Select the *Effect Source* layer, and in the Image Inspector, click the Clear button. The *Effect Source* and *Clone Layer* return to the default graphic.

Time to check out the results in Final Cut Pro.

9 Save the project and switch to Final Cut Pro.

10 Open the Effects Browser, select the Audi category, and drag the Gradient Contrast-Bad Film effect onto one of the PHNTM clips in the Timeline.

NOTE ▶ If necessary, quit and relaunch Final Cut Pro for the new effect to appear in the Effects Browser.

11 Select the clip with the applied effect, and in the Inspector, deselect the Correction 1 color correction.

By turning off the color correction, only your new effect affects the video clip.

12 Open the Gradient Editor, change the color of the color tags, add new tags, and adjust their locations. Drag the Intensity slider to create a customized look.

13 Select the Bad Film checkbox to activate it, and play the clip.

NOTE ▶ Because Final Cut Pro effects are applied directly to clips, they always expand or contract to fit the clip duration. Because the Bad Film effect is animated, it speeds up or slows down based on the clip length. You can set the animation speed to a fixed rate using a Loop End marker in Motion. See "Working with Markers in Templates" under the Motion 5 Help menu for more information.

14 Try turning on the Correction 1 color correction, and then adjusting your effect parameters for a still different look.

Congratulations! In this lesson, you covered a lot of ground working with titles, transitions, and effects. You learned how to rig, modify, and publish checkbox, pop-up, and slider widgets manually and in Rig Edit Mode. And along the way you learned a few tricks for building motion graphics projects in Motion.

Final Cut Generators

The last type of Motion project that is published to Final Cut Pro is the Final Cut generator.

Unlike title, transition, and effect projects, generator projects are empty by default. And in Final Cut Pro, instead of placing a generator project above a video clip (like a title), or between clips (like a transition), or directly on a video clip (like an effect), generators are applied just like video clips, as self-contained "blocks" that can be edited anywhere into the Timeline.

Generators are great for creating self-contained content, like an animated background, that doesn't rely on any video in the Timeline. You can add drop zones to generators in Motion so that the Final Cut Pro editor can add her own video. And, of course, you can rig generator projects with widgets to create all kinds of alternative looks for a Final Cut Pro editor to choose from. Check the Final Cut Pro Generators Browser for examples of generator content. Apply a few and check the Inspector to see that many of them have published parameters and widgets.

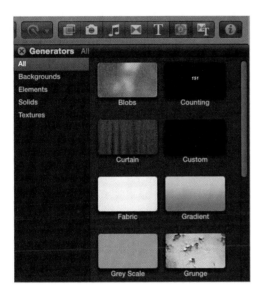

Finally, any standard Motion project, including projects created in earlier versions of Motion, can be published as generators, which means that any Motion project, present or past, can be used in Final Cut Pro X.

Lesson Review

1. What is the relationship between a rig and a widget?
2. Describe two ways to add a parameter to a widget.
3. What is the simplest type of widget and why?
4. How do you know if a parameter has been rigged?
5. What does the green placeholder layer in a Final Cut transition project represent?
6. When you finish rigging a widget, what do you have to do to make it available in Final Cut Pro X?
7. In Motion, how can you display a list of all published parameters?

8. You want to rig a transition so that you can choose from five color themes in Final Cut Pro. What type of widget should you choose?

9. You want to rig a generator so that the Final Cut Pro editor can rotate all the graphics at once to point in any direction. What type of widget should you use?

Answers

1. A rig is a container for widgets, much like a group is a container for layers. Before you can add a widget to a Motion project, you must first add a rig to contain the widget.

2. You can add a parameter to a widget manually by choosing Add to Rig > (*Rig name*) > Add to (*Widget name*), or automatically by clicking Start to enter Rig Edit Mode and changing the value of the parameter.

3. A checkbox is the simplest type of widget because it has only two states: selected or deselected. Each state is called a *snapshot* and contains parameter values that you select.

4. Next to the Animation menu of a parameter, a joystick icon indicates that the parameter is rigged.

5. A Final Cut transition contains a placeholder layer for each side of the edit point. The green layer, Transition A, represents the outgoing video clip; the red layer, Transition B, represents the incoming video clip.

6. You need to publish the widget to use it in Final Cut Pro X.

7. In the Layers list, select the project, and then in the Project Inspector, select the Publishing pane.

8. The pop-up widget allows you to set as many discrete snapshots as you'd like to place in a menu.

9. The slider widget lets you set up snapshots for maximum and minimum values and then choose any value between them by dragging the slider.

Keyboard Shortcuts

Command-Control-R	New rig

An Introduction to 3D

13

Lesson **13**

Building a 3D Scene

We live in a three-dimensional world, but Motion's world takes place on a flat, two-dimensional computer screen.

Yet even on this flat screen, Motion lets you create a virtual 3D world in which you can move and rotate layers in three-dimensional space and use cameras to look at the world from different angles.

In this lesson, you will learn the basics of manipulating layers and groups in 3D space, how to add a camera, and how to use the various 3D controls as you arrange scenes in a virtual 3D world.

Making 3D Transformations in the Canvas

At its most basic, working in 3D means that you can change the position and rotation of layers along three axes: the horizontal, or x-axis; the vertical, or y-axis; and the depth, or z-axis, which points straight out of your computer screen. You can transform layers using the Inspector or the HUD, or do so directly in the Canvas. You will use all these tools to arrange each layer of a group so that they form a "set." As on a Hollywood film set, the performers—Motion's layers—can be arranged on your 3D stage.

1   In Motion, open the Lessons > Lesson_13 > Lesson_13_Start project.

This project contains several layers organized into groups. It is similar to projects you worked with in earlier lessons but some important differences make it more effective for setup as a 3D scene. To see all the layers in the Layers list without scrolling, you can resize the layers.

2   In the Layers list, open all the groups. Click the Scale button, and then drag the slider to the left, shrinking the size of each layer in the list, until you can see them all.

In this project, you'll find groups that profile a skier and the events in which she has competed. Each group contains the title graphic and a photo from an event. This arrangement allows you to treat each image/text combination as a "set" made up of layers you can move and rotate individually, and then move and rotate together by transforming the group that contains them.

The *2010 Selections* and *2011 Jr Nationals* groups are turned off, so you see only the Skier group in the Canvas.

Each photo has an image mask applied, and all three image masks use the same source to create the mask: the *grunge-bk.psd* layer in the *Matte* group.

The last group contains the background video clip and is currently turned off so that you can focus on the other groups.

Although you've learned that layers typically start at different points in the project, all layers in this project start on the first frame of the project. This setup will come in handy when you arrange the layers and groups in 3D space, because you'll be able to see them all without moving the playhead.

3   Save the project to the Lesson_13 > Student_Saves folder.

Now that you understand the structure of the project, you can create depth in the scene by moving and rotating the layers in 3D space.

4   In the *Skier* group, select the *Vanessa* text/graphic layer, and press F1 to open the Properties pane of the Inspector.

The Inspector Transform parameters can position a layer up and down on the y-axis or side-to-side along the x-axis. They can also rotate a layer on the z-axis, like a propeller. But they can do a lot more.

5   For both the Position and Rotation properties, click the disclosure triangle next to the name to open additional parameters for each property.

When opened, the position parameters include Z-position, and the Rotation parameters include X and Y Rotation to allow full 3D transforms for each layer.

6   Drag in the value fields that appear to see how these values affect the layer. Undo after each change.

You may have noticed that subtracting values from the X position moves an object to the left, and adding to the X value moves an object to the right. Adding to the Y value moves an object up, and subtracting from the Y value moves an object down. You can move an object closer by adding to the Z value, or move it farther away by subtracting from the Z value. The center of the Canvas has coordinates as X=0, Y=0, Z=0, making it very easy to center objects by entering the zero values in the Inspector.

You can also make these 3D changes in the HUD and directly in the Canvas. To do so, you use a special tool.

7   Open the HUD, and in the toolbar, choose the Adjust 3D Transform tool, or press Q.

The HUD populates with the 3D Transform tools, and the center of the selected layer in the Canvas now contains three colored arrows and three hollow white circles.

8   Drag left on the leftmost Move control in the HUD, to bring the *Vanessa* text/graphic layer forward (toward you) along the z-axis. Keep your eye on the Inspector to set a value of about 200 pixels.

9   In the HUD, drag in the middle Move control to slide the layer up and over to the right a little, again watching the Inspector to see exactly which parameters are changing.

    The right Move control in the HUD moves the selected layer along either the x-axis or z-axis, but you don't need it here. This control is useful when you want to spread layers in space and keep them all on the same horizontal plane, like actors on a stage.

10 In the HUD, try dragging in the Rotate control, watching both the Canvas and the Inspector. The layer rotates along the x, y, and z axes, but in this exercise you just want to swing the layer on its y-axis. Press Command-Z to undo the changes.

11 In the Inspector, drag right on the Rotate control to set the Y Rotation value to 45 degrees.

You can make these same types of 3D transformations directly in the Canvas with the Adjust 3D Transform tool. Let's position and rotate the *Paulsen* text/graphic layer to offset it from the *Vanessa* layer.

12 In the Layers list, select the *Paulsen* text/graphic layer.

As you learned when adjusting the mountain gorilla text in Lesson 6, the colors of the three axis arrows—red, green, and blue, or RGB—map to the three axes of 3D space. The red arrow moves along the x, or horizontal, axis; the green arrow moves along the y, or vertical, axis; and the blue arrow moves along the z, or depth, axis. The blue arrow is pointing almost directly at you, so it looks more like a dot than an arrow.

You can drag an arrow to constrain movement to that axis alone.

13 Drag the blue arrow to the right and watch the Inspector to move the layer about 200 pixels forward along the z-axis. The selected arrow turns yellow. Notice that the status bar at the top of the Canvas displays the transform values and matches what is shown in the Inspector.

14 Drag the red arrow to the right to move this layer up against the side of Paulsen's face, and then drag the green arrow up to move the text layers closer together.

TIP ▶ You can also drag anywhere inside the bounding box to move along both x and y axes at the same time.

The hollow white circles at the 12, 3, and 9 o'clock positions are rotation handles.

15 Drag the y-axis rotation handle (at 9 o'clock) to the left to rotate the layer –45 degrees around the y-axis. Colored rotation bands appear to indicate the axis of rotation.

TIP ▶ Layers and groups rotate around their anchor points. Therefore, changing the location of the anchor point can have a dramatic impact on the rotation. For example, to swing a graphic of a door from the edge rather than from its center, you would move the anchor point to that edge.

You can see how easy it is to change the position and rotation of layers in 3D space using the Inspector, the HUD, and the Canvas. One more crucial step remains for making layers behave as though they live in a 3D world: converting the groups that contain them into 3D groups.

Converting 2D Groups to 3D

Layers only interact or intersect with each other—and respond to cameras or lights—when they are contained inside 3D groups. Fortunately, it's quite easy to switch a group from 2D to 3D.

Before you do so, however, you will work with the various axis modes in the HUD and Canvas. They can be handy when manipulating layers and groups.

Let's say you want to push the *Paulsen* text/graphic layer straight back in z-space, to move it behind the photo.

1   In the HUD, drag left and right on the left Move control, and then undo the change.

2   In the Canvas, drag left and right on the blue z-axis arrow, and then undo the change.

Notice that in both cases the layer does not move straight toward you or away from you. Rather, it moves along the layer's own z-axis, which is perpendicular to the surface of the layer.

3   In the HUD, drag around in the Rotate control, and then undo the change.

Notice in the Canvas that the colored arrows move as the layer moves: The red arrow stays horizontal with respect to the layer, the green arrow stays vertical with respect to the layer, and the blue arrow always points straight out from the plane of the layer. This is called Local Axis mode since you are adjusting the layer around its own, local set of axes.

4   In the HUD, from the Adjust Around pop-up menu, choose View Axis. In the Canvas, the blue arrow now points directly at you, even though the layer is rotated.

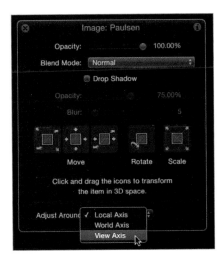

5   In the HUD, once again drag around in the Rotate control, watch the results, and then undo the change. This time, no matter how the layer moves, the axes remain fixed: Red is always horizontal, green is always vertical, and blue is always pointing straight out—with respect to the computer screen, or *your view* of the project.

NOTE ▶ The other option, World Axis, is currently the same as View Axis. That will change after you add a camera and begin to move in 3D space. The Inspector's Position and Rotation values are always based on the World Axis.

This axis mode makes it easier to push the layer directly away from you.

6   In the HUD, drag the left Move control to the right; or, in the Canvas, drag the blue arrow to the left to move the *Paulsen* text layer back in z-space to about –15 pixels.

NOTE ▶ Setting the Adjust Around pop-up menu to anything other than Local Axis on a 2D group will prevent you from adjusting the Z position of an object directly in the Canvas. You can, however, adjust the Z position using the HUD or Inspector.

The *V_Paulsen_1* layer is located at 0 pixels along the z-axis (you can select it and check that value in the Inspector), so the *Paulsen* text/graphic layer should be at least partially behind the photo now, but it still appears completely in front. This is because you are working in a 2D group, and layers in 2D groups do not interact with each other.

The compositing order of 2D group layers in the Canvas is dictated entirely by the layer order in the Layers list. Because the *Paulsen* text layer is above the *V_Paulsen_1* photo layer in the Layers list, it will always appear in front of the photo in the Canvas. How layers are positioned in front of and behind other layers is the fundamental difference between a 2D group and a 3D group.

Another way to see that the layers aren't yet truly 3D is to rotate the group.

7   Select the *Skier* group, and then in the Canvas, drag the top rotation handle down to tilt the group around its x-axis.

All the layers appear completely flat, and the mask doesn't tilt with the layers. To make layers interact with each other based on their positions in z-space rather than their layer order, you need to switch the group containing them to 3D.

8 Undo the group rotation.

9 In the Group pane of the Inspector, set the Type pop-up menu to 3D.

When the group type is changed to 3D, the icon to the left of the Layers list for that group changes from three flat rectangles to a stack of rectangles to indicate that it is now a 3D group. Notice the difference between the 3D icon and the icon on the *2010 Selections* group below it in the Layers list.

In the Canvas, the *Paulsen* text now intersects with the photo layer.

Let's return it to its previous location.

10 Use the HUD or Canvas to move the *Paulsen* text forward to about 200 pixels along the z-axis.

11 Once again, rotate the group down around the x-axis. The layers remain rotated and spread out in z-space when you look at them from a different angle.

You are finished building your first scene. You will use these same tools to arrange the other two scenes in a similar fashion.

12 Now that you're a bit more familiar with the tool, undo the group rotation, and turn off the *Skier* group.

13 Turn on the *2010 Selections* group and make it a 3D group.

> **TIP** ▶ You can also make a selected 2D group into a 3D group by clicking the 2D/3D icon in the Layers list, or choosing Object > 3D Group, or pressing Control-D.

To make sure these text graphics have the same rotations and z-positions as the ones in the first set, you can copy the values from the layers in the *Skier* group.

14 Select the *Vanessa* text/graphic layer. You want to start the *2010* text/graphic layer with the same position and rotation as the *Vanessa* layer.

15 Drag the word *Transform* from the Properties pane onto the *2010* layer in the Layers list.

The *2010* text layer takes on all the values from the *Transform* group of parameters. It is now about 200 pixels forward in z-space and rotated 45 degrees on the y-axis. Let's do the same for the *Selections* text layer.

16 Select the *Paulsen* layer, and drag the word *Transform* to the *Selections* layer.

With both graphics layers properly positioned and rotated with respect to each other, you only need to reposition them with respect to the photo.

17 Shift-click both the *2010* and *Selections* text layers to select them, and in the Canvas, drag them up so they are more fully centered with the skier in the photo. Now you just need to repeat the same process on the last set.

18 Turn off the *2010 Selections* group; then turn on the *2011 Jr Nationals* group and make it 3D. Drag the Transform properties from the *2010* text layer to the *2011* text layer and from *Selections* to *Jr Nationals*, and then reposition the layers as necessary. Save your work.

Terrific! Your 3D "sets" are now built. The next step is to spread them out in 3D space. For that task, it's very helpful to have a camera in the project.

Adding and Working with Cameras

A 3D environment without a camera is like a fast car without the keys. You can sit in it and look around, but you can't go anywhere.

> **NOTE ▶** Animating cameras is covered in more detail in Lesson 14.

In 3D mode, everything that you see in the Canvas represents the viewpoint of a camera, either the default reference cameras that view the scene from specific positions and orientations such as top, right side, and front; or a scene camera that you add to look at your scene from different points of view.

When you add a camera to a Motion project, a whole set of new tools, or *3D overlays*, become available. You can use these tools to manipulate the scene camera or to step away from the camera to get a different perspective on your 3D scene. You can even separate your view from the camera and rise above to get a bird's-eye view as you build your scene.

If you don't have any 3D groups in your project, adding a camera will automatically switch all your groups to 3D. Let's try it.

1   Close all the groups in the Layers list. You don't need to see the individual layers for the next steps.

2   Command-click each of the three 3D groups to select them, and then press Control-D to revert them to 2D groups.

3   In the toolbar, click the New Camera button or choose Object > New Camera. A dialog appears, warning you that cameras affect only 3D groups.

4   Click "Switch to 3D."

Several things happen:

▶ All the groups in the project are automatically switched to 3D.

▶ A new *Camera* layer appears at the top of the Layers list.

▶ The HUD transform controls now affect the camera.

▶ New tools appear in three corners of the Canvas.

These five new 3D overlays are available only when a camera is in the scene. You can choose specific 3D overlays to turn on or off, and you can toggle the visibility of all the 3D overlays.

5   In the upper right of the Canvas, click the "View and Overlay" pop-up menu.

The five 3D overlays are listed underneath the Show 3D Overlays command. The Inset view and 3D grid are not visible in the Canvas because they appear only under certain conditions.

NOTE ▶ If you do not see checkmarks next to Show 3D Overlays and every 3D overlay, choose each one until all 3D overlays are turned on.

By default, when you add a camera, you begin viewing the scene through the camera, as indicated by the words *Active Camera* at the top left of the Canvas. The camera is added and positioned so that your view of the scene does not change when you switch from 2D to 3D. Now that you have a camera, you can move it around.

6   In the HUD, use the 3D transform tools to move and rotate the camera. Notice that the changes are also made in the Properties Inspector. Undo after each change.

When you move the camera up and down or rotate it, a 3D grid appears in the Canvas. The grid represents the "floor" of the virtual world, with a red x-axis and a blue z-axis intersecting at 0, 0, 0—your virtual "home base." This grid can help you stay oriented as you move around in 3D space.

At the top right of the Canvas is a set of three icons with a camera icon to the left. The three icons are the 3D View tools—Pan, Orbit, and Dolly. The camera icon next to them indicates that these tools are manipulating the camera just as you did when using the HUD.

NOTE ▶ If you can use the HUD to manipulate the camera, why would you need the 3D View tools? In the HUD, the camera can be manipulated only if it is the selected layer. Often, a different layer or group will be selected because you are working on it (transforming it, animating it, or adding effects) and you want to move the camera to change your view of the scene. The 3D View tools allow you to move and rotate the camera even when the camera layer is not selected.

7   Drag the Pan, Orbit, and Dolly tools to see how they work. Notice the changes reflected in the Inspector. This time, do not undo your changes.

These tools include a handy feature to quickly reset the camera.

8   Double-click any one of the 3D View tools and look at the Inspector.

Double-clicking a 3D View tool resets the camera to 0, 0, 0 for both Position and Rotation, so it is once again looking at the center of your virtual world. Like Dorothy clicking the heels of her ruby slippers, no matter how far afield you may stray in 3D space, you can always come home with a simple double-click.

But what does it mean when the camera is at 0, 0, 0? You know the photo layer is at 0, 0, 0, so doesn't the camera have to back up a distance from the very center of the z-axis to "look at" the photo and have it fill the screen?

To understand where the camera is in relationship to the layers in your scene, you need to step away from the camera, or even fly above it. And that's the purpose of the 3D overlay at the bottom left of the Canvas, the 3D Compass.

9   Move your pointer over the arrows around the 3D Compass but don't press the mouse button. The arrow under the mouse lights up, and text appears, identifying the name of the view Motion will display if you click that part of the 3D Compass.

10   Click the top of the green arrow to go to the Top view. The scene rotates as you "fly" above it. You are now looking straight down the world's y-axis.

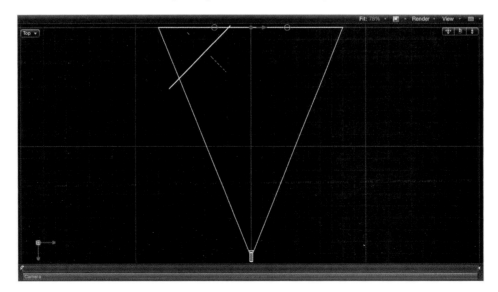

NOTE ▶ If you don't see the full camera outline, press Shift-Z to fit the scene to the Canvas.

Layers in Motion are always 2D—like playing cards—which is why the two rotated graphics layers look like a white X in the Canvas. You can't see a line for the photo layer because it aligns with the focal plane of the camera as represented by the base of the yellow isosceles triangle.

The red, green, and blue arrows are located at the center of the focal plane, which is why the camera's location is 0, 0, 0. In other words, the position of the camera is determined by its focal plane, not by its "body."

11 In the HUD, drag the Rotate control.

Notice that the camera rotates around the center of its focal plane. No matter how much you rotate the camera, it stays focused on the center of your virtual world. This behavior will come in handy when you animate your camera in the next lesson.

Notice also that a small window appears at the bottom right, the Inset view. It shows you how the scene looks from the camera's point of view—so you can adjust the camera from a different view, and still see the results from the camera's view.

You may wonder why the axes' arrow colors for the camera don't match the grid colors: The green arrow lines up with the blue grid line. If you look in the HUD, you can see that you are in View Axis mode—the mode in which z (blue) always points straight at you.

12 Undo the camera rotation, and then, in the HUD, change the View Axis to World Axis. The axes of the camera and the 3D grid now match.

Look at the 3D View tools at the top right of the Canvas. Now that you are not in the Active Camera view, the camera icon no longer appears next to these tools. Therefore, these tools can be used in Perspective view to pan, orbit, and dolly without moving the camera.

Let's select a more freeform view than the Top view and use the 3D view tools to move around. In addition to the Compass, you have another way to change your 3D view. The Camera pop-up menu at the top left of the Canvas displays the current view with a checkmark and allows you to change the view.

13 From the Camera pop-up menu, choose Perspective, and then use the 3D View tools to pan, orbit, and dolly the view.

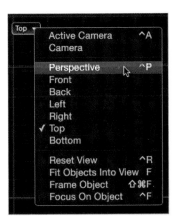

Notice that the camera has not moved, and neither have any of the layers. You have changed only your view of the scene by using one of the default reference cameras.

14 From the Camera menu, choose Reset View to return to your perspective view starting point.

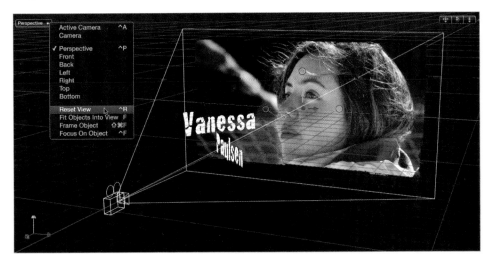

To go to the view looking through the camera, you use the Camera menu.

15 From the Camera menu, choose Active Camera, or press Control-A. Your view returns to the original camera view.

Now that you know how to turn on and use the 3D overlays to change your view of the scene and to manipulate the camera, you can arrange the groups in 3D space.

Arranging and Modifying Groups and Layers in 3D Space

In the next lesson, we will animate the camera to fly from one set to the next. But right now, all the groups are located at the same place: the center of the virtual world. So you'll spread them apart, and rotate them so that the camera must twist and turn as it moves from one group to the next.

To move groups in 3D space, you can use the 3D overlays and the Adjust 3D Transform tool. To see the impact of your changes from more than one angle, we'll use a view layout to display two angles in the Canvas.

After you spread out the groups and layers in 3D space, you may still need to do some work on them—transforming layers, and adding masks, filters, or behaviors. The Frame Object command will help you quickly find and modify elements. Finally, you will use a 2D group to add a background that stays put, no matter where the camera moves.

Arranging the Groups

The first task is to move two of the groups away from the camera and then rotate them to face it. Facing the camera isn't required, but it can create a pleasing arrangement that makes it easy for the camera to turn and see each group.

1   In the Layers list, select the activation checkboxes of the *Skier* and *2010 Selections* layers so that you can see them as you move them in 3D space.

The groups of layers are currently stacked on top of each other. To spread them apart, use different views to get a broader perspective.

2   In the HUD, set Adjust Around to Local Axis so you can move and rotate the groups more in line with the camera's view.

3   Click the 3D Compass to go to the Top view; then in the 3D View tools use the Dolly and Pan controls to move the camera and set icons to the upper right of the Canvas.

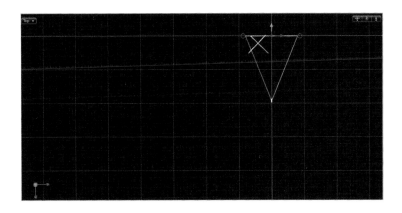

We'll leave the *Skier* group in front of the camera, move the *2010 Selections* group to the left and down, and move the *2011 Jr Nationals* group directly behind the camera.

4   In the Layers list, select the *2010 Selections* group, and in the Canvas, drag the red x-axis arrow to the left, using the status bar as a guide to move the group about –4000 pixels.

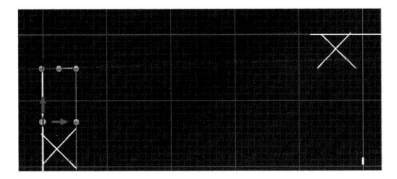

5   Drag the blue z-axis arrow down to move the group to about 1000 pixels, until it is roughly even with the camera.

6   In the Inspector, in the Y-Rotate field, type *90* to rotate the set counterclockwise and face the camera.

NOTE ▶ Locating the rotation handles in this view can be a little difficult, although you're welcome to try.

The *2011 Selections* group is now off-camera to the left, and facing the camera; so if the camera turned to look, it would see the elements of the group face-on.

Let's now move and rotate the *2011 Jr Nationals* group. To keep the Inset view from getting in the way, you will turn it off.

7   From the "View and Overlay" pop-up menu, choose Inset View to deactivate it.

8   Select the *2011 Jr Nationals* group. Drag the blue arrow down to move the group to about 3000 pixels; then in the Inspector rotate the group to 180 degrees in the Y direction to face the camera. This is your preliminary set arrangement. You can adjust it as you want, after you see how it looks with the camera animation.

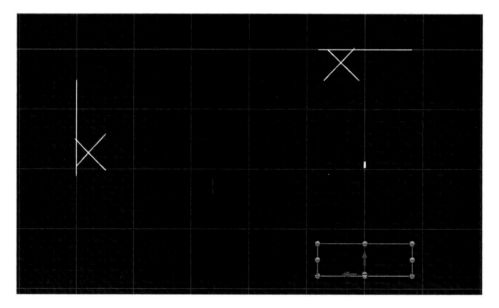

Now, you want to see what these groups look like from "ground level," but you want to keep this view onscreen as well, in case you want to use it to make changes.

You can display your scene from multiple angles simultaneously by choosing one of several view layouts. Each layout divides the Canvas into *viewports*. Each viewport can display the scene from a different position and orientation. You can display viewports by selecting the Active camera or one of the default reference cameras from the Camera menu.

9   At the upper right of the Canvas, from the View Layouts pop-up menu, choose the split horizontal view—the third option.

The Canvas splits into two viewports of the scene. The upper viewport shows the Top view you were working in, and it has a yellow border around it to indicate that it is the active view. The lower viewport shows the Right view by default, but you can change either viewport to whichever view you want.

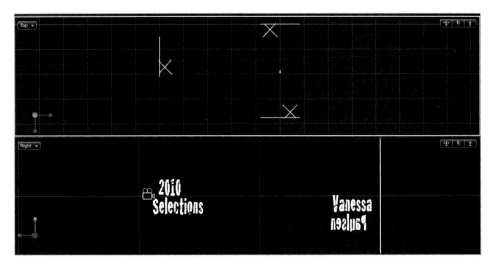

NOTE ▶ The active viewport is the one that animates during playback. You can make a viewport active by clicking inside it.

10 Use the Camera menu to set the upper viewport to the Active Camera view. Then press Shift-Z to fit the set in the viewport.

11 In the lower viewport, click the center of the 3D Compass to go to the Perspective view, and then use the 3D View tools to pan, orbit, and dolly the view until you can see all three sets in the viewport.

The text graphics for the sets you positioned and rotated are visible, but the photos are not. This is because all three photos are masked by the same graphic in the *Matte* group, and the graphic is still located at 0, 0, 0. So, it masks the *Skier* layer, but it's no longer aligned with the other two photo layers since you repositioned and rotated them.

To align the masks, we want a separate copy of the graphic to mask each photo layer, and we'll move each copy to the exact same location as each photo layer.

Modifying Layers in 3D Space

In this exercise, we will create copies of the graphic that was used as a mask and copy it to each of the three skiing photo groups. Then each copy will be aligned with the photo layer in that group. While you could drag the layers in the different Canvas windows to align them, there is a much faster way to move a layer to a precise location in 3D space.

1   Open the *Matte* group. Option-drag a copy of the *grunge-bk.psd* layer, first to the *Skier* group, and then the *Selections* group, and finally to the *Nationals* group. After it is copied to each of the three groups you've been working with, delete the *Matte* group.

The groups open, and a copy of the graphic is now located in the top layer of each group. In the lower viewport of the Canvas, all the photos appear without masks.

To move each *grunge* graphic layer to the same position and rotation of each photo, let's copy the parameters from the photo to the matte graphic.

2   In the *Skier* group, select and activate the *grunge-bk.psd copy* layer and look at the Properties pane of the Inspector. In the Perspective view, the layer is clearly in the wrong position; in the Inspector, you can see that it's nowhere close to 0, 0, 0—the location of the *V_Paulsen_1* photo.

You could click the Transform properties reset arrow to return the layer to 0, 0, 0 for both position and rotation, but that would also reset the scale, which you don't want to do. Besides, that approach won't work if the layer you want to match the graphic to isn't at 0, 0, 0.

3   Select the *V_Paulsen_1* photo layer.

4   In the Properties pane, Shift-click the words *Position* and *Rotation* to select them both, and then drag them onto the *grunge-bk.psd copy* layer. The Position and Rotation

values are copied to the graphic, and in the Active Camera view it lines up with the photo. Now you just need to apply it as the source for the image mask.

5   Open the *V_Paulsen_1* photo layer to reveal the image mask, and then drag the *grunge-bk.psd copy* layer onto the Image Mask. The photo in the Active Camera view is now properly masked by the graphic.

NOTE ▶ You can set the source of the image mask in three locations: by selecting the image mask, and then dragging the source layer to the well in the HUD; by dragging directly to the image mask in the Layers list; and by dragging into the Mask Source well in the Inspector.

This process of dragging parameters from the Inspector to a layer can be used to move any layer to align with any other layer in 3D space. It's quite powerful, and we'll use it again for the *2010 Selections* group. However, this group is a bit difficult to see in the Perspective view. It's on an angle and far away. You could use the 3D View tools to move closer, but there's a faster way to move the camera to frame any group or layer in 3D space.

6   Close the *Skier* group, and select the *V_Paulsen_2* photo layer inside the *2010 Selection* group.

7   In the upper viewport, from the Camera menu, choose Frame Object. The Active camera rotates to face the selected layer, and pans and dollies until its focal plane touches the layer, thereby framing the layer.

NOTE ▶ This command changes the position and orientation of the camera itself—not just a view—so be cautious when using it if the camera is already in a specific location you want to preserve, or if you have already animated the camera with behaviors or keyframes. In this case, the starting position of the camera is 0, 0, 0, so it's very easy to return "home" by double-clicking one of the 3D View tools or resetting the camera's Transform parameters in the Properties pane.

8   In the Properties pane, Shift-click the Position and Rotation parameters, and drag them inside the *2010 Selections* group onto the *grunge-bk.psd copy 1* layer.

NOTE ▶ The position and rotation of the *V_Paulsen_2 photo* layer is 0, 0, 0—even though the layer isn't close to the center of the virtual world. This is because the coordinates are relative to the group containing the layer. Although you moved the entire group and changed its position and rotation, you haven't changed the position or rotation of this layer with respect to the group that contains it.

9   Open the *V_Paulsen_2* photo layer, and drag the *grunge-bk.psd copy 1* layer onto the image mask. The photo now appears masked in the Active Camera view. There's just one more group to go.

10 Close the *2010 Selections* group, select the *V_Paulsen_3* photo layer in the *2011 Jr Nationals* group, and choose Frame Object from the Camera menu or press Command-Shift-F to frame the layer with the camera.

11 In the Properties pane, Shift-click the Position and Rotation parameters, and drag them inside the *2011 Jr Nationals* group onto the *grunge-bk.psd copy 2* layer.

12 Open the *V_Paulsen_3 photo* layer, and drag the *grunge-bk.psd copy 2* layer onto the image mask.

NOTE ▶ Feel free to adjust the Perspective view to look at all the sets.

All three photos now appear properly masked. To finish setting up the 3D scene, let's add a background.

Mixing 2D and 3D Groups

Motion lets you freely mix 2D and 3D groups in a 3D project. Because 2D groups aren't affected by the camera, you can use them to add elements that you always want to see, such as a watermark, station ID, or background element.

1   Close the *2011 Jr Nationals* group and turn on the visibility of the *Background* group.

In the Active Camera view, nothing changes where the camera is framing the *2011 Jr Nationals* group. But in the Perspective view, the background clouds appear behind the Skier group.

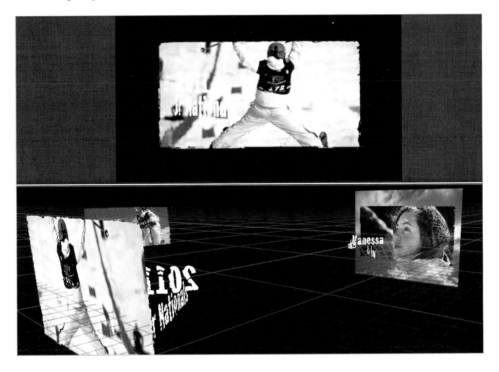

Because the Background group is a 3D group, the camera sees it in 3D space at a fixed location. But you want to see the background no matter where the camera moves.

2 Click the 2D/3D icon for the *Background* group to switch it to a 2D group. Now the Clouds video appears in the upper Active Camera window behind the *Jr Nationals* group, and also appears in the Perspective view, flat to the screen.

3 Try orbiting the camera with the 3D View tool in the Active Camera view.

No matter where the camera looks, the Clouds video stays still and always faces the viewer. However, you can still manipulate the position and rotation of 2D groups and their layers.

4 In the upper Active Camera window, double-click one of the 3D View tools to reset the camera to its default location at 0, 0, 0, framing the *Skier* group.

5 Open the *Background* group and select the *Clouds* layer.

6 Look to the left of the toolbar. If the Adjust 3D Transform tool is not selected, press Q to select it.

7 In the HUD, drag in the Move, Rotate, and Scale controls to transform the layer. After each adjustment, press Command-Z to undo it.

The layer moves and rotates in the Active Camera and Perspective views, which means you can position and rotate a layer in a 2D group as needed to set it up, but it won't move from that orientation when the camera moves.

Notice that no matter how far forward you move the layer along the z-axis, it never moves in front of the other groups. This is because 2D groups respect the layer order in the Layers list.

8   Close the *Background* group, select it, and choose Object > Bring to Front. The cloud now obscures all other groups because it's a 2D group at the top of the layer stack. If this group contained a small semitransparent watermark, corporate logo, or station ID in the corner of the screen, it would stay there as the camera moved.

9   Choose Object > Send to Back to return the *Background* group to the bottom of the layer stack and the back of the composition.

10 Save the project.

Throughout the lessons in this book, you've learned that creating 2D and 3D groups is a powerful compositing technique. It's more than just dropping layers into a "folder" for organization. That being said, with that power comes a few caveats. The most important caveat being rasterizing, also sometimes called pre-composing, which you'll examine in the next section.

Rasterizing Groups

Rasterization happens on both 2D and 3D groups when certain filters, masks, or blend modes are applied to a group. The result of rasterization is that the group is converted into a bitmap image, and that conversion impacts how groups interact with other project elements.

In this exercise, you'll discover the ways that rasterization is imposed on your group and how to identify rasterized groups.

1   At the upper right of the Canvas, from the View Layouts pop-up menu, choose the single view, the first option. Then press Shift-Z to fill the window.

2   In the Layers list, select the Skier group, and in the Inspector, set Blend Mode to Normal.

You just applied the quickest way to rasterize a group. Any time you change a 2D or 3D group's Blend Mode setting to anything other than Pass Through, the group is rasterized. It may not appear any different in the Canvas right now, but you can see indications that the group is rasterized.

Look at the icons to the left of the names of the *Skier* and *2010 Selections* groups, and notice how they differ.

You'll also see a small R icon next to the Blend Mode menu in the Inspector.

3   In the Inspector, return the *Skier* group's Blend Mode to Pass Through.

Now the icons look the same. Pass Through means that any blend modes applied to layers within a group will pass through to the groups beneath them.

4   Open the *Skier* group and select the *Vanessa* layer. In the HUD, set Blend Mode to Overlay to blend it with the photo layer and a bit with the clouds background.

Because the blend mode for the group containing this layer is set to Pass Through, the Overlay blend mode on the *Vanessa* layer passes through to the *Clouds* layer in the *Background* group beneath it. This is the default state for groups and blend modes.

However, certain operations applied to a group will cause that group to become rasterized—converted into a bitmap image—before it is composited with other groups. When a group is rasterized, any blend modes applied to layers within it will no longer pass through to the groups below.

5　Select the *Skiers* group, and in the Inspector, drag the slider to lower the Blending Opacity value.

The instant you change the Blending Opacity value from 100% a box surrounds the *Skier* group icon to indicate that the group is rasterized. The Overlay blend mode applied to the *Vanessa* text no longer affects the group underneath. The text is now white where it should be composited over the clouds background.

Certain operations applied to a group will trigger rasterization and, as a result, blend modes on layers in that group will not pass through to layers in the groups below.

There's often another way to accomplish the same result. In this example, you could change the opacity of each individual layer in the group rather than alter the group itself. However, for this project, no blend mode or opacity is needed.

6　Select the *Vanessa* layer. In the HUD, return Blend Mode to Normal, and then return the *Skier* group Opacity to 100%. Close the group, and save your work.

The text returns to the standard white color it had prior to changing its blend mode to Overlay.

NOTE ▸ The most common operations that trigger rasterization for a group include adding a mask, applying a filter, and changing blend modes or blending opacity at the group level. The Motion documentation's groups and rasterization chapter includes a list of all operations that trigger rasterization.

You now know about rasterization, how to use 3D overlays, manipulate a camera, arrange objects in 3D space, animate with camera behaviors, and mix 2D and 3D groups. Your scene is arranged, and you are ready to animate the camera.

Lesson Review

1. How can you automatically switch all groups in your project to 3D?

2. How do you add a camera?

3. Name three locations in which you can change the position and rotation of a layer or group in 3D space.

4. What's the difference between layers in a 2D group and in a 3D group?

5. Do the 3D View tools always control the camera?

6. Which tool is used to make 3D transformations directly in the Canvas, and which keyboard shortcut selects it?

7. How can you quickly move a camera to look at and frame a specific layer in 3D space?

8. In the HUD, how would you set the Adjust Around pop-up menu if you wanted the z-axis of a layer to always point straight at you, no matter how the layer or the camera was oriented?

9. If you applied an image mask to a layer that is positioned in 3D space, why wouldn't the image mask appear on the layer?

Answers

1. By adding a camera

2. In the toolbar, click the New Camera button, or choose Object > New Camera.

3. In the Inspector, the HUD, or the Canvas

4. Layers in 2D groups are not affected by the camera, and are composited based on stacking order in the Layers list.

5. No. The 3D View tools control the camera only when the window is set to a Camera view.

6. The Adjust 3D Transform tool allows you to transform the position and rotation of layers and groups in both the HUD and the Canvas. Press Q to select the Adjust 3D Transform tool.

7. Select the layer, and from the Camera menu, choose Frame Object, or press Shift-Command-F.

8. Set the Adjust Around pop-up menu to View Axis mode to orient the axes so that they reflect the orientation of your computer screen.

9. The image mask source is not aligned to the layer you are masking.

Keyboard Shortcuts

Q	Select the Adjust 3D Transform tool
Control-A	Select the Active Camera view from the Camera menu
Control-D	Toggle a group between 2D and 3D

14

Lesson Files   Motion5_Book_Files > Lessons > Lesson_14

Media   Motion5_Book_Files > Media > 3D

Time   This lesson takes approximately 90 minutes to complete.

Goals   Animate a camera with behaviors

Work with depth of field

Turn on and adjust reflections

Understand light types

Work with casting and receiving shadows

Animating Cameras and Using Advanced 3D Features

Now that you've arranged layers and groups into virtual sets in 3D, the real fun begins: animating the camera to fly from set to set, and examining each set before moving to the next.

In this lesson, you will animate your camera using behaviors, and explore several of the advanced 3D features of Motion, including limiting the camera's depth of field, turning on reflections, adding lights, and casting shadows.

Animating a Camera with Behaviors

In Lesson 13, you created a 3D scene that profiled a nationally-ranked skier. In this exercise, you will use two camera behaviors—Framing and Sweep—to animate the camera through that scene. The Framing behavior flies the camera to a new location in 3D space, and the Sweep behavior orbits the camera around a point of interest.

Using the Framing Behavior

The Framing behavior makes it easy to fly the camera to a specific layer, and even orients the camera to face the layer.

1   Navigate to Motion5_Book_Files > Lessons > Lesson_14, and open the Lesson_ 14_Start project. Then save it in the Student_Saves folder. This project is based on the project you completed in Lesson 13 with the addition of a few extra groups you'll use later. Let's quickly look at the project's structure.

   NOTE ▶ You can open this project from the Finder or directly from the Project Browser in Motion by clicking the Open Other button at the bottom of the Browser and navigating to the project in the Open window.

2   In the Layers list, select the camera, and use the 3D Compass to go to the Top view. Use the 3D View tools to dolly in and pan the scene, filling up the window with the three scenes and the camera you set up in the previous lesson.

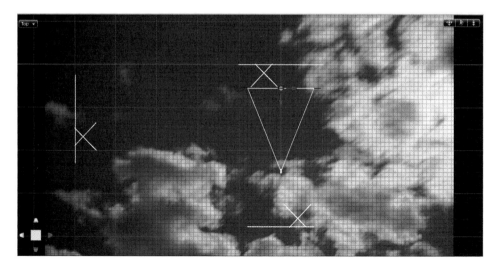

The three skiing groups are spread out in 3D space, each one containing a photo layer and two text/graphic layers that were rotated and positioned in front of the photos. The camera is located at 0, 0, 0—the center of the virtual world—framing the *Skier* group.

You'll animate the camera from this Top view. You want to move the camera from its current location to the *2010 Selections* group. The music that accompanies this project can provide some help in the timing of the behavior.

3   Enable the Play/Mute Audio button to hear the music in this project.

4   Play the project, and stop playback just after the first marker—at about 4:15. A dramatic musical crescendo here makes this a great time to end the camera move. You'll use the Framing behavior to time the camera move and end by viewing the *Selections* group.

5   In the Library, choose Behaviors, and then choose Camera. The six behaviors in this folder animate a camera in various ways. The preview area displays information and a sample animation that shows how each behavior works.

> **TIP** ▶ In addition to the Camera behaviors, cameras can be animated using Basic Motion behaviors such as Throw, Spin, Motion Path, and Point At. Parameter behaviors will also animate cameras. For example, try adding a Wriggle parameter behavior to the camera's position to create some camera shake.

6   Drag the Framing behavior onto the *Camera* layer in the Layers list. Click the Framing behavior (now under the *Camera* layer) to make the Canvas the active window. Then press Command-Option-Left Arrow to move to the first marker.

The behavior appears under the *Camera* layer, and like most behaviors, it is applied to the entire duration of the layer, so you also need to trim the In and Out points.

7   Press O to trim the Out point so the behavior ends at the marker. Drag the playhead back one second (around 3:00). Then press I to trim the behavior's In point to the playhead.

8   Set a play range around the behavior, starting a little before the In point and ending a little after the Out point. Resume playback to see the animation.

> **TIP** You can drag the play range In and Out points, but it may be faster to press Command-Option-I to set the play range In point and Command-Option-O to set the Out point.

> **TIP** While looping a short playback range, you may want to mute the audio by clicking the Play/Mute Audio button at the bottom left of the Canvas.

The camera doesn't move, because you need to give the Framing behavior a target to frame.

9   Drag the *2010 Selections* group from the Layers list to the Target well in the HUD.

> **TIP** You can also drag the target layer or group directly onto the Framing behavior underneath the *Camera* layer.

The camera now moves to the *2010 Selections* group, rotating as it moves so that when it arrives, it squarely faces the front of the group. The camera animation finishes sooner than the one-second duration of the behavior because the Framing behavior includes its own timing parameters. The default setting of 50% for the timing parameters means the behavior finishes halfway through its duration. It also starts and stops rather suddenly. You can adjust these default settings in the HUD.

10 In the HUD, drag the Position Transition Time and the Rotation Transition Time sliders to 100%. The camera now lands on the *Selections* group at the end of the behavior.

11 From the Transition pop-up menu, choose Ease In

The camera now animates smoothly at the start of the move. Let's see how things look from the camera's point of view.

12 Press Control-A to display the Active Camera view, and after viewing the animation, stop playback.

The camera move works well, and having photos in the scene—instead of videos—makes coordinating the camera move a lot easier. Because photos can be any duration, you can extend them through the entire length of the project and have the camera view them at any time. If you were using video clips, you would have to slide the clips along the Timeline to appear when the camera panned to them. To continue moving the camera, you will duplicate the Framing behavior you just added.

13 Move the playhead to the next musical hit at the second marker. This is where you want to end the next Framing behavior.

14 Rename the Framing behavior to *Frame Selections*. Press Command-D to duplicate it, and rename the copy *Frame Jr Nationals*.

15 Drag the *2011 Jr Nationals* group into the HUD well, and then press Shift-] (right bracket) to move the behavior's Out point to the playhead.

Because you copied the existing behavior, it already has the right duration and animation properties.

16 Press Option-X to reset the play range to the entire project, and then play it to see the camera animation.

The camera now animates quickly and smoothly to each of the scenes as they are introduced. It works well, but nothing moves during the time the camera looks at each scene. You can make things more dynamic by applying a Sweep behavior to keep the camera in motion as it looks at the layer or group it is framing.

Using the Sweep Behavior

The Sweep behavior animates a camera to rotate or "sweep" around the scene that it is framing—its point of interest—as if it was attached to the scene with a string and can't look away.

1   Before you continue, mute the audio by clicking the Play Mute/Audio button.

2   While playing the project with the camera selected, in the toolbar, click the Add
    Behavior pop-up menu, and choose Camera > Sweep.

The behavior is applied to the full project duration, and the HUD indicates that the
camera rotates from 0 to 30 degrees over the length of the behavior, which means the
camera points at the first group straight on, and then rotates as it frames each group.
Because you added Sweep after the Framing behaviors, the rotation is continuous.
Just as filters have a different effect on a layer depending on which filter is added first,
these behaviors can change the animation based on their layer order. You can best see
these differences by viewing the animation using the Top reference camera.

3   Use the 3D Compass to switch to the Top view, and continue playback.

    The animation might look better if the camera were to start with a slight rotation in
    the opposite direction.

4   In the HUD, set the Start slider to –15 degrees and the End slider to 15 degrees.

    The camera now reaches 0 degrees when it is directly facing the *2010 Selections* group,
    creating a more balanced look. If Sweep were applied *before* the Framing behaviors
    (and therefore placed under them in the Layers list), you would get a different result.

5   Reset the Start and End values to 0 and 30, respectively, and in the Layers list, drag the
    Sweep behavior under the two Framing behaviors.

Because the Framing behaviors are now applied *after* the Sweep behavior, they force the camera to frame each group face-on with no rotation, and the Sweep behavior restarts the rotation from 0 degrees. As a result, each group gets the same look: starting face-on and then rotating in the same direction.

Let's say that you want the camera to sweep in the opposite direction on the middle *2010 Selections* group. To do so, use separate Sweep behaviors.

In the Timing pane, you'll rename, duplicate, and trim the behaviors in the Timeline

6   Rename the Sweep behavior to *Sweep Skier*. Then duplicate it and rename the copy *Sweep Selections*.

7   Duplicate *Sweep Selections* and rename the copy *Sweep Nationals*.

8   In the Timeline, drag to trim each of the Sweep behaviors to fill the gaps between each Framing behavior. Trim *Sweep Skier* to fill the first gap, *Sweep Selections* to fill the middle gap, and *Sweep Nationals* to fill the final gap.

TIP ▶ Shift-drag to snap the In or Out point of the behavior to the In or Out point of the Framing behaviors.

9   Make sure the Start value for all the Sweep behaviors is set to 0, and then set the End value to 15 for *Skier*, –15 for *Selections*, and 20 for *Nationals*.

Because the Framing behavior is on top in the Layers list, the camera is forced to face each group. So, if you use a nonzero Start value for the sweep, the animation will jump. The negative value for Selections causes the camera to sweep in the opposite direction. And the larger value for *Nationals* is used because the final sweep lasts a bit longer.

10 Press Control-A to return to the Active Camera view, and play the project. The animation is looking more interesting. A few tweaks should finish it off.

11 Save your work.

Finessing Behaviors

In this exercise, you'll set an initial rotation of the first set so that it starts at an angle rather than squarely facing the camera. Then you will change the location and orientation of an entire group. Because the camera is animated with behaviors, it will still find and frame a target group no matter how you move it or rotate it.

1   Select the *Sweep Skier* behavior, and set the Start slider to –15 and the End slider to 0. The photo now turns to face the camera in a subtle reveal move.

> **TIP** You may need to use the Inspector to be exact; or you can use the HUD, if you're willing to settle for being close to the values. For the *2010 Selections* group, you can't adjust the Start value because the Framing behavior forces the camera to view the group face-on. However, you can rotate elements *inside* the group.

2   Select the *Sweep Selections* behavior, press Shift-I to move the playhead to the In point of the behavior, and open the Selections group.

You want to rotate the photo, but keep it aligned with the mask, so you also need to rotate the mask source.

3   Command-click the *V_Paulsen_2* photo layer and the *grunge-bk.psd copy 1* layer to select them, and in the Properties pane of the Inspector, set the Rotation Y value field to about –15 degrees.

This action rotates the photo and its mask while keeping the group framed in the camera. We'll do the same for the Nationals photo, but in the opposite direction.

4   Select the *Sweep Nationals* behavior. Press Shift-I to move the playhead to its In point, and open the *Jr Nationals* group. Command-click the V_Paulsen photo and *grunge-bk.psd copy* layers, and in the Inspector, rotate them 15 degrees.

5   Save your work and play the project. Each group now starts a little off-axis, and the camera sweeps in the opposite direction on the middle group.

The overall camera movement is a little repetitive: It sweeps, moves to the left, stops and sweeps, moves to the left, stops and sweeps. The result is that the photo and text graphics always appear to fly off to the right.

Because you framed each group using the Framing behavior, you can freely change the position and rotation of a group, and the camera will still frame it, which forces the camera to take a different route to the new destination. Moving a group can be a quick way to spice up the camera animation.

6   Stop playback, and move the playhead to about 5:00. Close all open groups, and use the 3D Compass to display the Right view, and from the Camera menu, choose Reset View.

At 5:00, the Selections scene is visible and facing the camera. Now let's transform the *Selections* group.

7   Use the 3D View controls to pan and zoom out of the Canvas until you see the entire *Selections* group, leaving a fair amount of space all around it.

8   Select the *2010 Selections* group, then choose the Adjust 3D Transform tool in the toolbar. In the HUD, set Adjust Around to Local Axis. In the Canvas, use the z-axis rotation handle (the blue ring) to rotate the group 90 degrees clockwise, and move it up about 700 pixels.

> **TIP** Open the Inspector as you work in the Canvas so you can view the parameters that are changing.

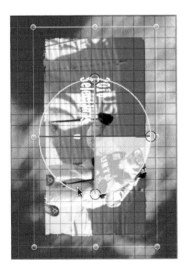

9   Select the camera so that you can see the focal plane outline, and then play the project in the Right view. The red line indicates the new motion path of the camera, which rotates on both its y and z axes as it moves up to frame the *Selections* group. It then rotates again to frame the *Jr Nationals* group.

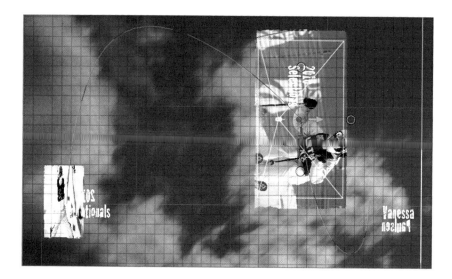

10 Press Control-A to return to the Active Camera view and see the result. The new camera animation creates a more dynamic transition between the groups, but the camera is now sweeping around the wrong axis for the *Selections* group. Also, the gridlines can be distracting because they won't appear in the final rendered animation.

11 To turn off the grid, from the "View and Overlay" pop-up menu, choose 3D Grid, or press Command-Shift-' (apostrophe).

12 Select the *Sweep Selections* behavior, and in the HUD, set Axis to Tilt X.

The Axis pop-up menu refers to the camera's axis of rotation. Because the camera had to rotate 90 degrees to frame the group, you needed to change the axis of rotation for the Sweep behavior.

13 Stop playback.

Well done. You've created and adjusted a camera animation in 3D space using behaviors. Next, you will discover some of the more advanced features you can use in a scene.

Using Advanced 3D Features

Motion offers several other features that can create atmosphere and add more realism to your motion graphics. You can limit the camera's depth of field so that layers outside a set distance are blurred and layers within the distance are sharply in focus. You can animate the camera's focus to shift from one layer to another. You can make layers reflect other layers. You can add several kinds of lights to a scene, and those lights can cast shadows.

Working with Depth of Field

By default, Motion's camera has infinite focus. By enabling depth of field (DOF), you can limit the focus distance and manipulate it in several ways.

By limiting the camera's depth of field, you will focus the viewer's attention on a specific area of the frame.

1   Position the playhead at the start of the project. From the Render pop-up menu at the top right of the Canvas, choose Depth of Field, or press Control-Option-D.

The text and the photo now have a little soft focus problem. You can use a command to quickly focus the camera on any selected layer or group.

2   Open the *Skier* group and select the *V_Paulsen_1* photo layer. From the Active Camera menu, choose Focus on Object, or press Control-F.

The photo snaps into focus, and the text layers are mostly in focus; but because both layers are rotated, the further from the photo layer they get, the less sharp they become. You can increase the blur on objects that are out of focus in two ways. The first is to adjust the layer placement.

3   In the *Skier* group, select the *Vanessa* text/graphic layer.

4   Press Q to activate the Adjust 3D Transform tool. In the HUD, set Adjust Around to View Axis.

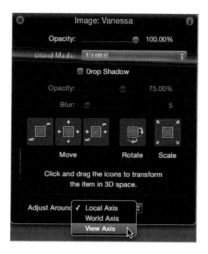

5   In the Canvas, drag the blue z-position arrow to the right until the Z position is around 500. Watch the status bar at the top of the Canvas to monitor the Z value if the Inspector is not open.

The blur increases as the layer moves away from the focused object (the photo layer, in this case).

Instead of moving layers, you could adjust the blur amount from the camera's Depth of Field controls in the Inspector.

6   Select the camera. Press F4 to view the Camera pane of the Inspector. Open the Depth of Field section, and increase the DOF Blur Amount to about 25.

What good is all this nice soft blurring if you can't rack focus like a real camera? You guessed it. Motion has a behavior for that. The Focus behavior can animate the focus from one object to the next. Let's start focused on the *Vanessa* text and then rack focus to the photo.

7   In the Layers list, select the *Vanessa* text layer, and from the Camera menu, choose Focus on Object. The *Vanessa* text sharpens into focus, and the photo goes out of focus.

8   In the Layers list, select the Camera layer.

9   In the toolbar, click the Add Behavior pop-up menu, and choose Camera > Focus. Trim the behavior's In point to 1:00 and the Out point to 2:00, and then drag the *V_Paulsen_1* layer to the well in the HUD.

10   Play the first few seconds of the project and watch as the focus shifts from the text layer to the *V_Paulsen_1* layer.

To continue this rack focus effect through the project, you would need to add additional Focus behaviors to ensure that the other scenes are sharp when the camera moves to them. Carefully positioning layers in and out of focus, as well as creating rack-focus camera effects, can give your composite a much more realistic appearance. Feel free to experiment with the other Depth of Field parameters and add the remaining Focus behaviors.

Turning On Reflections

Motion's layers can reflect other layers, and you can set this property on a layer-by-layer basis. The project has a large black rectangle that acts as a floor under the photos and can receive reflections.

1   From the Render pop-up menu, choose Depth of Field to disable it. Turning off Depth of Field speeds your workflow.

2   Reflections should already be chosen in this menu. If it's not, choose it now.

3   Open and enable the *Floors* group, and select the *Black Floor* layer.

4   In the Properties pane of the Inspector, select the Reflection checkbox, increase the Blur Amount to 10, and select the Falloff checkbox, if necessary.

The photos now look as if they are sitting on a shiny black floor. A lighter floor can create a different look for the reflections.

5   Turn off the *Black Floor* layer, and turn on the *White Floor* layer. Reflections are already enabled for this layer.

6   Experiment with altering the other Reflection parameters, including the Falloff and Blend Mode parameters.

> **TIP** ▶ Adding blur and falloff makes reflections look more realistic but also decreases playback performance and increases render times. You can set everything as you like, and then, to speed your workflow, turn off Reflections in the Render pop-up menu. You can still enable the rendering of reflections in the Export settings even if reflections are turned off in the project.

Using Lights and Shadows

Motion offers four types of lights that you can add to your project. You can adjust each light to create visually striking effects. Certain lights can also cast shadows, and you can choose which layers cast shadows and which layers receive shadows.

1　In the Layers list, turn on and open the *Lights* group. This project contains five lights.

2　Enable the *Ambient Light* layer.

This light is an ambient light type, as indicated in the HUD. Ambient light has no source and evenly lights everything in the scene. You can control only its color and intensity. It adds some overall light to the scene.

3　Select the *Center Point Light* layer and turn it on.

NOTE ▸ Rendering lights, shadows, and reflections is processor- and graphics card-intensive. Allow some time for your Canvas to update when you turn these effects on and off.

This light is a point light, which works much like a light bulb. It has a location and emits light in all directions. In the HUD, notice that this light now has a yellow/orange tint that adds some warmth as a fill light.

4　Select and enable the *Skier Spot* layer, and turn on the two remaining lights.

These three lights are spot light types as indicated in the HUD. They emit a cone of light that you can position, rotate, and adjust in several ways. The spotlights are positioned to illuminate each of the photos and text graphics. You may wonder why the text graphics are not casting shadows onto the photos.

5   Open the *Skier* group, select the *V_Paulsen_1* photo layer, and then in the Shadows section of the Inspector's Properties pane, select the Receive Shadows checkbox. You can choose whether each layer will cast a shadow and if it will receive shadows.

6   Select the *Skier Spot* light, press F4 to view the Light pane of the Inspector, and open the Shadows section.

For more realism, you can use the Uniform Softness checkbox to make the shadow blurrier as it gets farther from the source object.

NOTE ▸ Increasing shadow softness and turning off Uniform Softness will decrease playback performance and increase render times.

7   Experiment with different shadow settings for the lights, and try turning on Cast Shadows and Receive Shadows for different layers.

Exporting Advanced 3D Features

After you set up depth of field, reflections, lights, or shadows, you may want to turn them off in the Render pop-up menu to improve playback performance while you work. Even while they are turned off, you can choose which of these features you want to include in your final export.

1   Choose Share > Export Movie.

2   In the Export window, click the Render button.

Here you can select which of the 3D features you want to include in the exported movie. Each option can be turned on and off, or use the current Canvas setting, which is the default selected option.

Once your Render options are set, you can then click Next to move on to the export process. You'll have the opportunity to rename your file.

You've built and arranged sets in 3D space; animated cameras through 3D space using camera behaviors; and used some advanced 3D features, including depth of field, reflections, lights, and shadows. Now you're ready to enjoy building your own 3D motion graphics with Motion!

Lesson Review

1. Name two of the Camera behaviors.

2. Can the stacking order of Camera behaviors change the camera's animation?

3. You used a Framing behavior to frame a group. You then rotate the group 180 degrees around its y-axis and drag it down 1,000 pixels. How will this transformation affect the camera?

4. What types of behaviors, besides Camera behaviors, can you use to animate a camera?

5. How do you limit the camera's depth of field?

6. How do you turn on reflections for a layer?

7. You added a light and turned on shadows. Your text is throwing shadows onto the floor, which you want, but it is also throwing shadows onto another text layer, which you don't want. What do you do?

Answers

1. Framing, Sweep, Focus, Dolly, Zoom In/Out, Zoom Layer

2. Yes. For example, if the Framing behavior is on top of a Sweep behavior, it will force the camera to frame the target layer face-on, even if the sweep tries to rotate it.

3. The camera will also rotate 180 degrees and move down 1,000 pixels to properly frame the group.

4. Basic Motion, Parameter, and Simulation behaviors—basically, any behaviors that work on a layer will work on a camera.

5. From the Render pop-up menu, choose Depth of Field.

6. In the Properties pane of the Inspector, select the Reflections checkbox.

7. Select the text layer that is receiving the shadows, and in the Properties pane, deselect the Receive Shadows checkbox.

Keyboard Shortcuts

Option-L	Turn on lights
Control-Option-D	Turn on limited depth of field
Command-Shift-L	Add a new light
Control-Option-R	Turn on reflections
Control-Option-S	Turn on shadows
Command-Shift-' (apostrophe)	Toggle 3D grid visibility

Glossary

4:3 The standard display aspect ratio of a traditional television set. See *aspect ratio*.

8-bit For video, a bit depth at which color is sampled. Eight-bit color is common to DV and other standard-definition digital formats. Although some high-definition acquisition formats can record in 8-bit, they usually record in 10-bit resolution. Refers to 8 bits per color channel, making a total of 24 bits in an RGB image and 32 bits in an RGB image with an alpha channel.

16:9 The standard display aspect ratio of a high-definition television set. See *aspect ratio*.

64-bit For computer processors and programs, connotes that 64 bits of data can be processed in parallel or used for an individual data value. As a 64-bit application, Motion 5 is optimized for the current generation of high-performance processor and, as a result, can support deeper, more intricate multilayered effects.

action safe The area inside a border that is five percent smaller than the overall size of the video frame. Some or all of the Canvas image beyond this border will be cropped by the video display monitor or television. How much image is cropped differs between TV models and manufacturers. See *title safe*.

AIFF (Audio Interchange File Format) Apple's native uncompressed audio file format created for the Macintosh computer, commonly used for the storage and transmission of digitally sampled sound.

alpha channel An image channel in addition to the R, G, and B color channels that stores transparency information for compositing. In Motion, black represents 100 percent transparent, and white represents 100 percent opaque.

anamorphic An image shot in a wide-screen format and then squeezed into a 4:3 frame size.

anchor point In the Properties Inspector, the point that is used to center changes to a clip when using motion effects. A clip's anchor point does not have to be at its center.

animation The process of changing any number of variables, such as color, audio levels, or other effects, over time using keyframes or behaviors. See *keyframe.*

Apple ProRes 422 A codec that creates high-quality files optimized for efficient editing.

aspect ratio The width-to-height ratio of any viewing screen. Standard TV has an aspect ratio of 4:3; HDTV's is 16:9. See *high definition.*

audio mixing The process of adjusting the volume levels of all audio clips in an edited sequence—including the production audio, music, sound effects, voice-overs, and additional background ambience—to turn all of these clips into a harmonious whole.

audio sample rate The rate or frequency at which a sound is sampled to digitize it. The standard sampling rate for digital audio is 48 kHz; CD audio is sampled at 44.1 kHz.

audio waveform A graphical representation of the amplitude (loudness) of a sound over a period of time.

AVI A PC-compatible standard for digital video that is no longer officially supported by Microsoft but still frequently used. AVI supports fewer codecs than QuickTime. Some AVI codecs will not play in QuickTime and will be inaccessible in Motion without prior format conversion.

B

batch export The ability to export multiple clips and/or sequences with a single command by placing them in a queue. In Motion, the "Export using Compressor" option can be used to generate a batch export.

Bezier handles The "control handles" attached to a Bezier curve that allow you to change the shape of the curve.

black level The measurement of the black portion of the video signal. This level is represented by 7.5 IRE in the United States. Japanese NTSC and PAL black levels are represented by 0 IRE. See *NTSC; PAL*.

blanking The black border around the edges of a raw video image. This is the image created by the video camera CCDs—the photosensitive receptors that translate the lens image into digital information. The very edge of the picture is usually worthless. These black pixels should be cropped out of your image if you plan to composite it on top of other footage.

blend modes The methods used to combine overlapping elements. Blend modes use various mathematical formulas to combine pixels, thereby creating different effects between the elements. Also called composite modes or transfer modes.

blue screen A solid blue background placed behind a subject and photographed so that the subject can later be extracted and composited onto another image. See *green screen*.

broadcast safe The range of color that can be broadcast without distortion. According to the NTSC standards, this is defined as maximum allowable video at 100 IRE units and digital black at 0 IRE, or analog black at 7.5 IRE units.

cache An area of the computer's memory (RAM) dedicated to storing still images and digital movies in preparation for real-time playback.

C

Canvas The window in Motion in which you can view your edited sequence.

center point Defines a clip's location in the X/Y coordinate space in the Canvas.

chroma The color information contained in a video signal consisting of hue (the color itself) and saturation (intensity). See *hue; saturation*.

chroma-keying Electronically matting or inserting an image from one camera into the picture produced by another. The subject to be inserted is shot against a solid color background, and signals from the two sources are then merged. See *keying*.

clip A media file that may consist of video, audio, graphics, or any similar content that can be imported into Motion.

clipping Distortion that occurs during the playback or recording of digital audio due to an overly high volume level.

codec Abbreviation for *compression/decompression.* A program used to compress and decompress data such as audio and video files.

color correction A process in which the color of objects is evened out so that all shots in a given scene match.

color depth The possible range of colors that can be used in a movie or image. Higher color depths provide a wider range of colors but also require more disk space for a given image size. Broadcast video color depth is generally 24-bit, with 8 bits of color information per channel. Motion works natively with 8 bits per channel of red, green, and blue.

color matching Modifying the color of one shot to correspond with that of another.

component video A type of analog video signal in which the luminance and chrominance signals are recorded separately, thereby providing better video quality. The signal can be recorded in an analog form (Y, R-Y, B-Y) as in a Beta SP, or in a digital form (Y, Cr, Cb), as in a Digital Betacam.

composite The result of combining multiple visual elements—some moving, some still. As a verb it refers to the process of combining these elements, or *layers;* as a noun it refers to the final resulting image. It's also sometimes called a *comp.* In visual effects work, the goal of a composite is to create a single image that appears as if all the elements were captured by a single camera filming the scene. In motion graphics, the objective isn't so much to convince the audience that everything was shot "in camera" as it is to present a stylistic and coherent blend of elements. See *layers.*

composite video A type of analog video signal that combines all chroma and luma information into a single waveform capable of running through a single pair of wires. This can result in analog "artifacts" that adversely affect the quality of the video signal. See *chroma; luma.*

compression The process by which video, graphics, and audio files are reduced in size. The size reduction of a video file through the removal of perceptually redundant image data is referred to as a *lossy* compression scheme.

A *lossless* compression scheme uses a mathematical process and reduces the file size by consolidating redundant information without discarding it. Compression is irrelevant for clips imported into the Motion Canvas because all clips are decoded into fully uncompressed frames before caching to system RAM. Compression is, however, a consideration in the export of a composition to disk. See *codec.*

contrast The difference between the lightest and darkest values in an image. High-contrast images have a large range of values from the darkest shadow to the lightest highlight. Low-contrast images have a narrower range of values, resulting in a "flatter" look.

cut The simplest type of edit, where one clip ends and the next begins without any transition between them.

cutaway A shot related to the current subject that occurs in the same time frame—for instance, an interviewer's reaction to what is said in an interview. Also used to avoid technical problems in a shot.

DARS (Display Aspect Ratio Snapshot) A specific pixel dimension, such as 4:3 or 16:9, applied to a Smart Motion Template. Templates with matching DARS will adjust automatically when applied to a project in Final Cut Pro.

D

data rate The speed at which data can be transferred, or *must* be transferred to reproduce video. Often described in megabytes per second (Mbps), the higher a video file's data rate, the higher quality it will be, but it will require more system resources (processor speed, hard-disk space, and performance). During export, some codecs allow you to specify a maximum data rate for movie playback.

decibel (dB) A unit of measure for the loudness of audio.

decompression The process of creating a viewable image for playback from a compressed video, graphics, or audio file. Compare with *compression.*

desaturate To remove color from a clip. Desaturation of 100 percent results in a grayscale image.

dissolve A transition between two video clips in which the second clip fades up over the first one, eventually obscuring it.

drop-frame timecode NTSC timecode that skips ahead in time by two frame numbers each minute, except for minutes ending in *0,* so that the ending timecode agrees with the elapsed clock time. Although timecode numbers are skipped, actual video frames are not skipped. See *timecode.*

drop shadow An effect that creates an artificial shadow behind an image or text.

dub To copy an analog tape to the same media format.

DV (digital video) A digital video format standard created by a consortium of camcorder vendors that uses Motion JPEG video at a 720 x 480 resolution at 29.97 frames per second (NTSC), or 720 x 546 resolution at 25 fps (PAL), stored at a bit rate of 25 MB per second with 4:1:1 color sampling.

DVCAM A standard-definition digital videotape recorder format that records an 8-bit, 5:1 compressed component video signal with 4:1:1 color sampling. Recorded using quarter-inch tape. Supports two tracks of audio with 16-bit, 48 kHz audio sampling, or four tracks of audio with 12-bit, 48 kHz audio sampling.

DVCPRO Panasonic's native DV (digital video) component format that records an 8-bit, 5:1 compressed component video signal using 4:1:1 color sampling (PAL uses 4:2:0). This format supports two tracks of audio with 16-bit, 48 kHz audio sampling, or four tracks of audio with 12-bit, 48 kHz audio sampling. DVCPRO adds a longitudinal analog audio cue track and a control track to improve editing performance and user-friendliness in linear editing operations.

dynamic range The difference, in decibels, between the loudest and softest parts of a recording.

E

effects A general term used to describe filters and behaviors added to an object in Motion.

envelope The visual curve of an audio waveform's pan or level. Essentially the same as a keyframe curve (the term *envelope* coming from the audio engineering world; the term *curve* coming from the digital animation world). See *pan.*

fade The process of transitioning an object from fully transparent to fully opaque, or vice versa.

Favorite A custom effect that is used frequently. You can create Favorites from any element or group of elements in your Layers list.

field Half of an *interlaced video* frame consisting of the odd or the even scan lines.

FireWire The Apple trademark name for its implementation of the IEEE 1394 protocol used to connect external hard drives, cameras, and other digital devices to computers. It provides a fast interface to move large video and audio files to the computer's hard drive. FireWire exists as two standards: FireWire 400 and FireWire 800. FireWire 800 has twice the bandwidth of the traditional FireWire 400 and uses a different hardware connector.

frame A single still image from either video or film. For video, each frame may consist of two interlaced fields. See *interlaced video*.

frame blending A process of inserting blended frames to replace duplicated frames in slow-motion clips to make them play more smoothly.

frame rate The speed at which individual images of a moving sequence play. It's stated in terms of frames per second (fps). Film in 16mm or 35mm is usually shot at 24 fps; NTSC video is 29.97 fps; PAL video is 25 fps. HD can have several different frame rates.

frequency The number of times a sound or signal vibrates each second, measured in cycles per second, or *hertz*. Audio recordings consist of a vast collection of waveforms, using many different sound frequencies. Each frequency in a recording is associated with an audio pitch. The frequencies of an audio recording can be changed to disguise a voice or to correct an unwanted noise.

FxPlug 2 The Apple standard format for filters and effects. Motion includes more than 130 FxPlug 2 filters and generators and also accepts third-party effects. FxPlug 2 effects can support 64-bit processing and GPU acceleration, and may offer onscreen and dashboard controls.

gain In video, The electronic amplification of a video signal; in audio, the loudness of an audio signal as measured by the difference between the input signal and the output signal.

gamma A curve that describes how the middle tones of an image appear. Gamma is a nonlinear function often confused with *brightness* or *contrast*. Changing the value of the gamma affects midtones while mostly leaving the whites and blacks of the image unaltered. Gamma adjustment is often used to compensate for differences between acquisition formats.

garbage matte A matte that removes unwanted objects from an image. Also called a garbage mask.

generators Clips that are synthesized (or generated) by Motion. Generators can be used as different kinds of backgrounds and elements for visual design.

GPU (graphics processing unit) The central processor inside a modern computer graphics card.

gradient A generated image that changes smoothly from one color to another across the image.

grading The process of color-correcting footage to achieve a desired look.

green screen A solid green background placed behind a subject and photographed so that the subject can later be extracted and composited into another image. See also *blue screen.*

H

Hi8 A consumer analog videotape format with a video quality between VHS and DV resolutions.

high definition (HD) High definition was created to increase the number of pixels onscreen (a higher definition) as well as to solve many of the frame rate and cadence problems between film and video. There are two main types of HD footage. The highest is 1080, with a native resolution of 1920 x 1080. The other is 720, which has a native resolution of 1280 x 720. Both formats can have different frame rates and can be either progressive or interlaced.

high-key images Images that consist of mostly light values.

histogram A graph that displays the relative strength of all luminance values in a video frame, from black to super white. It is useful for comparing two clips in order to match their brightness values more closely. Available in the Levels filter.

hue A specific color or pigment, such as red.

In point The first frame of an object displayed in the Canvas.

I

insert edit To insert a clip into an existing sequence into the Timeline, and automatically move the other clips (or remaining frames of a clip) to the right to make room for it. An insert edit does not replace existing material.

interlaced video A video scanning method that first scans the odd picture lines (field 1) and then scans the even picture lines (field 2), and finally merges them into a single frame of video. Used in standard-definition video.

jiggle To move a parameter away from its current value, and then move it back to the original value. Used to force Motion to create a keyframe in Record Animation mode.

J

jog To move forward or backward through your video one frame at a time.

JPEG (Joint Photographic Experts Group) A popular image file format that lets you create highly compressed graphics files. The degree of compression can be varied. Less compression results in a higher-quality image.

jump cut A cut in which an abrupt change occurs between two shots, with no continuity from one to the other.

keyframe A point on the Timeline where a specific parameter value is set. Motion interpolates between keyframes to create in-between frames.

K

keying The process of creating a mask (key) to eliminate a specific background area in order to composite foreground elements against a different background. See *chroma-keying*.

layers Containers that group several objects in a Motion project. Layers can be nested inside other layers. Filters and behaviors applied to a layer will affect all the elements contained within it. Known in other applications as precompositions.

L

letterbox Describes when widescreen-ratio video images are fit within a standard 4:3 monitor, resulting in black bars at the top and the bottom of the picture.

linear editing A video-editing style in which a program is edited by copying shots one-by-one from the original source tapes to a master tape. Because the assembly is linear, any changes made to an earlier point on the tape result in the rest of the edited tape requiring reassembly from that point forward. See *nonlinear editing.*

low-key images Images that are made up of mostly dark values.

luma Short for *luminance.* A value describing the brightness information of the video signal without color (chroma). Equivalent to a color television broadcast viewed on a black-and-white television set.

Luma Keyer A filter used to key out a luminance value, creating a matte based on the brightest or darkest area of an image. Keying out a luminance value works best when your clip has a large discrepancy in exposure between the areas you want to key out and the foreground images you want to preserve. See *keying* and *matte.*

luminance See *luma.*

M

markers Indicators that can be placed on a clip or globally in a project to help you find a specific location while you edit. Can be used to sync action between two clips, identify beats of music, mark a reference word from a narrator, and so on.

mask An image, clip, or shape used to define areas of transparency in another clip. Acts like an external *alpha channel.* A mask is an application of a matte.

master shot A single, wide shot of dramatic action, often of an entire scene. While medium shots, over the shoulder shots, and close ups are often edited into the scene, the master shot provides "coverage."

matte An effect that uses information in one layer of video to affect another layer. Mattes are useful when you want to use one clip to selectively hide or reveal part of another—for example, to reveal parts of a video layer with a round spotlight shape. Matte filters can be used by themselves to mask out areas of a clip, or to create alpha channel information for a clip in order to create a transparent border around the clip that can be composited against other layers. See *alpha channel.*

media file A generic term for elements such as movies, sounds, and pictures.

midtones The middle brightness range of an image. Not the very brightest part, not the very darkest part.

mini-Timeline The small timeline at the base of the Canvas that solos the timing events for the selected object, filter, mask, or behavior.

mono audio An audio clip that contains a single track of sound. Sometimes mono audio is created by mixing equal amounts of audio channels 1 and 2 into one clip or audio track.

motion blur An effect that blurs any clip with keyframed motion applied to it, similar to blurred motion recorded by a camera.

motion path A path that appears in the Canvas showing the path a clip will travel based on *keyframe* points that are applied to the clip.

motion tracking A technique that involves selecting a particular region of an image and analyzing its motion over time.

MPEG (Moving Picture Experts Group) A group of compression standards for video and audio, which includes MPEG-1, MPEG-2, and MPEG-4.

MPEG-4 A global multimedia standard based on the QuickTime file format. Delivers scalable, high-quality audio and video streams over a wide range of bandwidths—from cell phone to broadband—and also supports 3D objects, sprites, text, and other media types.

N

non–drop frame timecode NTSC timecode that assigns a corresponding number for every frame of video, as opposed to drop-frame timecode that "drops frames" or skips numbers in order to keep in sync with NTSC video that runs at 29.97 frames per second.

noninterlaced video The standard representation of images on a computer and some HD video formats, also referred to as *progressive scan*. The monitor displays the image by drawing each line in order, one after the other, from top to bottom.

nonlinear editing A video-editing process that uses computer hard disks to store and randomly access media. It allows the editor to reorganize clips very quickly or change sections without recreating the entire program.

nonlinear editor (NLE) An editing platform (usually on a computer) used to perform nonlinear editing.

nonsquare pixel A pixel with a height that is different from its width. An NTSC pixel is taller than it is wide, and a PAL pixel is wider than it is tall.

NTSC (National Television Systems Committee) The standard of color TV broadcasting used mainly in North America, Mexico, and Japan, consisting of 525 lines per frame, 29.97 frames per second, and 720 x 486 pixels per frame. See *PAL*.

NTSC legal The range of color that can be broadcast free of distortion according to the NTSC standards, with maximum allowable video at 100 IRE units and black at 7.5 IRE units.

offset tracking A tracking process that is used when your reference pattern is obscured. With offset tracking, the track point follows the same path, but a new search region/reference pattern is used to acquire the tracking data.

opacity The degree to which an image is transparent, allowing images behind to show through. An opacity of 0 percent means an object is invisible; an opacity of 100 percent means the object is completely opaque.

optical flow Optical flow is a frame blending option that produces smoother retiming effects by estimating the motion between two frames of video and rendering an intermediate frame that interpolates the motion. However, optical flow requires more rendering time than other frame blending options. See *frame blending*.

Out point The last frame of an object displayed in the Canvas.

overscan The part of the video frame that cannot be seen on a TV or video display. Broadcast video is an overscan medium, meaning that the recorded frame size is usually larger than the viewable area on a video display. The overscan part of the picture is usually hidden behind the plastic bezel on the edge of a television set.

overwrite edit An edit in which one clip replaces an existing clip in a sequence. The overall duration of the sequence remains unchanged.

PAL (Phase Alternating Line) The European color TV broadcasting standard, consisting of 625 lines per frame, running at 25 frames per second and 720 x 576 pixels per frame. See *NTSC*.

P

pan To rotate a camera left or right without changing its position. The term has been adapted in computer graphics to refer to the movement of individual video elements.

pixel Abbreviation for *picture element*. One dot in a video or still image.

pixel aspect ratio The width-to-height ratio for the pixels that compose an image. Pixels on computer screens and in high-definition video are square (1:1 ratio). Pixels in standard-definition video are nonsquare.

playhead A navigational element that shows the current frame in the Timeline, Canvas, Keyframe Editor, or Audio Editor.

postproduction The phase of film, video, and audio production that begins after all the footage is shot.

premultiplication The process of multiplying the RGB channels in an image by their alpha channel.

preset A portion of a Motion project saved into the Favorites section of the Library.

QuickTime Apple's cross-platform multimedia technology. Widely used for editing, compositing, CD-ROM, Web video, and more.

Q

QuickTime streaming Apple's streaming-media addition to the QuickTime architecture. Used for viewing QuickTime content in real time on the Web.

real time Refers to the ability to play video content during preview at exactly the same frame rate as the final intended output. Can also refer to the ability to update parameters and instantly see the result of the change.

R

redo To reverse an undo, which restores the last change made to a project.

render The process by which a computer calculates final frames for a project. In Motion, rendering is performed in the GPU of the graphics card.

rig A container for widgets in a Motion project file.

RGB An abbreviation for *red, green,* and *blue,* which are the three primary colors of a color video image.

rotoscoping A frame-by-frame hand-painting technique to create imagery over time.

safe zones The two sets of lines representing action-safe and title-safe areas in the Canvas. See *action safe; title safe.*

sampling The process during which analog audio is converted into digital information. The sampling rate of an audio stream specifies how many samples are captured. Higher sample rates are able to more accurately reproduce higher-pitched sounds. Examples: 44.1 Kbytes, 48 Kbytes. Greater bit depths during sampling increase the dynamic range (changes in volume) of the audio.

saturation The purity of color. As saturation is decreased, the color moves toward gray.

scale An adjustable value that changes the overall image size of a clip. The proportion of the image may or may not be maintained.

scrub To move through a clip or sequence by dragging the playhead. Scrubbing is used to find a particular point or frame or to hear the audio.

SECAM (Sequential Couleur Avec Memoir) The French television standard for playback. As with PAL, the playback rate is 25 fps and the frame size is 720 x 546. Primarily a broadcast medium; editing for SECAM broadcasts is still performed in PAL.

Smart Motion Template A motion project designed specifically to be published to Final Cut Pro's effects browsers as a title, transition, effect, or generator.

SMPTE (Society of Motion Picture and Television Engineers) The organization responsible for establishing various broadcast video standards, such as the SMPTE standard timecode for video playback.

snapping The process by which the playhead or an object in the Canvas "snaps," or moves directly, to guides, markers, or edit points when it is moved close to them.

snapshot A set of parameter values applied to each state of a widget in a Motion project. For example, a checkbox widget has two snapshots: one for when it is selected, the other when it is deselected.

solo The process of temporarily disabling all objects other than the selected objects to improve real-time performance.

sound byte A short excerpt taken from an interview clip.

square pixel A pixel that has the same height as width. Computer monitors and certain HD formats have square pixels, but NTSC and PAL video do not.

stabilization The process of selecting a particular region of an image and analyzing its motion over time. Once analyzed, the motion data is inverted and applied to the clip, causing it to become stable. Clips need to be stabilized for a variety of reasons, ranging from weave created by an unsteady camera gate to a shaky camera move.

standard definition The term used to differentiate traditional television broadcast signals from high-definition signals. Standard-definition broadcast signals are usually 720 x 486 (NTSC) or 720 x 576 (PAL). See *high definition.*

stereo audio Sound that is separated into two left/right channels. Stereo pairs are linked and are always edited together. Audio-level changes are automatically made to both channels at the same time.

straight cut An edit in which both the video and audio tracks are cut together to the Timeline.

streaming The delivery of media over an intranet or the Internet.

super black Black that is darker than the levels allowed by the CCIR 601 engineering standard for video. The CCIR 601 standard for black is 7.5 IRE in the United States and 0 IRE for PAL and NTSC in Japan.

super white A value or degree of white that is brighter than the accepted normal value of 100 IRE allowed by the CCIR 601 standard.

T

talent An actor in a clip.

thumbnails Small square icons displaying a frame of the represented clip.

TIFF (Tagged Image File Format) A widely used bitmapped graphics file format that handles monochrome, grayscale, and 8- and 24-bit color resolutions.

tilt To pivot the camera up and down, which causes the image to move down or up in the frame.

time remapping The process of changing the playback speed of a clip over time. The equivalent of varying the crank speed of a film camera.

timecode A numbering system of electronic signals laid onto each frame of videotape that is used to identify specific frames of video. Each frame of video is labeled with hours, minutes, seconds, and frames (01:00:00:00). Timecode formats include drop frame, non–drop frame, time of day (TOD), or EBU (European Broadcast Union—for PAL projects).

timecode gap An area of tape with no timecode. Timecode gaps usually signify the end of all recorded material on a tape, but they may occur due to starting and stopping a camera or tape deck during recording.

Timeline A window in Motion for displaying and editing the timing events for all objects, filters, and behaviors.

title safe Part of the video image that is guaranteed to be visible on all televisions. The title-safe area is the inner 80 percent of the screen. To prevent text in your video from being hidden by the edge of a TV set, you should restrict any titles or text to the title-safe area.

tracking The process of analyzing the motion of one clip and applying that motion to another clip.

tracks Layers in the Timeline that contain the audio or video clips in a project.

transfer modes Another term for *blend modes.*

trimming To precisely add or subtract frames from the In or Out point of a clip. Trimming is used to fine-tune an edited sequence by carefully adjusting many edits in small ways.

U

underscan To display video on a computer or video monitor with a black border around the edge, so that no part of the frame is hidden from the viewer.

undo A feature that allows you to cancel out the last change made.

variable speed See *time remapping.*

Vectorscope A window in Final Cut Pro that graphically displays the color components of a video signal, precisely showing the range of colors in the signal and measuring their intensities and hues. It can be used to calibrate the color in video signals being captured from videotape, and to compare two clips for purposes of color correction.

video-in-text effect When a video image is matted inside the shape of text.

vignette A popular photographic effect in which the photo gradually darkens around the edges, usually in an oval shape.

VTR / VCR (videotape recorder/videocassette recorder) A tape machine used for recording pictures and sound on videotape.

VU meter (volume unit meter) An analog meter for monitoring audio levels.

WAV A sound file format developed by Microsoft and IBM.

white balance To make adjustments to a video signal being recorded in order to reproduce white as true white. For example, if the white in a shot is too green due to fluorescent lighting, white balancing adds enough magenta to make the white appear neutral.

white level An analog video signal's amplitude for the lightest white in a picture, represented by IRE units.

widget A checkbox, pop-up menu, or slider to which multiple parameters can be attached. The parameter values are set for each state, or snapshot, of the widget. See *snapshot.*

widescreen A format for shooting and projecting a movie in theaters in which the width dimension is larger than the height. With the advent of high-definition video, widescreen 16:9 video has come into popular use. See *16:9.*

widescreen mask filter Adds black bars across the top and bottom of a 4:3 image to crop it to a 16:9 format.

X

x-axis Refers to the x coordinate in Cartesian geometry. The x coordinate describes horizontal placement in motion effects.

Y

y-axis Refers to the y coordinate in Cartesian geometry. The y coordinate describes vertical placement in motion effects.

YUV The three-channel PAL video signal with one luminance (Y) and two chrominance color difference signals (UV). It is often misapplied to refer to NTSC video, which is YIQ.

Z

z-axis Refers to the z coordinate in Cartesian geometry. The z coordinate describes perpendicular placement in motion effects.

zoom To change the magnification of your Canvas or Timeline.

Index

Apple Certification
Fuel your mind.
Reach your potential.

Stand out from the crowd. Differentiate yourself and gain recognition for your expertise by earning Apple Certified Pro status to validate your Motion 5 skills.

This book prepares you to earn Apple Certified Pro—Motion 5 Level One status. You can pay to take the exam at an Apple Authorized Training Center (AATC). Level One certification attests to essential operational knowledge of the application.

Three Steps to Certification

1 Choose your certification path.
   More info: training.apple.com/certification.

2 All Apple Authorized Training Centers (AATCs) offer all Mac OS X and Pro Apps exams, even if they don't offer the corresponding course. To find the closest AATC, please visit training.apple.com/locations.

3 Register for and take your exam(s).

"Now when I go out to do corporate videos and I let them know I'm certified, I get job after job after job."

— Chip McAllister, Final Cut Pro Editor and Winner of The Amazing Race

Reasons to Become an Apple Certified Pro

- **Raise your earning potential.** Studies show that certified professionals can earn more than their non-certified peers.

- **Distinguish yourself from others in your industry.** Proven mastery of an application helps you stand out from the crowd.

- **Display your Apple Certification logo.** Each certification provides a logo to display on business cards, resumes and websites.

- **Publicize your Certifications.** Publish your certifications on the Apple Certified Professionals Registry to connect with schools, clients and employers.

Training Options

Apple's comprehensive curriculum addresses your needs, whether you're an IT or creative professional, educator, or student. Hands-on training is available through a worldwide network of Apple Authorized Training Centers (AATCs). Self-paced study is available through the Apple Pro Training Series books, which are also accessible as eBooks via the iBooks app. Video training and video training apps are also available for select titles. Visit training.apple.com to view all your learning options.

The Apple Pro Training Series

Apple Certified

Apple offers comprehensive certification programs for creative and IT professionals. The Apple Pro Training Series is the official training curriculum of the Apple Training and Certification program, used by Apple Authorized Training Centers around the world

Books

The critically acclaimed Apple Pro Training Series Books, are comprehensive, self-paced courses written by acknowledged experts in the field

OS X Lion Support Essentials

Apple Pro Training Series: OS X Lion Support Essentials: Supporting and Troubleshooting OS X Lion
9780321775078

The only Apple-certified book on OS X Lion, this best-seller will take you deep inside the latest big-cat operating system—covering everything from installation and configuration, customizing the operating system, supporting applications, setting up peripherals, and more.

OS X Lion Server Essentials

Apple Pro Training Series: OS X Lion Server Essentials: Using and Supporting OS X Lion Server
9780321775085

The only Apple-certified book on OS X Lion Server, this comprehensive reference takes support technicians and ardent Mac users deep inside this server operating system, covering everything from networking technologies to service administration, customizing users and groups, and more.

Final Cut Pro X

Apple Pro Training Series: Final Cut Pro X
9780321774675

Completely revised for Final Cut Pro X and featuring compelling new footage, this best-selling, Apple-certified guide from Diana Weynand starts with basic video editing techniques and takes readers all the way through Final Cut Pro's powerful features.

Final Cut Pro X Advanced Editing

Apple Pro Training Series: Final Cut Pro X Advanced Editing
9780321810229

In this Apple-authorized guide, director and filmmaker Michael Wohl teaches the advanced skills that editing professionals need to know most.

Final Cut Pro X Quick-Reference Guide

Apple Pro Training Series: Final Cut Pro X Quick-Reference Guide (E-Book)
9780132876346

This e-book is a compendium of Final Cut Pro best practices, tips, and quick-glance reminders, plus a great summary of what's new in Final Cut Pro X.

Motion 5

Apple Pro Training Series: Motion 5
9780321774682

Master trainer Mark Spencer starts with the fundamentals of motion graphics and quickly moves into compositing, animation, motion graphics design, visual effects design, and the world of 3D

Logic Pro 9 and Logic Express 9

Apple Pro Training Series: Logic Pro 9 and Logic Express 9
9780321636805

Record, edit, mix, and polish music files using Apple's pro audio software

Logic Pro 9 Advanced Music Production

Apple Pro Training Series: Logic Pro 9 Advanced Music Production
9780321647450

Go beyond the basics of creating and producing music with Logic Pro 9

Aperture 3

Apple Pro Training Series: Aperture 3
9780321647443

The best way to learn Aperture's powerful photo-editing, image retouching, proofing, publishing, and archiving features

iLife '11

Apple Training Series: iLife '11
9780321700971

Focused lessons take you step by step through all aspects of iLife

iWork

Apple Training Series: iWork 09
9780321618511

Focused lessons take you step by step through all aspects of Keynote, Pages, and Numbers.

Videos

The Apple Pro Video Series offers Apple-certified video training on key Apple technologies.

Apple Pro Video Series: Final Cut Pro X
9780321809629

Introducing the first Apple-Certified video on Final Cut Pro X. In this tutorial, Apple-mentor trainer Steve Martin, guides you through the new workflows, toolsets and features of Final Cut Pro X.

Apple Pro Video Series: Final Cut Pro X
9780132876308

Introducing the first Apple-Certified video on Final Cut Pro X. In this tutorial, Apple-mentor trainer Steve Martin, guides you through the new workflows, toolsets and features of Final Cut Pro X.

Apple Pro Video Training: Aperture 3
9780321749840

This Apple-certified guide to Aperture 3 includes over 3 hours of high quality video tutorials and a companion printed quick-reference guide that will get you up and running quickly, taking you step by step through Aperture's powerful editing, retouching, proofing, publishing and archiving features.

Apple Video Training: Pages for iPad, Online Video
9780321765147

In this Apple-certified guide to Pages for iPad, master trainer Rich Harrington takes you on a comprehensive tour.

Apple Video Training: Keynote for iPad, Online Video
9780132711708

In this Apple-certified guide to Keynote for iPad, master trainer Rich Harrington takes you on a comprehensive tour.

Apple Video Training: Numbers for iPad, Online Video
9780132711616

In this Apple-certified guide to Keynote for iPad, master trainer Rich Harrington takes you on a comprehensive tour.

Test your Mac skills with essential iPhone/iPad Apps

Whether you are preparing for Apple Certification exams or brushing up on your Mac skills in general, the new Test Yourself iPhone/iPad apps from Peachpit can help you prepare with confidence.

Test Yourself for Mac OS X v10.6 Server Essentials

Test Yourself for Mac OS X v10.6 Support Essentials

Test Yourself for Aperture 3 App

Introducing the Apple Pro Video iPhone/Ipad Apps

The Apple Pro Video Training iPhone and iPad Apps provide hours of high-quality video tutorials that provide a comprehensive tour of a wide variety of essential Apple topics.

Apple Pro Video Training for Aperture 3, iPhone Edition

Apple Pro Video Training for Aperture 3, iPad Edition

Video Training for Pages for iPad

Video Training for Keynote for iPad

Video Training for Numbers for iPad